Governance Stories

In contrast to conventional approaches to political science, this book develops an interpretative approach to governance theory. In their earlier book *Interpreting British Governance*, Bevir and Rhodes sought to understand changes in British government by setting out an interpretative approach to British political science, which focused on an aggregate analysis of British political traditions. Here, Bevir and Rhodes argue that situated agency, the analysis of people's webs of belief and actions located in the inherited traditions and practices that inform them, plays a key role in interpretative political science. This book:

- provides a theoretical defence of situated agency;
- compares their approach to British political science with other forms of enquiry, including post-structural and institutional analysis;
- provides a general account of governance as the context for ethnographic analyses of governance in action;
- includes studies of the 'Blair presidency', the National Health Service, government departments and the police.

This new volume presents a major challenge to present-day political science. It will be of interest to advanced students and researchers in political theory, public policy, British politics and British history.

Mark Bevir is Professor of Political Science at the University of California, Berkeley.

Roderick Rhodes is Professor of Political Science and Head of Program in the Research School of Social Sciences, Australian National University.

Routledge Advances in European Politics

Governance Stories

Mark Bevir and R. A. W. Rhodes

Routledge
Taylor & Francis Group

LONDON AND NEW YORK

First published 2006
by Routledge
2 Park Square, Milton Park, Abingdon, Oxon, OX14 4RN

Simultaneously published in the USA and Canada
by Routledge
270 Madison Ave, New York NY 10016

Routledge is an imprint of the Taylor & Francis Group

Transferred to Digital Printing 2007

© 2006 Mark Bevir and R. A. W. Rhodes

Typeset in Garamond by
Book Now Ltd

British Library Cataloguing in Publication Data
A catalogue record for this book is available from the British Library

Library of Congress Cataloging in Publication Data
Bevir, Mark
Governance stories/Mark Bevir and R. A. W. Rhodes.–1st ed.
    p. cm.–(Routledge advances in European politics)
Includes bibliographical references and index.
1. Political culture–Great Britain. 2. Great Britain–Politics and government. I. Rhodes, R. A. W. II. Title. III. Series.

JN231.B483 2006
306.2′0941–dc22   2005012449

ISBN10: 0–415–37660–2 (hbk)
ISBN10: 0–415–45977–X (pbk)

ISBN13: 978–0–415–37660–0 (hbk)
ISBN13: 978–0–415–45977–8 (pbk)

To Jenny from Rod

Contents

Illustrations

Tables

Figure

Preface and acknowledgements

In our earlier book, *Interpreting British Governance*, we outlined an interpretive approach to political science and used it to explore changes in British governance. We focused on reforms of the public sector. We emphasized the importance of interpreting governance by examining practices from the bottom up. We also bemoaned the lack of such studies. *Governance Stories* seeks to fill that gap with ethnographic fieldwork. Equally, we emphasized that practices of governance arise out of actions based on beliefs informed by traditions. *Governance Stories* locates its ethnographic work in a broader account of traditions in the study and practice of politics. We hope the results are edifying stories about some of the complex, conflicting practices of governance in Britain today.

We must acknowledge various debts. The Research School of Social Sciences, Australian National University (ANU) awarded Mark a Fellowship so we could collaborate with greater ease. The following commented on all or parts of the manuscript: Robert Adcock (Stanford), Jenny Fleming (ANU), Andrew Gamble (Sheffield), Brian Hardy (Leeds), Colin Hay (Birmingham), Anthony Mughan (Ohio State), Dave Richards (Sheffield), John Uhr (ANU), John Wanna (ANU) and Pat Weller (Griffith). Laura Bevir prepared the index. Tanya Liebrecht (Griffith), Carolyn Hendricks (ANU) and Karthik Srinivasan (Berkeley) provided research assistance. A special thank you to Jenny Fleming and Brian Hardy, each of whom was the co-author of one chapter (see below), for allowing us to use their work here. We are also grateful to Brian and Jenny for permission to use their primary research in the relevant chapters. We also owe a special debt of gratitude to the politicians and public officials without whom several chapters could not have been written; the views expressed are, of course, ours alone.

We have drawn on three essays previously published jointly and singly in 2003 and 2004. Some of the new material will appear separately in 2005 and 2006. We list below in date order the essays on which we draw:

'Searching for civil society: changing patterns of governance in Britain', *Public Administration*, 81(1), 2003: 41–62.

(with Brian Hardy), 'Beliefs and institutional change: the UK national health service', in J. Fleming and I. Holland (eds), *Government Reformed: Values, Institutions and the State*. Aldershot: Ashgate, 2003.

'Governance and interpretation: what are the implications of post-foundationalism?' *Public Administration*, 82(3), 2004: 605–25.

'Everyday life in a ministry: public administration as anthropology', *American Review of Public Administration*, 35(1), 2005: 3–26.

'Interpretation and its others', *Australian Journal of Political Science*, 40(2), 2005: 169–87.

'The Westminster model as tradition: the case of Australia', in J. Wanna, P. Weller and H. Patapan (eds), *Westminster's Legacies: Democracy and Responsible Government in Asia, Australasia and the Pacific*. Sydney: UNSW Press, 2005.

(with Jenny Fleming), 'Bureaucracy, contracts and networks: the unholy trinity and the police', *Australian and New Zealand Journal of Criminology*, 38(2), 2005.

'Traditions of political science in contemporary Britain', in R. Adcock, M. Bevir and S. Stimson (eds), *Modern Political Science: Anglo-American Exchanges since 1880*. Princeton, NJ: Princeton University Press, 2006 forthcoming.

Berkeley and Canberra
March 2005

1 Introduction

Meaning in action

How do we know what we know about British government? The easy answer to this question is that we describe key institutions like the prime minister, cabinet and the civil service using the conventional repertoire of social science theories to guide us. One problem with easy answers and conventional theories is they often reproduce sterile agendas and boring findings. To compare Tony Blair with Napoleon is to resurrect the presidentialization of the prime minister thesis yet again. We need some new spectacles.

This book argues that a philosophical analysis of meaning allied to historical analyses of traditions and ethnographic analyses of practices provides the new glasses. So, first, we deploy these new glasses to explore British political science and its characteristic accounts of British governance. In this chapter and the next, we begin by explaining how our glasses work and why we recommend them. Next, we look through these spectacles to tell stories about other approaches to political science, the Westminster model associated with many of them and our preferred account of governance. We question the unquestioned and expose inconsistencies in the dominant accounts of these subjects. Second, much as we love the peace and quiet of the library, we turn our attention to more detailed accounts of particular aspects of governance. Here we report our ethnographic fieldwork. We conducted long, taped, repeat interviews with ministers and top civil servants, not the five-minute forensic theatre beloved of journalists. We shadowed ministers and senior public servants for days at a time, not just in the hurly-burly of public life, but also in the night-time quiet of the private office. We used any and every available participant and non-participant method of observation to grasp some of the meanings of everyday life for ministers, civil servants, National Health Service managers and senior police officers. Our ethnographic stories concentrate, as our philosophical ideas require, on meaning in action.

Meaning in action

All political scientists offer interpretations of the world. Interpretive approaches differ from others in that they provide interpretations of interpretations. They concentrate on meanings, beliefs, languages, discourses and signs, as opposed to, say, laws and rules, correlations between social categories or deductive models. Of course, the distinction between interpretive approaches and others is not an all-or-nothing affair. Laws, social categories and models are, after all, matters of belief or language. So, proponents of an interpretive approach would allow that the study of laws, correlations and models could play a role in exploring practices. Likewise, sensible exponents of the new institutionalism, behaviouralism and rational choice allow that typologies, correlations and models can do explanatory work only when they refer to the beliefs and desires of the relevant actors. Nonetheless, there is a family of interpretive approaches to political science that stand out for their focus on meanings. The interpretive family includes not only our variant (Bevir 1999; Bevir and Rhodes 2003), but also discourse analysis (Howarth *et al.* 2000), poststructuralism (Burchell *et al.* 1991) and earlier forms of social constructivism (Berger and Luckman 1971). Also, it overlaps with other approaches, including those varieties of the new institutionalism concerned with the impact of ideas (see, for example, Berman 2001; Lieberman 2002; Finnemore and Sikkink 2001).

An interpretive approach is far from alone in paying attention to meanings. However, it is distinctive in that it typically takes a holistic view of meaning; it implies that political science is about meanings, as we might say, all the way down. An interpretive approach accounts for meanings by locating them in wider webs of meanings. It does so because, first, beliefs have a constitutive relationship to actions and, second, beliefs are inherently holistic (cf. Taylor 1971).

First, an interpretive approach holds that beliefs and practices are constitutive of each other. When other political scientists study voting behaviour using surveys of the attitudes of voters, or models of rational action given certain beliefs and preferences, they separate beliefs from actions in their search for a correlation or deductive link between the two. In contrast, an interpretive approach suggests that such surveys and models cannot tell us why, say, raising one's hand should amount to voting, or why there would be an uproar if someone forced someone else to raise their hand against their will, or why only certain people should be regarded as eligible to vote. We can explain these sorts of things only if we appeal to the inter-subjective beliefs that underpin the practice of concern to us. We need to know that voting is associated with making a free choice and so with a particular concept of the self. We need to know what counts as an infringement of free choice, and who is regarded as able to make such a choice. An interpretive approach holds that beliefs and practices are constitutive of one another. Practices could not exist if people did not have apt beliefs. Beliefs or meanings would not make sense without the practices to which they refer.

Second, an interpretive approach argues that meanings or beliefs are holistic. So we can make sense of someone's beliefs only by locating them in the wider web of other beliefs that provide their reasons for holding them. Even if other political scientists establish a correlation between a positive attitude to social justice and voting Labour, they still cannot claim people will vote Labour because of this attitude. After all, people who have a positive attitude to social justice might vote Conservative if they believe more strongly in conservative values or if they believe a Labour government will not implement its policies for promoting social justice. To explain why someone with a positive attitude to social justice votes Labour, we have to unpack the other relevant beliefs and desires linking that attitude to that vote. To explain an action, we cannot merely correlate it with an isolated attitude. Rather, we must interpret it as part of a web of beliefs and desires.

Many political scientists typically treat beliefs, meanings, ideas and norms as if they can be differentiated from actions and related individually to such actions. In contrast, an interpretive approach argues that meanings or beliefs form holistic webs that constitute actions and practices. This philosophical analysis of meaning in action informs several other notable features of an interpretive approach, including bottom-up inquiry and its denaturalizing critiques – that is, critiques that expose the contingency and unquestioned assumptions of other narratives.

Interpretive approaches share sympathy for bottom-up forms of social inquiry (Bang and Sørensen 1999). They usually believe that people in the same situation can hold different beliefs because their experiences of that situation can be laden with different prior theories. No abstract concept, such as a class or an institution, can properly explain people's beliefs, interests or actions. Such a concept can represent only proxy for the multiple and complex beliefs and actions of all those individuals we classify under it. An interpretive approach often concludes, for such reasons, that practices require bottom-up studies of the actions and beliefs out of which they emerge. They explore the ways in which social practices are created, sustained and transformed through the interplay and contest of the beliefs or meanings embedded in human activity. In this book, we offer just such bottom-up studies of governance in the chapters on the police, the NHS, life in a government department and the Blair presidency.

Another theme shared by interpretive approaches is an emphasis on the contingency of political life. Typically, an interpretive approach argues that people can interpret a situation in many ways. So, no practice or norm can fix the ways in which people will act, let alone how they will innovate when responding to new circumstances. An interpretive approach concludes that our practices are contingent. There is no fixed essence or necessary path of development explaining them. This emphasis on contingency explains why interpretive approaches so often criticize other theories. An interpretive approach suggests that political scientists efface the contingency of social life when they attempt to ground their theories in apparently given facts about the nature of reasoning, the path-dependence of institutions or the inexorability of social developments. So, its adherents try to show the contingency of those parts of political life that other political scientists represent as natural or inexorable (see, for example, Farmer 1995; Kass and Catron 1990). We will pursue just such a denaturalizing strategy in the ensuing chapters on British political science, the Westminster Model and governance.

Situated agency

The interpretive approach consists of a cluster of overlapping traditions. Important differences can appear among these traditions, in particular, about aggregating practices. An interpretive approach can seem to be confused about the nature of the meanings or beliefs that inform practices. Poststructuralists sometimes imply that meanings exist as quasi-structures governed by either a semiotic code or random fluctuations of power (see Foucault 1972, 1980). Others analyse meanings as the beliefs of individuals; they take an ideology, discourse or language to refer only to a cluster of inter-subjective beliefs.

When poststructuralists imply that meanings derive from quasi-structures, they usually do so because they want to emphasize how our beliefs and subjectivity are constructed out of social backgrounds. They want to reject a strong concept of autonomy. However, we prefer to distinguish between autonomy and agency. Autonomous individuals can, at least in principle, have experiences, reason, adopt beliefs and act, outside all contexts. On the other hand, agents can reason and act in novel ways, although they can do so only against the background of the contexts that influence them. Most poststructuralists reject autonomy because they believe all experiences and all reasoning embody theories; thus people can adopt beliefs only against the background of a prior set of theories, which at least initially must be made available to them by a social discourse or tradition. However, this rejection of autonomy does not entail a rejection of agency. We can accept that people always set out against the background of a social discourse or tradition and still think of them as agents who can act and reason in novel ways to modify this background. Even if a linguistic context forms the background to people's statements, and a social context forms the background to their actions and practices, the content of their statements and actions does not come directly from these contexts. It comes instead from the ways in which they replicate, use or respond to these contexts in accord with their intentions. An interpretive approach has no reason to throw agency out with autonomy. When we defend the capacity for agency, however, we do so recognizing that it always occurs within a social context that influences it. Agency is not autonomous. It is situated.

The idea of situated agency can resolve confusion among interpretive approaches about the aggregate study of practices. At the moment, poststructuralists sometimes rely on ideas such as discourse to recentre their accounts of practices.[1] They do so by treating meanings as given by quasi-structures. However, they also stress the contingency and particularity of beliefs. This emphasis appears to contradict their explanation of practices, which cannot be contingent and particular if they are determined by quasi-structures such as an episteme. The greater the emphasis we place on the contingency and particularity of beliefs, actions and practices, the harder it becomes to explain them by an aggregate concept or social process. Indeed, if an interpretive approach deploys discourse or paradigm to do explanatory work, these concepts imply a worrying neglect of agency. If a discourse claims to explain patterns of belief or speech, the implication is that the discourse fixes the content of the beliefs or intentions people can hold. What is more, if an interpretive approach uses discourse as an explanatory concept, it appears to adopt a determinism that barely can account for change. If individuals arrive at beliefs by a fixed and disembodied discourse, they lack the ability to modify that discourse. So any such changes appear inexplicable. Of course, poststructuralists often criticize structuralism for exhibiting just such determinism while insisting they themselves view such transformations as instabilities inherent in structures. However, this insistence merely elides the question of whether we are to understand such instabilities, contradictions and transformations as necessary qualities of a disembodied discourse or as contingent properties and products of individual subjects, their beliefs, their reasoning and their action.

An interpretive approach often struggles to recentre accounts of practices that have explanatory power. The problem can be resolved by the idea of situated agency. To reject autonomy is to accept that traditions and discourses influence individuals. Explanatory concepts must suggest, therefore, how social influences permeate beliefs and actions even when actors do not recognize such influence. To accept agency is, however, to imply people have the capacity to adopt beliefs and actions, even novel ones, for reasons of their own. In so doing they can transform the social background. The idea of tradition covers both inheriting beliefs and transforming them as they are handed down from generation to generation. It is evocative of a social structure in which individuals are born, which then acts as the background to their beliefs and actions even while they might adapt, develop and reject much of this inheritance. Similarly, an interpretive approach could usefully explore change by focusing on dilemmas. Change arises as situated agents respond to novel ideas or problems. It is a result of people's ability to adopt beliefs and perform actions through a reasoning that is embedded in the tradition they inherit.

Beliefs, traditions, dilemmas

Interpretive approaches typically are based on philosophical analyses of meaning in action. Our particular interpretive approach gives prominence to situated agency. We think of meanings as beliefs and, to explain webs of beliefs, we use the pragmatic concepts of tradition and dilemma. The concepts of belief, tradition and dilemma distinguish interpretivism from other approaches to political science. They also resolve debates among interpretive approaches about the nature of meaning and the ways we might recentre accounts of governance.

Why beliefs?

As early as the 1950s, philosophers forcefully criticized positivism. Political scientists often fail to take seriously the consequences of rejecting a positivist notion of pure experience. Some cling tenaciously to the positivist idea that we can explain human behaviour by objective social facts about people. In so doing, they remove the task of interpreting beliefs from the ambit of political science. Typically, many political scientists, when they reject positivism, only distance themselves from the idea of pure experience. They still avoid interpreting beliefs. They try to avoid such interpretation by reducing beliefs to abstract and deductive models or to intervening variables between social facts and actions.

However, once we reject the idea of pure experience, we undermine the positivist case against interpreting beliefs as part of webs of beliefs (Bevir 1999: 127–73). A rejection of pure experience implies that we cannot reduce meanings or beliefs to deductive models or intervening variables. When political scientists say that senior local government officers in charge of a department of social services have a vested interest in increasing their department's budget and employing more social workers, they use particular theories to identify these interests from the position of these officers. If others have a different set of theories, they might believe that someone in that position has different interests; they might equate their interests, for example, with loyalty to their elected boss and the efficient and speedy implementation of his or her policies. The important point here is that how the people we study see their position and their interests inevitably depends on their theories, which might differ significantly from our theories. Officials might possess theories that lead them to see their position as administrators serving the public interest, rather than as chief executives employing the best managerial practices of the private sector. Or they might see their interests as sustaining best professional practice in social work, not maximizing the turnover of caseloads.

To explain peoples' actions, we implicitly or explicitly invoke their beliefs and desires. When we reject positivism, we give up the possibility of identifying their beliefs by appealing to allegedly objective social facts about them. Instead, we give great prominence to the task of exploring the beliefs and meanings through which they construct their world, including the ways they understand their location, the norms that affect them and even their interests. Because people do not have pure experiences, their beliefs and desires are inextricably enmeshed with theories. Thus, political scientists cannot read-off beliefs and desires from objective social facts. Instead they have to interpret beliefs as part of webs of beliefs and, we would add, locate these webs against the background of traditions and dilemmas.

An emphasis on interpreting beliefs in their webs acts as a counter to the lukewarm positivism of much political science. Equally, it helps to remind us that meanings arise not as parts of disembodied quasi-structures like paradigms and epistemes, but rather as subjective and inter-subjective understandings. Meanings are always the beliefs of specific people. Of course, when we use belief in this way, we define the concept broadly to include the subconscious and unconscious as well as the conscious. For us, beliefs are not just big commitments people reach through deliberate reflection. They include the everyday tacit understandings on which people act without any noticeable deliberation. For example, the senior civil servants in Chapter 8 were socialized into the doctrines of the Westminster model on joining the service. Notions such as trust in and loyalty to one's minister are now taken for granted, commented on only in the rare breach. Our notion of belief is, then, a broad one that refers to all the understandings on which people act. We use the term 'belief', not 'language' or 'discourse', to remind ourselves that these understandings are the properties of situated agents, not disembodied quasi-structures.

Why traditions?

The form of explanation we adopt for beliefs, actions and practices revolves around the concepts of tradition and dilemma. The idea of a tradition captures the social context in which individuals both exercise their reason and act (Bevir 1999: 174–220). We define a tradition, therefore, as a set of understandings someone receives during socialization. A governmental tradition is a set of inherited beliefs about the institutions and history of government. Although tradition is unavoidable, it is so as a starting point, not as something that determines later performances. We are cautious about representing tradition as an unavoidable presence in everything people do in case we leave too slight a role for situated agency. In particular, we do not imply that tradition is constitutive of the beliefs people later come to hold or the actions they then perform. Instead, we see tradition mainly as a first influence on people. The content of the tradition will appear in their later actions only if their situated agency has not led them to change it, and every part of it is, in principle, open to such change.

Positivists sometimes hold that individuals are autonomous and avoid the influence of tradition. They suggest that people can arrive at beliefs through pure experiences, so we can explain why people held their beliefs by referring to those experiences. Yet once we reject positivism, we need a concept such as tradition to explain why people come to believe what they do. Because people cannot have pure experiences, they necessarily construe their experiences using theories they have inherited. People's experiences lead them to beliefs only because they already have access to theories in the form of tradition.

A social heritage is the necessary background to the beliefs people adopt and the actions they perform. Some political scientists adopt a strong version of this conclusion. They argue that a social structure, paradigm or episteme governs not only the actions people can perform successfully, but also their beliefs and desires. Strong structuralists argue that meanings and beliefs are the products of the internal relations of self-sufficient languages or paradigms. In contrast, when we stress situated agency, we suggest that social contexts only ever influence, as distinct from govern, the nature of individuals. We suggest that traditions are themselves products of situated agency. People are constantly confronting slightly novel circumstances that require them to apply tradition anew. When people confront the unfamiliar, they extend or change their heritage to encompass it, and as they do so, they develop that heritage. Every time individuals apply a tradition, they have to understand it afresh in present-day circumstances. By reflecting on it, they open it to innovation. Thus, situated agency can produce change even when people think they are sticking fast to a tradition they regard as sacrosanct.

A suitable emphasis on situated agency also makes us wary of essentialists who equate traditions with fixed essences around which they identify variations. A. V. Dicey and W. H. Greenleaf illustrate clearly the difference between an essentialist notion of tradition and our own. Dicey (1914: 62–9) divided the Victorian period into three parts. Between 1800 and 1830 was an era of legislative quiescence or an era of old Toryism. The Benthamite spirit of inquiry and governmental reform typified 1825–70. From 1865 to 1900 was the era of collectivism, irresistible yet unwelcome. There have been many challenges to Dicey's account of nineteenth-century administrative history, but his defence of individualism against collectivism continues to influence interpretations of British government. Greenleaf (1983: 15–20) describes the British political tradition, for example, as the dialectic between libertarianism and collectivism. But Greenleaf's categories of individualism and collectivism are too ahistorical. Although they come into being in the nineteenth century, after that they remain static. They act as fixed ideal types into which individual thinkers and texts are then forced. In contrast, an emphasis on situated agency encourages a view of tradition as a starting point for a historical story. It suggests that later instances cannot be constructed by comparison with the allegedly essential features of a putative tradition.

A certain relationship should exist between beliefs and practices if they are to make up a tradition. For a start, the relevant beliefs and practices should have passed from generation to generation. Such socialization may not be intentional. The continuity lies in the themes developed and passed on over time, rather than any self-conscious sense of continuity. As beliefs pass from generation to generation, so each cohort adapts and extends the themes linking the beliefs. Although we should be able to trace a historical line from the start of a tradition to its current finish, the changes introduced by successive generations might even result in beginning and end having nothing in common apart from the links over time. Nonetheless, an abstract set of beliefs and practices that were not passed on would be a summary at one point in time, not a tradition. Such a set would not relate moments in time to one another by showing their historical continuity. A tradition should consist of a series of instances that resemble one another because they exercised a formative influence on one another.

As well as suitable connections through time, traditions should embody appropriate conceptual links. The beliefs and practices that one generation passes on to another should display minimal consistency. A tradition could not have provided someone with a starting point unless its parts formed a minimally coherent set. Traditions cannot be made up of purely random beliefs and actions that successive individuals happen to have held in common.

Although the beliefs in a tradition must be related to one another both temporally and conceptually, their substantive content is unimportant. Because tradition is unavoidable, all beliefs and practices must have their roots in tradition. Our idea of tradition differs, therefore, from that of political scientists who associate the term with customary, unquestioned ways of behaving or with the entrenched folklore of pre-modern societies (cf. Oakeshott 1962: 123, 128–9). At the heart of our notion of tradition are situated agents using their local reasoning consciously and subconsciously to modify their contingent heritage.

Why dilemmas?

The form of explanation we adopt for beliefs, actions and practices revolves around the idea of dilemma as well as that of tradition. A dilemma captures the way in which situated agents are able to bring about changes in beliefs, traditions and practices (Bevir 1999: 221–64). An emphasis on situated agency suggests change originates in the responses or decisions of individuals. Whenever someone adopts a new belief or action, they have to adjust their existing beliefs and practices to make way for the newcomer. To accept a new belief is thus to pose a dilemma that asks questions of existing traditions. A dilemma arises for an individual or group when a new idea stands in opposition to existing beliefs or practices and so forces a reconsideration of the existing beliefs and associated tradition. Political scientists can explain change in traditions and practices, therefore, by referring to the relevant dilemmas. Traditions change as individuals make a series of variations to them in response to any number of specific dilemmas.

For example, the dilemma posed by the increasing size and scale of government fuelled changes in the British constitution. It no longer seemed credible to conceive of the constitution as rooted in a minimalist, caretaker role for the state. The dominant Liberal interpretation of that constitution was Dicey's formalist, normativist style of public law; it stressed a rule-oriented conception of public law. The key functions of constitutional law were adjudication and control of the executive. This stress on the separation of powers and the subordination of government to law confronted the functionalist style in public law that emphasized law as part of the apparatus of government, playing a regulatory and facilitative role and sustaining an instrumentalist social policy (Loughlin 1992: 60). The Liberal view of the constitution and its key doctrines of parliamentary sovereignty and ministerial accountability was decisively transformed by the functionalist or

Whitehall view of the constitution with its emphasis on executive power and the role of the executive as the guardian of the national interest – a precursor of the 'strong state'.

It is important to recognize that political scientists cannot straight-forwardly identify dilemmas with what they take to be allegedly objective pressures within the world. People vary their beliefs or actions in response to any new idea that they come to hold as true. They do so irrespective of whether the new idea reflects real pressures, or, to be precise, irrespective of whether or not it reflects pressures that political scientists believe to be real. In explain-ing change, political scientists cannot privilege their academic accounts of the world. What matters is the subjective or inter-subjective understandings of political actors. Of course, there is often much overlap between the pressures that political scientists believe to be real and the dilemmas that trouble political actors.

It is also important to recognize that although dilemmas often arise from people's experiences, this need not be the case. Dilemmas can arise from theoretical and moral reflection as well as from experiences of worldly pressures. The new belief that poses a dilemma can lie anywhere on a spectrum from views with little theoretical content to complex theoretical constructs that have only remote links to views about the real world. Globalization is a good example. Globalization is one dilemma that admits of many interpre-tations. Colin Hay (2002) distinguishes between the economic outcomes of globalization and effects of the discourse of globalization. A prominent discourse of globalization includes the theory that high taxation drives capital away, a theory for which there is little academic evidence. Nonetheless, politicians act as if there were a link between taxation and capital mobility; they reduce taxes. In this way, the social construction of globalization becomes crucial to explaining political actions irrespective of our views about its adequacy as an account of the world.

A related point to make here is that dilemmas do not have given, or even correct, solutions. When people confront a new event or belief, they neces-sarily change traditions creatively. It might look as if a tradition can tell people how to act in response to dilemmas. At most, however, it provides a guide to what they might do. It does not provide rules fixing what they must do. A tradition can provide hints on how its adherents might respond to a dilemma. But the only way to check if an individual's actions are consistent with the beliefs of a tradition is to ask whether that individual and other adherents of the tradition are happy with those actions. Because individuals respond creatively to dilemmas, it follows that we will recognize change everywhere. Indeed, even when people think they are merely continuing a settled tradition or practice, they might well be developing, adjusting and changing it. Traditions and practices could be fixed and static only if people never met and faced novel circumstances. But, of course, people are always meeting new circumstances. The state and political institutions are in per-petual motion.

Although dilemmas do not determine particular solutions, we can understand the solutions at which people arrive by the character of both the dilemma and their existing beliefs. To hold on to a new idea, people must develop their existing beliefs to make room for it. The new idea will open ways of adjusting and close down others. People have to hook it on to their existing beliefs, and their existing beliefs will present some opportunities and not others. People can integrate a new belief into their existing beliefs only by relating themes to their existing understandings. Change thus involves a pushing and pulling of a dilemma and a tradition to bring them together.

A summary of the argument

In this chapter, we described an interpretive approach that provides accounts of beliefs and practices that are interpretations of interpretations. We used the everyday words belief, tradition and dilemma to expand on our notion of 'situated agency'.

In Chapter 2, we look at several misconceptions about such an approach: that it focuses on beliefs or discourses, not actions or practices; that it ignores concepts of social structure; that it seeks to understand actions and practices, not to explain them; that it is concerned exclusively with qualitative techniques of data generation; that it must accept actors' own accounts of their beliefs; that it is incapable of producing policy-relevant knowledge; and that it is incapable of producing objective knowledge. Thereafter we work with this interpretive approach to offer a series of narratives about British political science and British governance.

In Part I, we concentrate on the work that the idea of tradition can do in understanding British political science. An interpretive approach inspires criticisms of many other approaches to political science for effacing the contingency of social life. For example, political scientists talk of the path-dependence of institutions or inexorable social developments such as class conflict. In Part I, we show the contingency of those parts of political life that other political scientists represent as natural, notably political science itself, the Westminster Model and governance. We probe for unquestioned assumptions and debates between traditions. In so doing we create the space for an interpretive approach and decentred studies of governance.

In Chapter 3, we denaturalize the dominant tradition in British political science. The dominant tradition in British political science has been bewitched by modernist empiricism and the aura of professionalism. We show there are several other traditions in British political science: for example, Idealism and Socialism. Each is alive and vital. However, the dominant tradition's narrative about the professionalization of British political science seeks to write out other traditions from the history of the discipline. This goal is facilitated both by state policies and funding and by mainstream political scientists' pursuit of state recognition and approval.

In the first section of the chapter we contrast the modernist-empiricist account of the development of British political science with its historicist alternative before documenting the rival traditions. We describe the Idealist and Socialist traditions, identifying some – but by no means all – of the variety in each tradition. For socialism we distinguish between the post-Marxists with their stress on the linguistic turn and the more conventional socialists with their emphasis on political economy. The final section of the chapter focuses on the question, how did we get here? It argues each tradition in its own way changed in response to the dilemmas posed by both changing intellectual agendas (for example, behaviouralism, Thatcherism) and changing state agendas (for example, 'the preference for relevance').

Chapter 4 critically examines the Westminster model, showing how local traditions changed these ideas when they were transplanted to the dominions and colonies. Australia provides a sharp illustration of this transmutation. We begin by identifying two uses of the phrase 'Westminster model': as historical description and as normative guide to constitutional design. We argue that each has manifold defects. So, we look at the Westminster model as an Australian governmental tradition. We argue that present-day Australian government is the heir to several traditions and each tradition constructs the structure of government differently. There are at least four traditions – the colonial heritage, responsible government, federalism and neo-liberalism. The meaning of Westminster depends on the spectacles, or tradition, through which it is constructed and observed. None are dead traditions. Australia is not now and has never been a Westminster system. Indeed, there is no single agreed definition of a Westminster system that it could be measured against. Westminster is a constructed notion. It does not have an essential core. It is contestable in all its features, the meaning of which varies from tradition to tradition. We conclude the Westminster model is alive and well among the Australian political elite because it provides a legitimating myth justifying the Commonwealth's search to centralize political power.

In Chapter 5, we turn our critical gaze to the idea of governance. We dispute there is a given, natural account of governance. There is no essentialist notion of governance, but at least four conceptions, each rooted in a distinctive tradition. The chapter describes the relevant traditions – Tory, Liberal, Whig and Socialist – and the different notions of governance associated with each tradition: intermediate institutions, marketizing public services, reinventing the constitution, and trust and negotiation. We explain these distinct conceptions of governance as responses to the dilemmas of inflation and state overload. We relate governance to the actions of many individuals; describe the conflicting but overlapping stories that inform the actions of these individuals; and use the concept of tradition to explain why these actors construct their worlds, and so governance, as they do. Individuals inherit traditions and they enact and remake these traditions in their everyday lives. We argue governing structures can only be understood through the beliefs and actions of individuals located in traditions. Historical analysis is the way to uncover the traditions that shape these stories. Political ethnography enables us to tell the stories of different individuals.

In Part II, we turn to our ethnographic fieldwork and practices of governance. In Chapter 1 we argued that people in the same situation can hold different beliefs, so an interpretive approach must explore the ways in which social practices are created, sustained and transformed. Ethnography reconstructs the meanings of social actors by recovering other people's stories from practices, actions, texts, interviews and speeches. It encompasses many ways of collecting qualitative data about beliefs and practices – for example, diary analysis, shadowing, elite interviewing, participant accounts. Part II provides such studies of governance in the Blair presidency, a government department, the NHS and the police.

In Chapter 6, we turn our attention to the argument about the 'Blair presidency'. We find the analogy unhelpful. After reviewing the relevant academic literature, we turn to prime ministerial and ministerial diaries and memoirs and interviews with senior ministers and civil servants. We ask the deceptively simple question, how do they understand the relationship between prime minister, ministers and their departments? There is an obvious answer. 'It depends.' There is no one phrase, no one theory, which covers all the circumstances. The prime minister wins, loses and draws as one might expect given the contingent and volatile nature of high politics. The language civil servants and ministers most often deploy to describe these varied outcomes is the classical one of the British constitution as the Westminster model. Time after time people use the language of cabinet governmental and ministerial accountability to describe what happened and why.

In Chapter 7, we look at everyday life in a government department. We seek to answer two questions. What do we know about the work of ministers and permanent secretaries? How do we know what we know about these topics? To do so, we survey briefly the existing literature on ministers and top civil servants, we describe the scope and methods of one ethnographic study, and we report some early findings based on that study.

In Chapter 8, we focus on the National Health Service (NHS). We examine how the beliefs of key decision-makers in the NHS evolved since the foundation of the NHS. We narrate a historical story that emphasizes the diverse, changing traditions of practitioners – doctors, managers and politicians. In doing so, we draw mainly on official documents, the written accounts of participants and interviews. We also focus on a key dilemma: the perceived conflict between beliefs of doctors about medical autonomy and the beliefs of managers and politicians about responsible financial or corporate management. The perceived conflict between these beliefs has strongly influenced institutional formation and change throughout the history of the NHS.

In Chapter 9, we turn our attention to the reform of the police. Why is reform continuous? The short answer is because each round of reforms is plagued with unintended consequences. So, why don't the reforms work?

Most accounts of police reform stress the conservatism of 'police culture'. We do not. Serving police officers as well as academics see the reforms of the past twenty years as a shift from command and control bureaucracy through markets to networks. We argue that these ideas are seen as incompatible and the perceived conflict between them simply makes it too easy for dynamic conservatism to win out. We do not argue for or against bureaucracy, contracts or networks. Our point is that the police believe the structures mix like oil and water, posing dilemmas for them and so producing unintended consequences. We look behind the scepticism of managers and sworn officers to show that the conflicts between the ideas that distinguish each governing structure create dilemmas that render all reforms contingent, and sometimes nugatory.

Finally, in Chapter 10, we explore the family resemblances among our governance stories. Governance arises from the bottom-up. It is a product of diverse practices that are themselves composed of multiple individuals acting amidst conflicting webs of beliefs rooted in overlapping traditions. In this chapter, we step back from our stories and ask, what do they tell us about British governance in general? The answer is that they challenge the craving for generality so characteristic of many accounts of governance, enact an approach to the study of governance, and provide lessons for reforming governance. Governance cannot be reduced to a list of general features, let alone essential properties, which characterize it in each and every instance. Governance cannot be explained by the social logic of (say) functional differentiation in advanced industrial societies. Instead, our stories provide snap-shots of different aspects of governance. We identify the family resemblances, none of which are always present, and explain them as the product of contingent actions rooted in competing traditions.

All too often critics dismiss an interpretive approach as fuzzy, subjective and impressionistic. They want to defend a political science that relies on hard data, experimental testing and methodological rigour. In this book, we reject the false idols of hard data and methodological rigour as a bewitching effect of positivist philosophy. We choose philosophical rigour and a defence of objective knowledge grounded in comparing rival stories. We give examples of the data, methods and epistemology associated with such an approach. Whatever else our approach may be, it is not conventional. Our portrait of British government is not one of prime ministerial power. Rather, it is a portrait of a story-telling administrative and political elite, who hold beliefs and engage in practices rooted in the Westminster model, and who use rituals to domesticate crises. We hope it is an edifying account of British government; we hope it is accurate, comprehensive, coherent and open. With due apologies to *Star Trek* and Mr Spock, 'it is political science, but not as we know it'.

2 Interpretation and its others

Interpretation is ubiquitous. Even accounts of the physical world are, in a sense, interpretations. However, if accounts of the physical world are interpretations, accounts of actions and practices are interpretations of interpretations. Beliefs, languages and discourses are ways of making sense of the world; they are interpretations. So, when we analyse actions or practices as embodiments of beliefs, languages or discourses, we interpret interpretations. An interpretive approach rests, first, on a philosophical analysis of meaning in action. An analysis of the constitutive relation of meanings to actions implies that we can grasp actions properly only by looking at the meanings or beliefs embodied in them. It prompts us to offer interpretations of interpretations. An interpretive approach rests, second, on a philosophical analysis of the holistic nature of meanings. An analysis of meanings as holistic rather than tied to individual referents implies we can grasp meanings only as part of wider webs of beliefs.

There are many misconceptions about interpretive approaches. Sometimes these misconceptions wrongly identify an interpretive approach with a particular object of inquiry rather than a philosophical analysis of meaning in action. They set up dichotomies between those objects allegedly studied by proponents of an interpretive approach and those studied by other political scientists. They contrast interpretation with several spurious others. So, allegedly, interpretation focuses on meanings not practices, on beliefs not rhetoric, on discourse not power. Alternatively, these misconceptions wrongly equate an interpretive approach with a particular mode of inquiry rather than a philosophical analysis of meaning in action. They set up dichotomies between the modes of inquiry of an interpretive approach and those of other political scientists. Interpretation is, in these accounts, about understanding not explanation, elucidation not critique, or empathy not rigour. A final misconception claims that an interpretive approach is relativist. Of course present-day proponents of an interpretive approach often draw explicitly on postfoundationalism. Nonetheless, to hurl a charge of relativism at them is simply to ignore the attempts made to spell out postfoundational epistemologies that are not relativist in a pernicious sense. In this chapter, we challenge these misconceptions about an interpretive approach.[1]

Interpretation and common sense

We begin by asking if an interpretive approach is mere common sense. All political scientists inevitably draw on philosophical theories and an interpretive approach is one such theory. Any study of anything, whether governance in Britain or family life in the Amazon, embodies philosophical theories about the nature of the objects being studied, the forms of explanation appropriate to these objects and the ways we might justify knowledge of them. An interpretive approach consists of philosophical theories about meaning in action and situated agency. So, an interpretive approach derives from philosophical analyses of the concepts of meaning and agency.

In a sense, therefore, interpretivism is indeed merely common sense. An interpretive approach derives from a philosophical analysis of the concepts that make up our everyday way of discussing human action. It uses this analysis as part of the 'battle against the bewitchment of our intelligence by means of language' (Wittgenstein 1972a: para. 109). It returns us to our everyday concepts as a challenge to positivist attempts to discuss actions as if they were akin to the physical phenomena studied by natural scientists. It also draws on common sense – our everyday concepts – to remind us of what is lost when we use formal, deductive models. So, political scientists who have never been bewitched by such alternative languages will consider an interpretive approach a fairly close fit to a practice developed using our everyday concepts. However, political scientists who adopt a 'scientific' language will oppose an interpretive approach. They will described it critically as a species of common sense and supplant it with an allegedly superior scientific language. An interpretive approach returns us to our everyday concepts and rejects claims there is a superior scientific language.

An interpretive approach derives from analyses of everyday concepts. Such analyses give concepts a greater clarity, coherence and rigour than they otherwise might possess. This analysis might worry political scientists indebted to the Whiggish distrust of abstract principles. Whiggism occupies a prominent place in the British study of politics (see Chapter 3). Its exponents would deride the explicit analyses that inform an interpretive approach as vapid abstractions rather than intimations of lived practice. This criticism is misplaced. Whenever somebody writes an account of British governance, they necessarily rely on a set of background theories, admittedly sometimes badly defined or even confused ones. As such, intellectual honesty surely commits them to defending their theories against incompatible alternatives. Even when an approach to political science is implicit, it has a normative force. It claims, even if only by implication, that it is appropriate to the study of the relevant object, be it parliament or social movements, and better than other, incompatible approaches. Although an interpretive approach contains beliefs that are incompatible with some alternatives, most proponents of an interpretive approach hold epistemologies that explicitly allow for, and even encourage, research programmes other than their own. They allow for diversity and disagreement, and are not committed to the given truth of the one agenda.

Interpretation and practices

One common misconception about an interpretive approach is that it concerns only beliefs or discourses, not actions or practices. This misconception implies that an interpretive approach might be a reasonable way of recovering the froth of political ideas, but it does not help us to understand the real world lurking underneath such froth. This misconception only makes sense, however, if we draw a false dichotomy between beliefs and actions. If beliefs and actions were unrelated to one another, it might make sense to suggest that we could recover one without exploring the other. In contrast, an interpretive approach rests on the claim that beliefs are constitutive of actions. It implies that we can properly understand actions only by recovering the beliefs that animate them. Far from neglecting practices, proponents of an interpretive approach explore meanings or beliefs to get a better grasp on the practices that embody them. For example, in Chapter 8 we show that the actions of doctors in the National Health Service (NHS) cannot be grasped without looking at the beliefs of the medical model of health. Its central beliefs see physiological factors ('genes and germs'), not psychosocial factors, as the main causes of illness. So, medical practices favour treating and curing individuals and downplay prevention and rehabilitation. Only a spurious attempt to define actions apart from beliefs or meanings could sustain the misconception that an interpretive approach neglects actions and practices.

Critics might object that concepts such as belief, tradition and dilemma are too abstract. They ignore the way meanings are always embedded in habits and social interactions. But we use the notion of tradition to capture the embedded nature of individuals and their beliefs. What is more, although tradition refers mainly to beliefs, we explicitly argue that beliefs need not be conscious or rational. An interpretive approach allows that beliefs and traditions do not exist as disembodied entities but become concrete in actions and practices. Its exponents suggest we can ascribe beliefs to people, including perhaps ourselves, only through an interpretation of actions, including, of course, speech-acts.

Although an interpretive approach explores practices by unpacking the relevant beliefs, it does perhaps conceive of practices in a different way from other political scientists. The difference appears in the way other political scientists often prefer to see practices as institutions (March and Olsen 1989). One difference arises over what it means to say practices, institutions or traditions are concrete social realities. Our definition of tradition makes it clear, for example, that we do not conceive of particular traditions or practices as natural or discrete chunks of social reality. Traditions do not have clear boundaries by which we might make them discrete entities. They do not possess natural or given limits by which we might separate them out from the general flux of human life. For example, the boundaries of a political party are not fixed by those attending weekly committee meetings. They also might cover those who attend once a year for the annual general meeting, those who wander in to the MP's surgery for help, those who go to fund-raising events organized by the party or those who participate in direct action over a political grievance. For a researcher using an interpretive approach, the limits of a practice are a pragmatic decision justified by the purposes of the inquiry. Practices are concrete social realities, but they are not natural kinds. So, it is political scientists as observers who separate particular practices, and they do so to suit their research purposes.

Perhaps proponents of an interpretive approach also differ from other political scientists in their analysis of the conventions, shared understandings or interactions that appear in practices. Although practices display conventions, this does not mean conventions constitute practices. No doubt many participants often seek to conform to the conventions of a practice. Even so, first, they do not always do so and, second, even when they do, they still might misunderstand the conventions. So, conventions cannot really be constitutive of practices. The situated agency of the participants constitutes practices and such agency is creative, not rule governed. Individuals are situated agents who necessarily interpret the conventions that characterize the practices in which they are engaged, and who can vary the conventions. This appeal to situated agency does not imply that all people are heroic individuals who have a great impact on the historical direction of a practice. It implies only that they have the capacity to modify their inheritance and so act in novel ways. When they do, they are unlikely significantly to alter a practice unless others also adjust. Even then, the changes in the practice are unlikely to correspond to any they might have intended. Practices rarely, if ever, depend directly on the actions of any given individual. They do consist of nothing but the changing actions and interactions of various individuals.

Interpretation and structures

For many political scientists, this analysis of practices contrasts sharply with approaches that rely on concepts of social structure. At issue here is how political scientists should think about the nature of social contexts and their impact upon the beliefs and actions of individuals. We have stressed situated agency, arguing that traditions only influence but do not define, or even limit, the beliefs individuals come to adopt and so the actions individuals attempt to perform. We have also emphasized that traditions are not natural kinds, arguing that observers construct them out of an undifferentiated context in order to explain that which interests them. Critical realists and others have suggested these emphases neglect the influence and the constraining effect that cultural schemes or structures exercise upon individuals (see McAnulla 2004; Reckwitz 2002).

An interpretive approach can allow for both the influence and the constraining effects of social contexts. It just refuses to reify practices or traditions by treating them as structures or cultural schemes. To begin, although we defend the capacity of the individual for situated agency, we reject the idea of the autonomous individual. People only ever can come to hold beliefs or perform actions against the background of a tradition that influences them. Appeals to traditions go a long way to explaining why individuals hold the beliefs they do and act in the way they do. Although we argue tradition does not constrain beliefs, we recognize that practices have a limiting effect on actions. Individuals are situated agents – they possess a creative ability to adopt beliefs or attempt actions for reasons of their own. However, their actions do not always necessarily succeed. The consequences of their actions depend on how others act. Practices thus constrain the actions people can successfully take.

An interpretive approach allows, therefore, that traditions influence people, and practices constrain the actions people can perform successfully. Where it might differ from critical realism is in the logical content it attributes to such concepts. So, we prefer the terms 'tradition' and 'practice' to 'cultural scheme' and 'structure' precisely because we are worried that the latter two appear to neglect situated agency and to reify social contexts. Of course, there are differences among critical realists, so we are unsure how much conflict there is with an interpretive approach.[2] To the extent that they accept structures are emergent properties of individual actions, any disagreement is minimal.

The term 'tradition' captures our analysis of individuals who inherit a set of beliefs that constitutes the background to their later reasoning and so inevitably influences them even though they might transform it over time through their local reasoning. The term 'cultural scheme' can appear, in contrast, to suggest a disembodied structure of concepts or ideas that sets clear limits to the beliefs and agency of individuals by fixing the ways they experience the world. Similarly, the term 'practice' captures our analysis of how actions are constrained by social contexts. Practices constrain the actions people perform if they enter into the subjective reasoning of the actors. A civil servant's belief that he or she will be fired for whistle-blowing might act as a reason for his or her keeping silent. Practices also constrain the effectiveness of actions because they consist of the actions of others. Politicians might try to lower inflation only to find the actions of business organizations and citizens prevent them. While an interpretive approach sees practices as constraints, it does so in ways that reduce practices to the contingent actions of other individuals. In contrast, the term 'structure' invokes a disembodied object that constrains people in its own right, rather as the Pacific Ocean stops us driving back and forth between Berkeley and Canberra.

Interpretation and explanation

Another related misconception is that interpretive approaches aim only to understand actions and practices rather than to explain them. The dichotomy between understanding and explanation again makes sense only if we falsely separate actions from beliefs. An interpretive approach rests on a philosophical analysis of actions as meaningful because they are constituted by beliefs. This analysis implies that other political scientists go awry when they attempt to explain actions in ways that do not appeal to beliefs. For an interpretive approach, any adequate explanation of actions or practices must refer to the beliefs that animate them. To understand the relevant beliefs is to explain the action or practice. What is more, when proponents of an interpretive approach suggest that meanings or beliefs are inherently holistic, they suggest we can explain meanings or beliefs by locating them as part of the web of those other meanings or beliefs that give them their character. To locate beliefs in webs of beliefs, and to locate webs of beliefs against the background of traditions and dilemmas, is to explain those beliefs and the actions and practices they inspire.

An interpretive approach explains actions and practices by beliefs, and it explains beliefs by traditions and dilemmas. This version of explanation differs from that often found among political scientists. The philosophical analysis of meaning in action that informs an interpretive approach suggests the human sciences rely on a distinctive form of explanation, which we describe as narrative (Bevir 1999: 304–6). When we explain actions by reference to beliefs and desires, we rely on a concept of choice and on criteria of reasonableness that have no place in natural science. So, the natural and human sciences use different concepts of causation. This difference does not mean the human sciences have no interest in causal analysis. To the contrary, the human sciences explain actions and practices in narratives that point to the beliefs and desires that cause the actions. Typologies, correlations and models can do explanatory work in the human sciences only if they are unpacked as such narratives.

Narratives are the way we explain actions and practices. They play a dual role in interpretive studies. First, when we offer an interpretation of governance, we offer a narrative. Second, the actors in our narrative have their own interpretations of their actions and practices, and these accounts also include narrative explanations. We deliberately use narrative to describe both what we offer and what we study. To say that we offer narratives of narratives restates the philosophical analysis of political science as interpretations of interpretations.

Narratives distinguish an interpretive approach from those approaches that introduce meanings or beliefs as 'ideational variables' alongside other variables (as in, for example, Gerring 1999; Wendt 1999). We would argue that other variables only do explanatory work if they are unpacked as beliefs. Equally, we would argue that it is a mistake to ask how we should specify the precise links between independent variables. Critics might worry that actions and beliefs, or alternatively beliefs and traditions, cannot be distinguished properly from one another. They might complain that these objects are not independent of each other as they should be in explanations. They might conclude that an interpretive approach only offers redescriptions. However, an interpretive approach rests on a philosophical analysis of meaning in action that invalidates the methodological rigour – the specification of independent variables – that animates their criticism. This philosophical analysis implies that actions are intentional, which means they are necessarily performed for reasons or beliefs. Similarly, this philosophical analysis implies that people are not autonomous, so they necessarily reach beliefs against the background of tradition. The manner in which they do so can and does vary, but they always so inherit beliefs. These philosophical arguments provide the causal mechanisms at work in our explanations. They show that actions and beliefs, and beliefs and traditions, are entwined. Thus, when political scientists try to specify them independently of one another, they are misled by a spurious concept of scientific rigour into adopting a form of explanation that is inappropriate for political science.

Critics might ask what criteria we have for identifying traditions and dilemmas if we do not operationalize them as independent variables. It is important to avoid thinking about traditions as if they are a series of discrete and identifiable entities. To avoid such essentialist accounts, it is best to think of an undifferentiated social context, which researchers slice up to explain whatever set of beliefs or actions happens to interest them. Traditions are artefacts, always interpreted by the observer. Political scientists select a topic, and they ask which are the relevant traditions for explaining the objects thus covered. For example, in Chapter 4, we examine how the meaning of the Westminster model changes depending on whether the political and administrative elite is wearing the spectacles of either the responsible government or the federal tradition. We focus on these traditions because our research question focuses on the changing beliefs of that elite. We adopt a top-down view. Were we to adopt a bottom-up view of constitutional change, then these traditions would tell us little about, say, the beliefs of indigenous Australians on the role of the constitution in sustaining political exclusion and oppression. Of course, any analysis will require that political scientists highlight some traditions more than others. There are always many ways of slicing the undifferentiated social background. Equally, the justification for the way one constructs a tradition lies in the claim that this way best explains what interests one.

Interpretation and method

Yet another misconception equates an interpretive approach exclusively with certain techniques of data generation (and on the misleading distinction between 'qualitative' and 'quantitative' methods, see Schwartz-Shea and Yanow 2002). An interpretive approach is wrongly limited to textual readings and small-scale observations. It is wrongly said to exclude survey research and quantitative studies. In fact, an approach that offers interpretations of interpretations does not necessarily favour particular methods. To the contrary, proponents of an interpretive approach might construct their interpretations using data generated by various techniques. They might draw on participant observation, interviews, questionnaires, mass surveys, statistical analysis and formal models as well as reading memoirs, newspapers, and official and unofficial documents. An interpretive approach rests on a philosophical analysis. This analysis does not prescribe a particular methodological toolkit for generating data. Instead, it prescribes a particular way of treating data of any type. An interpretive approach suggests that political scientists should treat data in ways consistent with the philosophical analysis of the task of interpreting interpretations. Proponents of an interpretive approach argue political scientists should treat data as evidence of the meanings or beliefs embedded in actions. Political scientists should not try to bypass meanings or beliefs by reducing them to given principles of rationality, fixed norms or social categories.

Although proponents of an interpretive approach are comfortable with a wide range of sources of data, they do argue that we should treat such data in a different way from that favoured by many political scientists. The difference can be illustrated by the example of political participation. An interpretive approach implies that studies of changes in participation rates make sense when we agree on the meaning of participation. It could be limited to electoral turnout and party membership or it could encompass the many forms of civic engagement, including direct involvement in street-level policymaking (Bang and Sørensen 1999). Participation occurs in the context of a web of meanings drawn from many sources, including the law, party ideology and beliefs about citizenship. If political scientists operationalize participation, specify its content and treat it as a variable, they risk obscuring these several meanings, which vary dramatically across time and place. In effect, they risk imposing their definition of participation on those they study in a way that would fail to do justice to the several, contesting beliefs (see, for example, Seyd 2005). We do not deny that surveys and statistical studies of participation rates produce useful data. We insist only that such data be treated as evidence of people's beliefs, rather than as a variable in objectified models, norms or categories.

The interpretive view of how we should treat data does, of course, have some implications for methods of data collection. It leads, in particular, to a greater emphasis upon qualitative methods than is usual among political scientists (cf. Yanow 1999). Suppose the data provided by comparing and codifying the formal constitutional documents of Westminster systems leads us to attribute a set of beliefs to their political leaders. Because such data encourages us to generalize from common patterns to individual circumstances, it elides differences between people, lumping together people who act in broadly similar ways for different reasons. Hence an interpretive approach favours decentred analysis or detailed studies of the beliefs of the relevant people by means of textual analysis, participant observation and in-depth interviews. Much present-day political science ignores or even denigrates such methods, preferring abstract models, typologies and correlations. In contrast, an interpretive approach does not require an exclusive use of any one type of data or method. However, it does redress the balance in favour of the qualitative analysis more often associated with anthropology and history than with political science.

Interpretation and rhetoric

The case for anthropological and historical studies should not be confused with the claim that political scientists must accept actors' own accounts of their beliefs, let alone the claim that actors' beliefs are always conscious and reasoned. Obviously people's statements about what they believe offer significant evidence about what they believe. However, people can be deliberately misleading. Obviously too, people do act on political commitments they have agonized over. However, people also act on habitual, unreflective beliefs about the nature of the world and about what is right in a given context. So, we might explain an action using beliefs other than the stated beliefs of the actors.

Another misconception is, therefore, that interpretive approaches cannot deal adequately with rhetoric (see Dowding 2004). We can explore uses of rhetoric using forms of explanation based on the concepts of belief, tradition and dilemma. When people use a rhetorical pattern, they do so because they believe it will help secure a desired response to their ideas. So, a political scientist can explain people's rhetoric by identifying their relevant beliefs and preferences about different patterns of rhetoric, their appropriateness and their probable effectiveness. To do so, the political scientist locates people's beliefs about rhetoric, whether conscious, preconscious or unconscious, in their wider webs of beliefs before then relating these wider webs of beliefs to appropriate traditions and dilemmas. For example, as we show in Chapter 7, top civil servants invoke the notion of ministerial responsibility, believing their primary duty is to the minister. In classic Weberian fashion, the doctrine of ministerial responsibility means that civil servants follow orders that politicians give them. Such beliefs sustain the anonymity and political impartiality of civil servants and are legitimated by the Whig tradition and the Westminster model.

Critics might worry that if we are to invoke beliefs other than those stated by the actors, we need criteria for identifying beliefs (see Brown 2002). They worry that we guess at people's beliefs rather than finding hard evidence of them. Proponents of an interpretive approach might reply that all experiences, including our experiences of others' beliefs, are guesses in that they are theory-laden. People always construct the content of their experiences through the prior theories they bring to bear on them. Political scientists are not mere recorders of a given external world. All too often, this insistence on the constructed nature of experience gets assimilated to a postmodern denial of any object outside the 'text'. We would deny we are trapped in texts. Rather, we use philosophical reasoning to defend a commitment to the existence of general classes of objects, including beliefs. We then use inference to the best explanation to defend a commitment to the existence of a particular case of such objects.

Whenever we act, we commit ourselves to certain concepts. For example, if we use a pen to fill in our tax form, take it to the tax office and pay by cheque, we commit ourselves to beliefs about the existence of certain objects, such as forms and money. We also commit ourselves to beliefs about the nature of these objects – for example, that paying tax avoids interest and fines for late or non-payment, and that others accept authorized cheques as discharging our liabilities. Finally, we often commit ourselves to beliefs about ourselves – for example, that we can act so as to pay, or not to pay, taxes. Philosophy can go to work on the concepts we thus commit ourselves to in our actions. It can analyse the implications of these concepts to provide an account of the classes of objects with which we populate the world and the forms of reasoning appropriate to such objects. For example, our acceptance of tax forms and use of pens suggests we populate the world with physical objects; our convictions about the utility of money suggest we populate the world with objects that acquire significance through intersubjective beliefs; and our convictions about our ability to act for reasons of our own suggests we populate the world with beliefs.

While philosophical reflection on the ideas embedded in our actions provides us with good reasons for proposing the existence of beliefs, actions and practices, it cannot justify assuming particular beliefs, actions or practices in any particular case. Nonetheless, we can justify ascribing particular beliefs to people by claiming that doing so best explains facts on which we agree. Although political scientists do not have direct access to people's beliefs, they can justify ascribing beliefs to people by saying that doing so best explains the evidence. For example, philosophical reasoning gives us grounds for assuming British politicians and civil servants hold beliefs. This assumption raises the question of what are these beliefs. Political scientists can answer this question by, for example, ascribing beliefs about effective service delivery to them. We can justify this reasoning by showing that civil servants spend more time managing services than advising on policy. The ascribed beliefs make sense of the agreed facts about their workload. In short, we infer from the best explanation that we are justified in attributing particular beliefs to political actors.

Interpretation and power

A related misconception appears in debates among those who advocate an interpretive approach. Poststructuralists sometimes imply that other interpretive approaches are insensitive to the ways in which relations of power constitute individuals including their beliefs. However, the concept of tradition does much the same work here as does the poststructuralist one of power. Tradition asserts that individuals, far from being autonomous, always come into being in a social context, which influences the beliefs they come to hold. People inherit concepts, values and practices from society. They can reflect on this inheritance and even modify it, but they can do so only in the context of the beliefs they have already inherited. So, our concept of tradition does much the same work as that of 'power' if the latter is conceived as the influence society inevitably exerts on individuals. We prefer the concept of tradition for two reasons. First, if we use the term 'power' here, we deprive it of explanatory and critical force. If power is everywhere, to point to its presence in any given case fails to provide any critical or explanatory leverage. Second, the notion of tradition emphasizes our commitment to situated agency. Appeals to power as constitutive of subjectivity appear to us to deny the agency of the subject. Poststructuralists are in danger of opposing agency as well as autonomy. It is a mistake to conceive of traditions or discourses as reified quasi-structures that somehow determine the beliefs people can come to hold.

The concept of tradition can do critical work akin to that of a poststructuralist concept of power. We do not believe that tradition is ever uniform. Rather, we try to disaggregate it into conflicting strands. Nor do we think it is ever natural. Rather, we expose unquestioned assumptions and inconsistencies to show how it arises as a contingent product of struggles over different ways of conceiving of, and responding to, constructed dilemmas. We also do not believe that political conflicts and contests are confined to government. Rather, we use the word governance to stress that such contests take place throughout society. We explore the civil service, hospitals and police. Others might prefer to explore the media, accounting and schools. Because of our notion of tradition, we often intend our narratives to be critiques. Our narratives often unmask the partiality of a political interpretation by showing how it arose against the background of a particular tradition. And our narratives also reveal the contingency of traditions by showing them to be just one among several historical possibilities. For example, whereas Liberals define governance as the inherent rationality of market reforms, and Whigs think it evolved out of existing practices, and socialists define it as joining-up, we narrate each of these varied perspectives as the contingent product of a particular tradition. We seek to reveal the contingency and contestability of narratives that present themselves as natural and fixed.

Interpretation and policy

If critiques are to have purchase, they need to be accompanied by an alternative, by a set of beliefs or actions arguably better than those being criticized. For many, effective critique presupposes the ability to suggest alternative public policies. Another misconception about an interpretive approach is that it is incapable of generating such policy-relevant knowledge. Critics suggest policy-relevant knowledge comes from prediction based on models and correlations between independent variables. The issue of policy advice dramatically reveals a tension between the positivist notion of scientific expertise and the wish to develop stories that are transferable and useful.

Before addressing this issue directly, we need to confront the notion that scientific expertise and prediction are the correct way of thinking about the advice political scientists might offer to practitioners. We reject the possibility of prediction – defined in contrast to the looser idea of informed conjecture – because it is incompatible with the narrative form of explanation. Change is a product of the ways in which people modify inherited traditions and practices, and the ways in which they do so are open-ended and so not amenable to prediction.

Because traditions and practices are not fixed, we cannot know in advance how people will develop their beliefs and actions in response to a dilemma. Therefore, political scientists cannot predict how people will respond to a dilemma. Whatever limits they build into their predictions, people could arrive at new beliefs and actions outside those limits. Political scientists cannot make predictions. All they can offer are informed conjectures that seek to explain practices and actions by pointing to the conditional connections between actions, beliefs, traditions and dilemmas. Their conjectures are stories, understood as provisional narratives about possible futures.

At this point we can directly address the issue of how an interpretive approach can contribute to policy advice. Most policy-oriented work on governance seeks to improve the ability of the state to manage the markets, bureaucracies and networks that have flourished since the 1980s (see Chapter 5). This work treats hierarchies, markets and networks as fixed structures that governments can manipulate if they use the right tools. An interpretive approach undercuts this idea of a set of tools that we can use to manage governance. Because governance is constructed differently, contingently and continuously, we cannot have tool kits with which to manage it. Hence an interpretive approach encourages us to foreswear management techniques and strategies but, and the point is crucial, to replace such tools with learning by telling stories and listening to them (see Chapter 10). While statistics, models and claims to expertise can have a place in such stories, we should not become too preoccupied with them. Instead, we should recognize that they too are narratives about how people have acted or will react given their beliefs and desires. No matter what rigour or expertise we bring to bear, all we can do is tell a story and judge what the future might bring.

Interpretation and truth

Arguably the most prevalent misconception about an interpretive approach is that it is inherently relativist. This misconception is puzzling because it ignores the numerous efforts of proponents of an interpretive approach to state their epistemological position (Bevir 1999: 78–126). Nonetheless, because it remains so prevalent, we want to devote some space to outlining our preferred epistemology and so dispelling the misconception.

All political scientists confront epistemological issues about how to evaluate narratives, models, correlations and typologies. An interpretive approach can address these issues by drawing on its holistic analysis of meaning. Holism undermines the idea that we can effectively vindicate or refute isolated claims to knowledge. Other political scientists, especially those still attracted to positivism, often imply that we can justify claims to truth using logics of vindication or refutation.[3] Logics of vindication would tell us how to determine whether a statement is true. Logics of refutation would tell us how to determine whether a statement is false. Verificationists argue that we can decode all reasonable theories into a series of observational statements, and we can determine if these are true because they refer to pure perceptions. They conclude that a theory is true if it consists of observational statements that are true. Or, it is more or less probably true according to the nature and number of observational statements that are in accord with it.

Falsificationists deny that positive observations can prove a theory to be true no matter how many we obtain. They defend an ideal of refutation, arguing that the objective status of theories derives from our ability to make observations that show other statements to be false. We need not worry much about differences between verificationists and falsificationists because both ground objectivity or truth in confrontations with basic facts. All logics of vindication and refutation believe that ultimately we can confront accounts of the world with basic facts in a test to prove them to be either true or false, or not-false or false. Their proponents defend the idea of basic facts by arguing that we have pure experiences of the external world. They disagree about whether the pure experiences that decide issues of truth are the particular experiences of individuals or the inter-subjective experiences of a community. But they almost always defend some sort of pure experience as the grounds of their logics of vindication or refutation.

Philosophical holism implies, in contrast, that we do not have pure experiences. The nature of a perception depends on the prior web of beliefs of the perceiver. A sensation becomes the object of a perception or an experience only when an intelligence identifies it as a particular sensation both distinct from, and in relation to, other sensations. People become aware of a sensation only if they attend to it, and if they attend to it, they identify it in the context of their current beliefs. Perceptions always incorporate prior categories. Even everyday experiences incorporate a wide range of realist assumptions, including: objects exist independently of our perceiving them, objects persist over time, other people can perceive them and they sometimes act causally upon one another. To insist on the role of prior categories in perception is not to argue that categories determine experiences. It is to argue only that categories influence how people experience sensations. People use prior categories to make sense of the sensations associated with objects. Experiences cannot be pure since they always embody prior categories. Moreover, because experience entails prior categories, evaluation cannot rely on logics of vindication or refutation. If an experience disproved a favourite statement, one could rescue the statement by insisting that the experience was based on a false theory.

Thus, holism leads many proponents of an interpretive approach to reject the idea of truth as absolute certainty. Because meanings are holistic, experiences always embody prior theories, so we cannot determine conclusively whether an individual statement is true or false since any such determination has to take for granted various theoretical assumptions embodied in our experiences. An interpretive approach adopts a holism that implies all knowledge could be mistaken. However, to reject the idea of absolute certainty is not necessarily to adopt a relativist position. As proponents of an interpretive approach, we repudiate relativism. We define objectivity as evaluation by comparing rival stories using reasonable criteria. Sometimes there might be no way of deciding between two or more interpretations, but this will not always be the case. Even when it is the case, we still will be able to decide between these two or more interpretations and many inferior ones.

Objectivity arises from our criticizing and comparing rival interpretations in terms of agreed facts. A fact is a piece of evidence that nearly everyone in the given community would accept as true. This definition of a fact follows from recognition of the role of theory in observation. Because theory enters into observation, we cannot describe a fact as a statement of how things are. Observation and description entail categorization. For example, when an opposition MP speaks to the prime minister in the chamber of the House of Commons, we categorize the event as question time. Such categorization also entails decisions about what other instances fall into that category. So, when any MP speaks to any minister in the chamber, this event resembles question time, but is rarely categorized as question time. Facts always entail prior categories, so they are not certain truths.

Narratives explain shared facts by postulating significant relationships, connections or similarities between them. A fact acquires a particular character as a result of its relationship to other facts. Narratives reveal the particular character of facts by uncovering their relationships to one another. Indeed, when narratives reveal the particular character of a fact, they help to define the content of that fact. In this sense, narratives do not just reveal the character of facts; they also create their character, and guide our decisions as to what counts as a fact. Because there are no pure observations, political scientists partly construct the character of a fact through the theories that they incorporate in their observations. Thus, we cannot say simply that such and such a narrative either does or does not fit the facts. Instead, we must compare bundles of narratives, or, if you prefer, theories, in terms of their success in relating various facts to one another by highlighting pertinent similarities and differences, continuities and disjunctions.

Objectivity arises from using agreed facts to compare and criticize rival narratives. Criticism plays a pivotal role in such an evaluation. The existence of criticism means no narrative can determine which facts it will encounter. Critics of a narrative can point to facts that its proponents have not considered. They can highlight what they take to be facts that contradict the narrative. In short, the narrative must meet the tests set by its critics. So, proponents of an interpretive approach defend objective knowledge as comparison between rival stories.

This notion of objective knowledge raises the question of what criteria decide between rival stories. We propose devising criteria from rules of thumb that treat objective behaviour as intellectual honesty in responding to criticism. The first rule is that objective behaviour requires taking criticism seriously. If people do not take criticism seriously, we will consider them biased. Nonetheless, as we have seen, they could respond to a fact or argument against their narrative by denying the fact or argument, or deploying a speculative theory to reconcile the fact or argument with their view. Thus, the second rule is that objective behaviour presupposes a preference for established standards of evidence and reason. It also assumes that challenges to these established standards rest on impersonal and consistent criteria of evidence and reason. This rule limits those occasions when people can reject a fact or argument that contradicts their narrative. The third rule is that objective behaviour implies a preference for positive speculative responses that generate exciting new stories, not ones that merely block-off criticism of existing stories. This rule limits the occasions on which people can have recourse to speculative theories to reconcile a narrative with seemingly contrary evidence. We should try to modify our narratives in ways that extend their range and vigour.

Our account of intellectual honesty gives rise to criteria for comparing stories. Because we should respect established standards of evidence and reason, we will prefer narratives that are accurate, comprehensive and consistent. Our standards of evidence require us to try to support our narratives by reference to as many clearly identified facts as we can. An accurate narrative fits the facts supporting it closely. A comprehensive narrative fits many facts with few exceptions. Similarly, our standards of reasoning require us to make our narratives intelligible and coherent. A consistent narrative holds together without going against principles of logic. Because we should favour positive speculative responses, we will prefer narratives that are progressive, fruitful and open. A progressive narrative is one characterized by positive speculative responses that introduce new ideas not previously connected with that interpretation. A fruitful narrative is one in which the new ideas contained in speculative responses characteristically receive support from the facts. Because fruitful progress derives largely from postulating speculative responses to criticism, the more a narrative cuts itself off from all possible criticism, the more it becomes a dead end, unable to sustain further progress. An open narrative is one that encourages and engages criticism.

Proponents of an interpretive approach can defend accounts of objective knowledge as a comparison of rival narratives. Positivist political scientists might reject such an epistemology as relativist because it gives us no reason to assume the narratives that we select as objective will correspond to truth. They might argue that, even if we agree on the facts and we have criteria for comparing narratives, we still cannot declare any narrative to be true. After all, facts might be widely accepted without being true. We would agree that our epistemology does not allow us to ascribe truth, understood as certainty, to objective knowledge. In our view, however, that is not a problem. It merely restates what should be a commonplace – knowledge is provisional. We would suggest that, although we cannot be certain of the truth of any particular statement, our epistemology allows us to have some confidence in the accuracy or truth of those narratives we select as objective. Here we would point out that our perceptions must be more or less reliable because human practices occur in natural and social environments. Our knowledge provides us with an understanding of the world, our understanding of the world guides our actions in the world and our actions in the world work out more or less as we expect. Because we must act in the world, the actions we perform successfully are limited by the nature of the world. Because our narratives and perceptions inform our actions, our narratives and perceptions too are constrained by the nature of the world. Thus, the successes we have in acting in the world – chairing a committee, voting in an election, giving a speech – all suggest that our perceptions are broadly reliable. Because we can rely on the broad content of our perceptions, we have good reason to assume the facts on which we agree are reliable, for facts are simply exemplary perceptions. Finally, because we have good reason to assume that accepted facts are broadly reliable, the best available narratives based on these facts are secure. In sum, we can relate objective narratives to truth because our ability to find our way around in the world vouches for the basic accuracy of our perceptions.

Our preferred epistemology is constructivist with a realist gesture. It overlaps with constructivism, emphasizing that political scientists, as observers, in part construct facts through their theories. It portrays knowledge as objective, but as an epistemic practice not a relation to the world. Our constructivism is clear from our analysis of facts as shared agreements, not pure perceptions, and in our stress on comparing stories rather than perception, as the basis of objective knowledge. Objective knowledge is entirely a function of a human practice. It consists of a suitable relation to shared and constructed facts, as opposed to a suitable fit to the world. However, is this constructed knowledge a reasonable fit with the world? The question misses the point. It asks for a certainty we cannot have. But another part of the answer is to make a realist gesture towards the nature of our being in the world. Our ability to act in the world suggests that our knowledge, beliefs and perceptions are not wildly random or wholly unreliable, even if they are also not infallible.

Conclusion

When critics contrast an interpretive approach with spurious others, they are often groping for a way of expressing their sense that an interpretive approach lacks rigour. They invoke the same basic dichotomy. They want to dismiss interpretation as fuzzy, subjective and impressionistic. They want to defend a political science that supposedly relies on hard data, experimental testing and methodological rigour. In this chapter, we have challenged this dichotomy in part by giving details of the data, methods and epistemology associated with an interpretive approach. More importantly, we have given reasons to doubt the false idols of hard data, experimental tests and rigorous methods.

Critics of interpretivism rarely avow positivism. Surely, though, their idols of hard data, experimental tests and methodological rigour lose all allure if one renounces the positivist faith in pure experience? If we cannot have pure experiences, all data are soft because they presuppose prior theories that are themselves contestable. If all data are soft, we cannot evaluate particular narratives or theories by means of experimental tests against such data. All knowledge arises, rather, from comparisons between rival theories or narratives that are based on at least partly constructed facts. As such, we also might challenge the idol of methodological rigour. Often methodological rigour is held up as a way of generating secure facts that others can replicate and accept. In our view, however, methods and the facts they construct should be evaluated together as parts of larger narratives or theories. We will accept methods as 'rigorous' – or to use a more apt term 'appropriate' – only if we adopt philosophical theories that imply the relevant methods are suitable for the objects to which they are applied. That is to say, judgements about rigour or appropriateness always depend on logically prior judgements about philosophical rigour or appropriateness. In our view, the idol of methodological rigour acts to obscure prior philosophical issues, pre-judging such issues in favour of positivism. An interpretive approach, in contrast, gives primary importance to philosophical rigour. It highlights the importance of ensuring that political science corresponds to the logical requirements of our concepts. It consequently rejects the stress on methodological rigour as a bewitching effect of a positivist philosophy.

Part I
Interpreting traditions

3 British political sciences

We have rejected verificationism and falsificationism. We have argued instead that objective knowledge arises from a comparison of rival narratives or webs of beliefs. This account of objective knowledge might appear unsatisfactory as a guide on how to deal with the high levels of incommensurability existing between different approaches to political science. If we disagree about the relative merits of narratives, we could look for a common platform – ways of reasoning, standards of evidence and agreed facts – which we could use to compare the narratives. However, different approaches to political science often instantiate rival forms of reasoning that inspire varied standards of evidence and even different concepts of a fact. The nature of objective knowledge is part of what is at issue between them. Does this mean we have no way to decide between different approaches to political science? We will argue it does not. Rather, the several narratives of the history of political science constitute an arena in which to evaluate different approaches to political science.

Approaches to political science seek to understand and explain human beliefs, actions and practices. The history of political science is a history of beliefs, actions and practices. So, any approach to political science presumably includes the claim, at least implicitly, that it might be applied successfully to the history of the discipline. That is to say, if interpretivism, institutionalism, rational choice or any other approach purports to offer a general analysis of human life, it should be able to show that it works with respect to the part of human life that is the history of political science. When we use an approach to political science to tell a history of political science, we use it to tell a narrative about the rise, development and character of rival approaches. Not only do alternative approaches to political science need to produce adequate histories of political science, they also have to engage with one another by telling a historical story about one another. Each approach will provide an account of the experience and fate of the others. The reasonableness of an approach will consist in its ability to provide a better account of the developments, problems and incoherence of other approaches than these others can provide of themselves.

In the next three chapters we deploy our interpretive approach to traditions of political science. We tell stories about modernist empiricism, the Westminster

Model and governance. These narratives act as critiques. Political scientists often present their preferred approaches or analyses as being based on given facts or neutral reason. Our narratives act as critiques in that they unmask such approaches and analyses, revealing their partiality and their contingency. They unmask their partiality by showing them to be just one among a field of possible approaches and analyses. They unmask their contingency by showing how they arose against the background of a particular inherited tradition. What is more, when our narratives unmask the partiality and contingency of various approaches and analyses within political science, they portray these approaches and analyses as mistaken about their own nature. Typically these approaches and analyses understand themselves as based on pure inquiries into given facts or reason. We show, to the contrary, that they arose as people developed and modified particular traditions in response to particular dilemmas. The next three chapters provide a series of critiques of prominent accounts of British politics.

The history of political science

In this chapter, we question the unquestioned and the arbitrary in present-day accounts of British political science. We suggest that positivism and its natural science aspirations exercised a bewitching effect that masked the several traditions, each with a distinctive version of the enterprise. British political science has a dominant self-image based on both its Whig inheritance and a narrative of professionalization. This narrative tells how a Whig heritage evolved into a more mature, largely autonomous, professional and suitably cautious discipline. Perhaps paradoxically, it also contrasts the restraint of the British discipline with the excessive scientism and professionalism of its American counterpart. It concludes with a portrait of a professional discipline producing modernist empiricist knowledge; that is, knowledge reached through atomization, comparison, classification and even quantification.

The British Academy's study of the British contribution to political science in the twentieth century (Hayward *et al.* 1999) illustrates this portrait. From beginning to end, the British Academy's view of British political science is restrained and, to a degree, in awe of the equivalent American enterprise. One editor of the volume even claims that when British and European colleagues are attuned to one another it is because they focus on the same American core – there is a transatlantic hegemony (Barry 1999: 461–2). This conclusion – in a volume that suggests Britain has no indigenous Marxist tradition, while ignoring present-day theories of the state, and that contains a mere three passing comments on postmodernism – is surprising and revealing by turns.[1]

The British Academy volume provides a naturalizing perspective. It implies that political science has a given empirical domain – politics – and a shared intellectual agenda – to make this domain the object of empirical study. It focuses on the establishment of an autonomous discipline, and tells of an initial optimism evolving into a more stolid professionalism. It highlights the emergence of professional norms and institutions. Instead of playing a revisionist role, it often reinforces received disciplinary identities. It celebrates established scholars and ideas, such as Sammy Finer in comparative politics or the English School in international relations. It gives scant attention to participants in other traditions. They may be institutionally in the discipline, but they are not of the discipline because they are not part of the memories that frame contemporary identities.

Jack Hayward (1991b) – an editor of the British Academy volume – provides perhaps the most influential mainstream account of the development of British political science.[2] He identifies three stages in the development of British political science since the formation of the Political Studies Association (PSA) in 1950. The first decade saw 'a retrospective Whig inclination to complacent description of traditions inherited from the past', perhaps even 'atheoretical empiricism'. Stage two, between 1961 and 1974, was an 'enthusiastic and optimistic phase of technocratic reformism' exemplified by the work of social scientists for government inquiries into the civil service and local government. Finally, since 1975, the discipline has been characterized by a 'sceptical professionalism', with leading political scientists commenting on, for example, the problems of overloaded government or the costs of adversary politics. For Hayward, British political science has remained insular despite, an eye-catching phrase, 'homoeopathic doses of American political science' (1991a: 104). He does not hesitate to prick American pretensions to a science of politics, commenting, in another striking aphorism, that political scientists have 'the capacity to offer some hindsight, a little insight, and almost no foresight'. He concludes that British political studies adapted 'in a piecemeal and incremental fashion' to the 'concerns of American political scientists but without their concomitant theoretical self-consciousness' (Hayward 1999: 31).

There is, therefore, an accepted 'story' of a British approach to politics that has its roots in the Whig tradition and that has made piecemeal adjustments to American theories, fashions and research methods.[3] An interpretive approach might prompt a historicist critique of the narrative of professionalization. It might make us more sensitive to various traditions of political science found in Britain, and to the contingency of their historical development. So, we argue, first, there are several traditions in British political science. These include the modernist empiricism, which often informs the narrative of professionalization, as well as idealist and socialist traditions. The narrative of professionalization seeks to write out the latter traditions from the history of the discipline. State policies and funding, coupled with mainstream political scientists' pursuit of state recognition and approval, facilitate this goal. In contrast, we denaturalize the narrative of professionalization by showing it is just one among many possible stories.

We argue, second, each tradition in British political science changed in response to the dilemmas posed by changing intellectual and state agendas, but there were great differences in their responses. The changes were contingent responses to particular dilemmas. The narrative of professionalization seeks to tame such contingency by suggesting a smooth process of development that can be explained by the internal dictates of a logic of professionalization. In contrast, we seek to denaturalize the narrative of professionalization by showing how it embodies just one possible response to various dilemmas.

Modernist empiricism

An interpretive approach encourages us to highlight several traditions of political science in Britain, many of which are ignored or marginalized by the dominant narrative of professionalization (see Table 3.1). As examples, we highlight idealism and socialism as well as the Whig and behavioural strands that have contributed so much to the dominant modernist empiricism. No survey of British political science that focused solely on modernist empiricism can pretend to be accurate or comprehensive. Nonetheless, we might begin by recounting the fortunes of a mainstream modernist empiricism as its Whiggish inheritance encountered behaviouralism and Thatcherism.

Sometimes commentators treat the Whig tradition as a hangover from the past. There are, however, several reasons for querying this treatment. The Whig tradition persists, in particular, because it constituted the tradition against the background of which British political scientists forged mainstream modernist empiricism (see Bevir 2005: chapter 1; Kavanagh 2006; Kenny

Table 3.1 Traditions in the study of British political science

Traditions	Idealism		Modernist-empiricist		Socialism	
Characteristics			Whig	Behavioural		
Definition of politics	The activity of attending to the general arrangements of a set of people whom chance or choice have brought together. (Oakeshott 1962: 112)		Government – the unending task of making and changing the rules and policies for any human society so that it may survive. (Moodie 1984: 32)	The ways in which 'values' are allocated in an authoritative manner by the community. (Blondel 1969: 6)	The specific articulation of class struggle. (Miliband 1977: 19)	
Present-day variants	Conservative idealism	Social human-ism	New institutional-ism as 'the emperor's new clothes'		Post-Marxism	Political economy
Examples	Greenleaf (1983)	Skinner (1998)	See Table 3.2, especially Finer (1997)		Laclau (1990)	Jessop (1990, 2001)

2006). Atomization, analysis, classification, comparison and correlation gradually dominated. Nineteenth-century theorists evoked history to postulate the beliefs, reason or character by which they interpreted politics. When modernist empiricists, such as Sammy Finer, turned to history, they were more likely to evoke social and institutional regularities and to construct typologies than they were to interpret meanings.

Even when modernist empiricism brought novel methods and logics of inquiry to British political science, British political scientists still remained greatly indebted to Whiggism in defining the objects of their inquiries. Whig historiography resulted in the more ahistorical idea of the Westminster model, and a vague concern with British exceptionalism remained widespread, perhaps even contributing to a complacent insularity. Of course, there was some tension between the new modernist logics of inquiry and the older Whiggish objects of inquiry. This tension helps to explain, in turn, the gradual rise of new areas of inquiry, including electoral behaviour, policy networks and, most recently, governance, all of which had little, if any, place in the nineteenth-century study of politics.

The persistence of Whiggism in modernist empiricism appears starkly in Vernon Bogdanor's (1999) forceful apologia. He conceives of British political scientists in terms of the Whig account of English exceptionalism. Like earlier Whigs, he sees the study of politics as methodologically eclectic, moderate and sensitive to local contexts. He contrasts just such a British tradition with the dogmatism, scientism and rationalism of an American political science in thrall to rigid conceptual structures and programmatic manifestos. He argues the main characteristics of the Whig tradition are its aversion to 'over-arching theory' and 'positivism'. Whiggish writers are the fundamental influences on British political science; for example, Dicey, 'who sought to discover what it was that distinguished the British constitution from codified constitutions'. Another favourite is Walter Bagehot, who 'sought to understand political "forms" through the analysis of political "forces"'. British political scientists are 'eclectic'; 'they have rarely concentrated on just one form of analysis because it seems fashionable'. At its best, British political science 'has combined deep historical knowledge with breadth of perspective'. American social science undoubtedly had an influence, but there is 'an indigenous British approach to politics, a definite intellectual tradition, and one that is worth preserving' (Bogdanor 1999: 149, 150, 175, 176–7, 178).

Bogdanor draws too sharp a distinction between British and American approaches to the study of politics. The overlap between the two is as great as the disjunction and from this overlap stems the bewitching effect of professionalism. If British political scientists were uncomfortable with the hypothesis testing and deductive methods of behaviouralism, they were at ease with the atomization, classification and measurement of modernist empiricism. They treated institutions such as legislatures, constitutions and policy networks as discrete objects to be compared, measured and classified. What is more, their modernist empiricism overlapped with behaviouralism at various junctures. Both adopted comparisons across time and space as a means of uncovering regularities and probabilistic explanations to be tested against neutral evidence. These overlaps provided a channel through which many British political scientists could indeed take a dose of behaviouralism.

David Sanders (1995) captures the meaning of behaviouralism in British political science. He associates it with, first, a particular take on empirical theory. Theory is 'a set of interconnected abstract statements, consisting of assumptions, definitions and empirically testable hypotheses, which purports to describe and explain the occurrence of a given phenomenon or set of phenomena'. Second, he associates it with that type of explanation that requires 'the specification of the minimum non-tautological antecedent necessary and sufficient conditions required' for a phenomenon to occur (Sanders 1995: 60).

Jean Blondel was among the leading supporters of such behaviouralism. His approach to comparative government was 'general and analytical', considering 'the general conditions which lead to the development of types of political systems' (Blondel 1969: ix–x; see also Blondel 1990: xvi, 4). So, 'one is inclined to look for "causes" and, more generally, for regularities'. The use of quantification to identify such regularities is, he continues, an important ambition, since in its absence political science is 'descriptive', 'superficial' and indistinguishable from journalism (Blondel 1981: 107, 168, 109). However, even Blondel qualified his behaviouralist ambitions in a way that echoed the concerns of mainstream modernist empiricists. He admitted that politics was '"messy" and somewhat unscientific', even adding, 'the development of quantification in political science does depend in part on an "act of faith"'. Blondel argued, therefore, that general or universal theories were too ambitious: '"middle range" or "partial systems" comparisons' are the best way of tackling 'the persistent problem of political institutions'. Comparative government requires a general analysis of such institutions as political parties, legislatures, bureaucracies, the military and the judiciary. Blondel focused on middle range comparisons employing quantification whenever possible to identify and explain genuine cross-national regularities (Blondel 1981: 163, 178–85, 190, 197; 1990: 357–9).

Key words characterize Blondel's approach to comparative government: for example, 'quantification', 'systematic' and 'regularities'. They have a dual significance. They are not only the objectives of his comparative method, but also criticisms of other methods, most notably case studies. They convey his behaviouralist suspicions of the continuing strength within British political science of a sceptical and atheoretical Whiggism. Blondel explicitly contrasted his preferred nomothetic approach of quantitative, middle range analysis as a source of systematic thinking and generalizations, with an idiographic approach that was mainly descriptive and focused on the unique (Blondel 1969: 5, 1981: 67). In short, Blondel, with his emphasis on facts and the search for regularities, is a fine example of modernist empiricism after it has taken a dose of behaviouralism.[4]

Thatcherism provided a much greater challenge to modernist empiricism in Britain than had behaviouralism. It marginalized political science, and its rise challenged the old Whig nostrums of consensus, gradualism and the capacity of British institutions to evolve and cope with crises. There were several battlegrounds. None posed a bigger challenge than the new public management (NPM). The impetus and ideas behind the Thatcher government's NPM reforms came from economists, management consultants and New Right think tanks. They were the source of policy innovations. They challenged many nostrums of British political science, forcing a rethink of, for example, the theory of bureaucracy. Political scientists were essentially bystanders. They did not create and promote such new ideas. Challenged by Thatcherism and NPM, students of public administration in particular were losing their institutional base in the universities. They had difficulty finding a new role and constructing a coherent intellectual identity.

Modernist empiricists responded to the dilemmas posed by Thatcherism with a new literature on governance (see Chapter 5). This literature suggested the New Right had fallen prey to an economistic dogma, which had failed to bring the promised results. It did so by highlighting the unintended consequences of NPM, especially the perceived weaknesses of marketization. Once again, British political scientists presented themselves as cautious, professional, agnostics; they commented judiciously on the gap between aspirations and achievements in policy areas such as privatization, public expenditure and civil service reform.

The governance narrative initially described the pattern of public administration that had arisen unintentionally out of the reforms of the Thatcher government. In this narrative, the reforms had created a series of networks, not pure markets, and these networks were poorly coordinated, increasingly difficult for government to control, and perhaps worryingly unaccountable. The economists and management consultants had failed. They had pursued a formal dogmatic faith in markets, when, as political scientists now explained, what mattered was getting the right mix of hierarchies, markets and networks. The governance literature also informed various attempts to atomize the rising networks from their particular contexts and thereby construct analytic classifications. At times, these classifications even purported to identify appropriate managerial strategies for the different categories of classification.

Although the literature on governance traced weaknesses in the Thatcher government reforms, it remained within an entrenched modernist empiricism. It is important to recognize here that the impact of Thatcherism as a political movement was not matched in Britain by the impact of rational choice theory as an intellectual movement. Rational choice theory remained a minority interest among political scientists.[5] The majority dismissed it as an example of the excesses of American scientism. It was considered an intellectual exercise of little relevance to the real world. Also, it was tarnished by its association with the New Right.

The absence of rational choice theory does much to explain British responses to the new institutionalism. The first point to note is that many

British political scientists denied any novelty to the new institutionalism (see, for example, Rhodes 1997: 78–9). They argued, in Britain, neither the behavioural revolution nor rational choice had swept the study of institutions away. Hence they often took the rise of the new institutionalism in America to be a vindication of their British modernist empiricism, with its scepticism toward universal theory, against the deplorable scientism characterizing American political science.

Even today, when British political scientists drape themselves in the new institutionalism, it often acts merely as a cloak of convenience. Case studies of institutions can be dressed up as a revitalized institutionalism and British political scientists can claim they wear the latest fashionable clothes. But, in fact, they are the emperor's new clothes. If you look closely little has changed: we are in the altogether. Vivien Lowndes is one prominent example of a British political scientist who espouses the new institutionalism. She makes probably the strongest possible claim for it when she argues it is not a theory, but an organizing perspective, which provokes questions and yields fresh insights. It is not associated with any one theory and its strength lies in its multi-theoretic character (Lowndes 2002: 108). So understood, the new institutionalism is, at least in Britain, little more than a cloak with which Whigs and modernist empiricists can pursue the kinds of work they long have done unruffled by the pretensions of behaviouralism and rational choice.

What does the research done in the mainstream of British political science look like? There is simply no space to summarize the diversity of such research and, of course, it is dangerous to claim one author can exemplify a tradition. Nonetheless, Sammy Finer's three-volume history of government combines a Whiggish sensitivity to history with a modernist empiricist belief in comparisons across time and space, regularities and neutral evidence. As Hayward observes, Finer is either 'the last trump reasserting an old institutionalism' or 'the resounding affirmation of the potentialities of a new historical institutionalism within British political science' (Hayward 1999: 35).

Looking back at the evolution of political science, Finer argued, as early as 1954, that, although the predictions offered by political science 'are short term and have a low degree of probability', it is still a science 'because it can offer reasons and causes for events once those events have happened' (1980a: 361, 363). Latterly he took the even more cautious view of political science as '*interpreting* a body of factual knowledge' or 'making a *pattern* out of it'. He still welcomed the proliferation of professional theories and techniques that had come to constitute 'a rich armoury into which we can dip to select the appropriate weapon' to study our chosen question or problem.

Finer's (1997) *The History of Government* combines this modern armoury with history in an attempt to explain how states came to be what they are with a specific emphasis on the creation of the modern European nation state. He searches for regularities across time and countries in an exercise in diachronic comparison. *The History of Government* sets out to establish the distribution of the selected forms of government throughout history, analyse each according to a standard format and assess its general character, strengths and weaknesses according to a standardized set of criteria. It identifies similarities and differences between the forms of government using a standardized typology (Finer 1997 Volume 1: 1). The typology is complex as the summary outline in Table 3.2 shows. The book then provides, true to its title, a history of government from ancient monarchies (about 1700 BC) to AD 1875. The result may be old institutionalism or it may be new institutionalism, but, coupled with the typology, it is a fine example of an eclectic modernist empiricism at work.

The history of modernist empiricism in Britain fits moderately well with the narrative of professionalization. Modernist empiricism arose, at least in

Table 3.2 Finer's typology and variables summarized

---

1. There are four basic clusters of variables.
   (a) Territory
   (b) Type
   (c) Possession of an army and/or bureaucracy
   (d) Limitations on activities.
2. Each cluster breaks down into sub-variables.
   (a) Territory breaks down into:
       (i) City
       (ii) National and
       (iii) Empire.
   (b) Type breaks down into ten combinations of:
       (i) palace
       (ii) nobility
       (iii) church and
       (iv) forum.
   (c) These types are in turn discriminated by the nature of their decision-making and decision-implementing personnel.
       (i) Decision-making breaks down into:
           A. Dominant personnel
           B. Characteristic political processes
           C. Legitimacy basis.
       (ii) Decision-implementing breaks down into:
           A. Bureaucracies:
               Developed
               Emergent and
               Rudimentary.
           B. Armed Forces:
               Community-in-arms
               Notables and
               Standing armies.
   (d) Constraints are:
       (i) Substantive and
       (ii) Procedural
       (iii) Horizontal (central government) and
       (iv) Vertical (centre to locality).

Source: Finer (1997 Volume 1: 35, 37, 60–1, 65, 72, 78).

part, out of the Whig tradition and it later assimilated various American 'revolutions' from behaviouralism to new institutionalism. However, we have told this narrative without reference to any supposed logic of professionalization. We told the story of how one particular tradition developed as its exponents responded to intellectual challenges from abroad and elsewhere. By doing so, we have tried to expose the contingency of what has become the mainstream of British political science. We have also tried to create space to explore the rival claims of other, alternative traditions, which are written out of the narrative of professionalization. So, we now explore the idealist and socialist traditions.

Idealism

Whiggism and idealism overlapped in many complex ways during the late nineteenth century (den Otter 2006). The emergence of modernist empiricism and behaviouralism meant that idealism got pushed toward the margins of political science. It kept a strong presence only in the subfield of political theory. Even so, idealism was not static. Although pluralists such as Ernest Barker and A. D. Lindsay challenged the pivotal role earlier idealists ascribed to the state, their pluralism was less a rejection of idealism than a refashioning after World War One. In addition, the disillusionment that followed World War One led many later theorists to reject the earlier idealists' concepts of the absolute. R. G. Collingwood, John Macmurray, Michael Oakeshott and many others qualified or even rejected the idea of an absolute mind immanent in the world. As a result, it is perhaps questionable whether they should be described as idealists. Still, they remained indebted to many other themes associated with idealism – a vitalist analysis of human behaviour, a thick concept of the person, a positive concept of freedom and often a concern with community (see Bevir and O'Brien 2003).

In the 1960s and 1970s, idealist themes characterized two rather different approaches to the study of politics. The first approach was a conservative idealism associated mainly with Oakeshott. The second was a diffuse social humanism found in the work of political theorists such as Charles Taylor and Quentin Skinner.

The inheritors of idealism challenged behaviouralism for its neglect of meanings, contexts and history. Oakeshott argued political education required the 'genuine historical study' of a 'tradition of behaviour'. He then adopted a conservative analysis of tradition as a resource to which one should typically feel allegiance. Indeed, he almost treats political traditions as 'natural', animating particular polities that can take from them unambiguously correct lessons for their current practices. He does so despite his explicit comments against such an analysis of tradition. Oakeshott thus defined the task of the political scientist as being 'to understand a tradition', which is 'participation in a conversation', 'initiation into an inheritance' and 'an exploration of its intimations' (Oakeshott 1962: 59–60, 62–5).

During the 1970s and 1980s, W. H. Greenleaf and Nevil Johnson, two of Oakeshott's disciples, continued to develop the master's position to encompass developments in British political science. Greenleaf made the point bluntly when he argued that although 'the concept of a genuine social science has had its ups and downs, and it still survives . . . we are as far from its achievement as we were when Spencer (or Bacon for that matter) first put pen to paper' (1983a: 286). Indeed, he opines, these 'continuous attempts . . . serve only to demonstrate . . . the inherent futility of the enterprise'.

Johnson (1989) similarly wrote a book entitled *The Limits of Political Science*. He found the study of politics wanting, whether in the guise of journalism or political science. Journalism was 'naively descriptive and empirical, and too deeply immersed in the ebb and flow of current affairs to permit either accurate description or cool judgement'. He denounced political science for its American-inspired 'thoroughgoing positivism'. It displayed a 'remarkable naivety in the perception of the diversity of human conduct and culture, combined with a readiness to dress up uninteresting conclusions in fancy technical clothes and portentous jargon'. The belief in the utility of the social sciences in general and political science in particular is 'confused', 'vulgar' and 'mistaken' (Johnson 1989: 55, 81, 104–5). Johnson argued the study of politics should allow, rather, that 'a political association exists only within specific traditions'. 'Political association entails institutions to express its form'. Moreover, since 'institutions serve as means of communicating and transmitting values', institutions express human purpose (Johnson 1989: 129, 131, 112; Johnson 1975). The aim of the study of politics is to 'gain a reflective and critical understanding of some of the varieties of human political experience'. So, 'explanatory work in politics is likely to refer chiefly to institutions and must rely extensively on the methods of historical research'. It does not seek 'to formulate statements of regularity or generalizations claiming to apply universally'. History is 'the source of experience' while philosophy is 'the means of its critical appraisal' (Johnson 1989: 117, 122–3).

Social humanists such as Taylor and Skinner were equally critical of positivist approaches to political science. Taylor's Oxford doctoral thesis was a defence of a vitalist analysis of human behaviour against mechanism (published as Taylor 1964).[6] After that he wrote a series of essays explicitly challenging behaviouralism and its leading tenets. He argued, in 'Interpretation and the sciences of man', that beliefs, meanings and language were constitutive of human actions and practices. The social sciences were unavoidably hermeneutical. His argument entailed a break with 'mainstream social science' and its empiricist and positivist epistemology. In particular, 'we cannot measure such sciences against the requirements of a science of verification; we cannot judge them by their predictive capacity' (Taylor 1971: 51).

In 'Neutrality in political science', Taylor (1967: 48, 27, 46) extended his argument to take direct aim at 'the cult of neutrality'. Behaviouralists defended the superiority of their approach by arguing that older approaches were always permeated by value positions. So, their frameworks were never scientific. They always served the interests of a normative or ideological theory. Behaviouralists proposed instead to turn the study of politics into a technocratic 'policy science', akin to engineering or medicine, which would 'show us how to attain our goals'. However, Taylor pointed out that when behaviouralists constructed theoretical frameworks to delimit the proper area of scientific inquiry, they too made fundamental choices that entailed normative commitments. The work of Harold Lasswell, David Easton and Gabriel Almond hid their norms. Referring to Lasswell's *Power and Society* (Lasswell and Kaplan 1950), Taylor pointed out that 'we come out with a full-dress justification of democracy [...] in a work which claims neutrality'. In general, Taylor suggested that conceptual frameworks always depended on theory, and theory could not be constructed apart from values. The ties binding theoretical frameworks and values also opened the possibility of seeing some values as especially meaningful responses to particular empirical contexts.

Although social humanists emphasized meanings and contexts in a similar fashion to conservative idealists, they took a different view of tradition, language and community as the relevant contexts. Social humanists placed far greater emphasis on the contingency and diversity of the contexts and languages present within any given society. We have already seen how Taylor argued that political studies closed off the comparison of, and even judgement between, rival moral frameworks in society. Likewise, Skinner emphasized the plurality of languages or ideologies found in a society at any given time. At times social humanists also suggested traditions or languages were open-ended. There was no single correct way to apply them or extend them on any particular occasion.

It was, however, the conservative idealism associated with Oakeshott that appeared in Johnson and Greenleaf's studies of British politics. Difference, discontinuity and dispersal were all elided. Johnson represented the British constitution as rooted in the 'extraordinary and basically unbroken continuity of conventional political habits', even suggesting it '*is* these political habits and little else'. The core notion in this inheritance is, he adds, 'the complete dominance of one particular body of ideas about government, namely what we usually call the idea of parliamentary government'. He even maintained there is 'no alternative or competing political tradition to fall back on, no different view of the basis on which political authority might rest' (Johnson 1977: 30).

Although Greenleaf (1983: 13, citing Oakeshott 1962: 61) declared that a tradition of behaviour was 'a tricky thing to get to know', he asserted, 'the British political tradition as it has developed in modern times' is 'constituted by a dialectic between the two opposing tendencies' of libertarianism and collectivism. In his view, there was no sharp distinction between these two strands of the British tradition. They were 'an impressionistic working hypothesis of an historical kind', which could be used to pull together the diverse practices and ideas of British political life. Libertarianism meant four things: an inalienable title to a realm of self-regarding action; a limited role for government; the dispersion of power; and the Rule of Law. Collectivism stood in contrast to this individuality; it was concerned with the public good, social justice, positive government and the concentration of state power. Greenleaf viewed the past century and a half as one of government growth, and so of the triumph of collectivism over individualism. Most of his four volumes is taken up with documenting this claim and answering the question of why a libertarian, individualist society sustaining a limited conception of government had been in so many ways and to such a degree replaced by a positive state pursuing explicit policies of widespread intervention in the name of social justice and the public good. Greenleaf, like Oakeshott and Johnson, implied traditions give us unambiguous answers to problems, and the British tradition tells us we should oppose state action.

It was this opposition to state action that led to Oakeshott becoming a guru in the 1980s, appealing to all shades of Conservatism (see, for example, Gilmour 1992: 98; Mount 1992: 74–5; Willetts 1992: 72–3). His distinction between the state as a civil and an enterprise association became a mantra for those seeking to justify the minimalist state. Thus, for Ian Gilmour (1978: 92–100, 1992: 272–3) an enterprise association is 'human beings joined in pursuing some common substantive interest, in seeking the satisfaction of some common want or in promoting some common substantive interest'. Persons in a civil association 'are not joined in any undertaking to promote a common interest . . . but in recognition of non-instrumental rules indifferent to any interest', that is, common rules and a common government in the context of which they pursue diverse purposes. However, while Conservatives favoured civil association and limited state intervention, they rarely invoked the idealist philosophy with which Oakeshott had sustained his argument.

At the time Conservatives adopted Oakeshott, social humanists were expressing strong disquiet at an aggressive liberal individualism widely associated with the New Right. They invoked ideals of fellowship, community and citizenship as antidotes to the selfishness and social dislocation they saw in the New Right. Most obviously, Taylor, who had by then returned to Canada, developed a communitarian philosophy. He appealed to community as a necessary corrective to a society based solely on impersonal contracts and self-interest (Taylor 1989). What is more, his concept of community again expressed the concerns with diversity and difference that characterized social humanists' accounts of context. His work on multiculturalism in Canada sought to allow for 'deep diversity' by recognizing a 'plurality of ways of belonging' to the community (Taylor 1993: 181–3).

Skinner moved cautiously away from his earlier opposition to our using past texts to resolve our problems.[7] He began to reconstruct a republican notion of liberty according to which 'we must take our duties seriously, and instead of trying to evade anything more than "the minimum demands of social life" we must seek to discharge our public obligations as wholeheartedly as possible' (Skinner 1990: 308). Before long, he announced his ambition was 'to question this liberal hegemony'. He attempted to re-enter the 'intellectual world' of English republicans, such as Harrington, who had espoused a neo-roman theory of the free state and free citizens (Skinner 1998: x; see also Skinner 2003).

Socialism

Britain has a long-standing, distinguished socialist tradition of political analysis. It remains a powerful presence, with its own publishers such as Verso, Lawrence and Wishart and Pluto, its own journals such as *New Left Review*, *Marxism Today* and *The Socialist Register*, its own key figures including Perry Anderson, Stuart Hall, Bob Jessop, Gareth Stedman Jones, Tom Nairn and E. P. Thompson, and arguably its own debates such as those over labour historiography and the relation of structure to agency.

British socialists have long rejected the professional aspirations and alleged neutrality of modernist empiricism. For them, the accolade of science should be applied, if anywhere, to Marxism. Colin Leys (1983: chapter 1) criticizes political science because it claims to be value free, it has a pluralist conception of politics, it discusses politics in isolation from economics, it fails to think about the present historically and it ignores the effects and social origins of ideas. Leys views politics as a struggle between the interests of labour and capital, and the political system as shaped by the needs of capital. Typically, British socialists responded to behaviouralism, especially its aspiration to a universal scientific theory, primarily by denouncing it in just this way. Equally, socialists sometimes deployed behaviouralist techniques to gather data for their alternative narratives. Ralph Miliband (1969, 1970) built much of his Marxist critique of the British state on behaviouralist empirical data (see also Dearlove and Saunders 1984; Kingdom 1991).

Thatcherism constituted a far more significant dilemma for socialists than behaviouralism. British socialists typically adopted a certain historiography, arguing capitalism possessed an innate trajectory defined by its inner laws. Early opposition to capitalism was a naïve Luddism. As social critics and others came to terms with a capitalism generated independently of their beliefs, so the workers acquired greater class-consciousness and began to aim at class cohesion as a means of winning political power. Their class-consciousness grew in Chartism, the trade unions, the Labour Party and the welfare state. This historiography defined a research agenda based on topics such as class, production, trades unions, the Labour Party and the state. However, Thatcherism signalled the end to the historical march forward of labour.[8] It also cast doubt on a historiography in which labour's rise appeared as the dominant story of modernity. Socialism was on the defensive, if not vanquished.

We might distinguish two main strands in the socialist response to Thatcherism. The first is the socialist school of political economy, with its realist claims that the world exists independently of our knowledge of it, and social structures have causal impact on history and politics. Typically, it sought to explain Thatcherism using concepts drawn from the research agenda tied to the old historiography. The second is post-Marxism, which has been influenced by 'the linguistic turn' and at times by post-structuralism. It rejected many of the concepts associated with the old historiography, turning instead to traditions, languages and discourses as its main objects of inquiry.

Socialist political economy consists of several attempts to rethink and reapply Marxist social and economic analysis. It might seem that if there was ever a time to claim that Marxist approaches were irrelevant, it would be in today's post-communist world, but nothing could be further from the truth. For example, Andrew Gamble and his colleagues (1999) marshal sixteen essays to reawaken interest in 'a legacy of critical social theory and social analysis which remains a key resource for today's social scientists'. If historical materialism and economic determinism have been relegated to the dustbin of history, what is left? Gamble (1999: 7, 3, 4, 6) believes Marxism 'continues to pose key questions about the origins, character and lines of development of the economic and social systems of the modern world'. David Marsh notes the varieties of Marxism, but argues, first, that most modern Marxists reject econ-omism and structuralism, preferring to emphasize contingency and accept a key role for agents; they no longer privilege class, acknowledging the crucial role of other bases of structured inequality. Second – and this is perhaps where such work differs from post-Marxism – 'almost all Marxists broadly share a realist epistemological position'. He argues Marxism still offers three things to political science: explanations of the periodic crises of capitalism, an analy-sis of structured inequality and a normative engagement with that inequality (Marsh 1999: 325–6, 332–3).

Realist epistemologies are often deployed by British socialists to defend a realist ontology of social structures. Once socialists assign a causal role to structures, they can argue the capitalist economy, as one such structure, con-strains the development of society and the state. Socialist political economy recently has paid great attention, therefore, to the relation of structure to agency. Bob Jessop's 'strategic-relational approach' is one of the more innova-tive attempts to conceptualize this relation. Jessop (1990, 2001) argues against all those approaches to state theory predicated on a distinction between structure and agency. He treats structure and agency only as an analytical distinction; they do not exist apart from one another. Rather we must look at the relationship of structure to action and action to structure. So, 'structures are thereby treated analytically as strategic in their form, content and operation; and actions are thereby treated analytically as structured, more or less context sensitive, and structuring'. This approach involves examining both 'how a given structure may privilege some actors, some identities, some strategies . . . some actions over others', and 'the ways . . . in which actors . . . take account of this differential privileging through "strategic-context analy-sis"' (Jessop 2001: 1223). In other words, individuals intending to realize certain objectives and outcomes make a strategic assessment of the context in which they find themselves. However, that context is not neutral. It too is strategically selective in the sense that it privileges certain strategies over others. Individuals learn from their actions and adjust their strategies. The context is changed by their actions, so individuals have to adjust to a different context. Institutions or functions no longer define the state. It is a site of strategic selectivity, a 'dialectic of structures and strategies' (Jessop 1990: 129).

The strategic-relational approach and critical realism have provided socialist political economy with concepts by which to explore Thatcherism and related shifts in British politics. We can explore these ideas in the debate between Hall and Jessop about the analysis of Thatcherism. Drawing on the work of Gramsci and the notion of hegemonic projects, Stuart Hall tells the story of Thatcherism replacing the existing social democratic ideology with its own vision, creating a new historic hegemonic project described as 'authoritarian populism'. The populism encompassed, 'the resonant themes of organic Toryism – nation, family, duty, authority, standards, traditionalism – with the aggressive themes of a revived neoliberalism – self-interest, competitive individualism, anti-statism'. The authoritarian covered the 'intensification of state control over every sphere of economic life', 'decline of the institutions of political democracy' and 'curtailment of . . . "formal" liberties'. So, the 1980s were characterized by centralization, the 'handbagging' of intermediate institutions, the refusal to consult with interest groups and state coercion. Thatcherism stigmatized the enemy within – for example, big unions and big government – while creating a new historic bloc from sections of the dominant and dominated classes (Hall 1983: 29, 1980: 161).

Jessop and his colleagues (1988) criticize this analysis because of its one-sided focus on the ideological at the expense of its economic and political aspects. They argue for a focus on both the specific institutional forms that link state, civil society and the economy and on the distinctive form of the state system. They use the ideas of social base, accumulation strategy, state strategy and hegemonic project to develop their analysis of Thatcherism. So, Thatcherism involves creating a new social base through its project of popular capitalism (for example, the sale of public housing); an accumulation strategy of privatization, deregulation and marketization; an authoritarian and centralizing state strategy; and a two-nations hegemonic project. As one might expect, the analysis pays attention 'not only to the social forces acting in and through the state but also to the ways in which the rules and resources of political action are altered by changes in the state itself' (Jessop *et al*. 1988: 161).

Post-Marxists typically pursue cultural analyses similar to that provided by Hall of Thatcherism. Some follow Hall in expressing an almost humanist opposition to the structuralist legacy in post-structuralism. Gareth Stedman-Jones, who has long since shed his own structuralist cloak, complained of 'the stultifying effect of the survival, sometimes in disguised form and often barely self-aware, of a residue of reductionist and determinist assumptions dating from the 1970s' (Stedman-Jones 1996: 24). He sought to move post-Marxism away from 'the legacy of Foucault' toward a closer engagement with social humanists such as Skinner. No doubt, as Stedman-Jones implies, many post-Marxists pursue studies of languages, discourses, and traditions, with little awareness of the underlying theoretical issues. Equally, some post-Marxists, notably Ernesto Laclau, are more sympathetic toward – even openly supportive of – the structuralist legacy in post-structuralism (Laclau 1990; Laclau and Mouffe 1985).

Laclau's version of discourse theory resembles many idealist and post-idealist approaches to politics in that it understands actions, practices and institutions as analogous to written and spoken texts; to discuss them adequately, one has to engage with the meanings they embody. It resembles the idealist inheritance too in its concern to explore such meanings by locating them in the historical context of a tradition, language or ideology. However, Laclau draws on structural linguistics in a way few of those indebted to idealism do. Hence, he often conceives of the relevant context as the relations between the semantic units within the discourse. These relations are unstable. But they allow little, if any, room for human agency.

Laclau's debt to post-structuralism has undermined many of the characteristic themes of Marxist thinking. His emphasis on the role of discourses and on historical contingency leaves little room for any Marxist social analysis with its basic materialism. Similarly, his rejection of the privileging of class, and so presumably of Marx's analysis of capitalism, allied to his hostility to any notion of human nature, leaves little room for a Marxist ethics or politics. Why, after all, should anybody support radical struggles if these do not serve to end ills such as exploitation or to realize human potentialities? Laclau here confuses recognition of the ubiquity of hegemony with an argument for democratic hegemony. What is needed for the latter is an account of why we should prefer democratic hegemony to any other form of hegemony.

One area where Laclau does use Marxist themes is in his use, following Gramsci and Hall, of the term 'hegemony'. He concentrates on the hegemonic role of discourses and the possibilities for counter-hegemonic struggles. In his view, hegemonic projects set out to construct nodal points which serve partially to fix meanings and so to elide the historically contingent and politically constructed nature of a particular discourse. Yet, while hegemonic projects thus strive to fix discourses, any discursive configuration will contain social antagonisms. An antagonism is conceived here as a 'blockage of identity' that occurs when the presence of an '"Other" prevents me from being myself' (Laclau and Mouffe 1985: 113, 115). To use Laclau's (1990: 26) phrases, 'the constitutive nature of antagonisms' leads to a consequent 'radical contingency of all objectivity' and this contingency then creates a space for counter-hegemonic discourses.

Most of the empirical work by post-Marxists focuses on political identities associated with gender and race. There is little work addressed to topics such as parliament, political parties, interest groups, and administrative and local politics. One exception is Stephen Griggs and David Howarth's (2000) analysis of the campaign against Manchester airport's second runway. They take interests and identities alike to be contingent and politically constructed. In their case study of the runway, they then ask how the local village residents and direct action protestors overcame their collective action problem. Their explanation has three elements. First, there was strong group identity in that all were affected by the environmental costs of the runway. Second, there was a social network and political entrepreneurs. Third, new political identities were forged – 'the Vegans and the Volvos'. Middle-class protestors saw democratic channels as unreliable and so supported more radical forms of protest. This alliance worked because the pro-runway campaign stigmatized both residents and protestors alike and used heavy-handed tactics. Yet the protestors lost. Once evicted, the eco-warriors moved on to the next protest site. Residents split over whether to mount a national-level campaign or concentrate on the public inquiry.

The governance of political science

We have shown there are several traditions of political science in contemporary Britain. Each tradition has changed as its exponents have responded to various dilemmas. It is important to recognize, in addition, that the fate of the traditions is intimately bound up with the broader social and political context. In Britain, the state is the only major source of funds for political scientists. The development of contemporary political science cannot be grasped apart from its governance. The state helped to define political science through its higher education policy, which favours some disciplines over others, by providing incentives for only certain types of research, and by its own definition of significant problems, for example, through the media.

The relationship between political science and the state is, of course, symbiotic. On one hand, political scientists help to develop the ideas and techniques of governance that the state uses to try to stimulate, regulate and control various activities within civil society. On the other hand, university education and research, including political science, is one of the areas the state typically seeks to stimulate, regulate and control using just these ideas and techniques.

Modernist empiricists typically scorned narratives of social conditions and moral character for atomistic and analytic studies of private opinions, behaviour and institutions. The resulting objectification of opinion, behaviour and institutions characteristically acted as a prelude to their governance. The state permeated new areas of civil society and private life. As it did so, it sought to tame not only its subjects but also its own policies. The state sought to monitor its own impact on education, employment, health and housing. As the state expanded its activities, politics and administration became continuous social processes at the intersection of state and society. The changing role of the state overlapped with the emergence of studies of policy and implementation. Mackenzie (1955) tellingly inaugurated the study of pressure groups in Britain by arguing that party programmes mattered less than the continuing process of adjusting policies.

The constant extension of the state's knowledge and activity led to fears of state-overload, bureaucracy and inefficiency. These fears then provided part of the rationale for the new public management. The state increasingly struggled to objectify, monitor and control not only its impact on society, but also its internal procedures. It began to rely on financial management and competition to secure accountability, and on regulation to ensure that competition worked appropriately. When the New Right deregulated and privatized functions of the state, it often used techniques such as auditing and contract to monitor and control the agencies substituting for the state. Also, now that New Labour uses the state to enable individuals and organizations to take active responsibility for themselves, it defines appropriate forms of responsible action and monitors and responds to outcomes. In both cases, while individuals appear as agents responsible for their own position, the state still promotes a particular concept of responsibility by giving them skills and opportunities to find employment, to protect their health or to provide for their future. When modernist empiricists explore these developments, they describe the emergence of new patterns of governance associated with, say, self-governing and inter-organizational structures (Pierre 2000). In doing so, they objectify these structures, ascribing specific characteristics to them, and encouraging the state to steer them by adopting techniques such as negotiation and an indirect style of management based on trust (see, for example, Ferlie and Pettigrew 1996; Kickert *et al.* 1997).

So, state actors have come to believe that policy-relevant knowledge takes the form of modernist empiricist or even positivist studies. The major state departments contract a vast amount of applied research from British universities, but even pure research is state-funded through the Economic and Social Research Council (ESRC). The ESRC and its predecessor, the Social Science Research Council (SSRC), provide a clear example of the governance of political science at work. The SSRC was created in 1965 specifically to promote 'policy-relevant research'. Their strategic plans, annual reports and other official publications have chanted the mantra of 'policy-relevant research' ever since. One of its four current strategic objectives is 'to increase the impact of the ESRC's research on policy and practice'. It sets 'thematic priorities' to guide its research funding and all applications must indicate to which priority they will contribute.[9] It proudly proclaims, 'all our decisions involve users – from public, private and voluntary sectors – as members of our Boards, and Council itself, as participants in our priority setting and programme and award selection'. There is an Evidence Network, launched in 2000 with £3 million worth of funding to pursue evidence-based policy and practice. There is a Connect Club – a select group of policymakers and business people who 'receive regular targeted information on ESRC research in their field of concern'. There are also Concordats with seven government departments for 'establishing collaboration and feeding in the outputs of ESRC research'. Nor is the effort to accommodate users limited to research. For postgraduate training, there is LINK, the Teaching Company Scheme and Collaborative Research Studentships, all of which involve working with business.[10]

Political scientists may conspire in their own fate by playing the grants-manship game. Even though the ESRC has been the face of government to academia for much of its existence, nonetheless many modernist empiricists and positivists agree with the official discourse. They can invoke the norms and regulations of the governance of political science to press their particular research agendas on to their more sceptical colleagues. For example, Keith Dowding (2001: 90) wants 'to persuade British political scientists to think seriously about the way in which they go about their business' because they need 'to use . . . the social science methods they are required to teach in their departments if they want ESRC recognition for their masters and doctoral instruction'. Modernist empiricists have a symbiotic relationship with the state. Behaviouralism sometimes can encourage policy-relevant research because it gives political scientists a toolkit for providing policy analysis. 'Evidence-based policymaking' under New Labour returns such research to centre stage. The professionalization narrative of political science not only responds to the dilemma posed by state power, but also legitimizes the active involvement of political scientists with the state.

Idealists and socialists, in contrast, can be pushed aside by the state's preference for relevance. They often reject the idea that political scientists can provide such policy-relevant knowledge. Among the idealists, Johnson notes the ESRC's 'very marked shift in priorities towards practical and policy oriented research' and rails against both 'the illusion of utility' and the 'embarrassing' results for social research (Johnson 1989: 93, 97). Moreover, even when socialist political economy does claim to provide scientific know-ledge, it is often designed to mobilize opposition to the state rather than to enhance the effectiveness of the state. The problem for idealists and socialists is how to describe their work so it fits with the expressed preference of govern-ment departments for research rooted in modernist empiricism. The ESRC's thematic priorities may not exclude their work but equally they do not signal an open door.

Conclusions

We have argued there are several traditions in British political science: for example, modernist empiricism, idealism and socialism. We have also argued proponents of these traditions modified them more or less drastically in response to the dilemmas posed by changing intellectual agendas, such as behaviouralism or neoliberalism, but there were great differences in their responses. Our narrative contrasts with the modernist empiricist one of the professionalization of British political science. The narrative of professional-ization writes out other traditions from the history of the discipline and domesticates change. It presents modernist empiricist modes of knowing as inevitable, natural or reasonable. We have sought to denaturalize modernist empiricism by recounting it as just one contingent tradition among others. In our view, the reasonableness of interpretivism consists, first, in the coherence of its philosophical premises, and second the powerful narratives it can offer about alternative approaches. Interpretivism can narrate more adequate histories of modernist empiricism, behaviouralism, rational choice and the new institutionalism than these approaches can provide of themselves.

The pertinent question with which to draw this chapter to a close is 'whither British political science?' There are two obvious points with which to start. First, political scientists will set out against various overlapping and competing traditions, which they will modify in response to dilemmas. Political scientists will walk no single path. Second, exponents of the narrative of professionalization will seek to contain that diversity, to write out other traditions from the history of the discipline. No doubt they will be aided both by state policies and funding and by their own pursuit of state recognition and approval.

Perhaps we might see radical change. In anthropology, as Fred Inglis (2000: 112) points out, there has been a lethal attack on positivism and physicalism alike. He opines that the work of philosophers such as Taylor, and also Peter Winch and Alasdair McIntyre, means that using the methods of the natural sciences in the human sciences is 'comically improper'. Similarly, students of international relations in Britain have begun to confront their 'comically improper' shortcomings (cf. Hay 2002: chapter 6, and references therein). But it is fair to conclude that many political scientists have yet to do so. So, one possible avenue of change is for a broad interpretive church to replace modernist empiricism. A broad interpretive church might unite many idealists and socialists. Conservative idealists, social humanists and post-Marxists all offer historicist critiques of positivism. They debunk typologies, correlations, models and classifications as objectifications that hide the historicity of the objects they depict and the modes by which they do so. Some socialist political economists too have begun to take seriously the role of ideas as causal and even perhaps constitutive aspects of economic policies and practices (see, for example, Hay 2002).

The prospect may exist for British political scientists to take an 'interpretive turn'. But any such turn would collide with the entrenched modernist empiricism of the mainstream, which will hang on grimly; no doubt hoping 'postmodernism' – it will be the pejorative label used to describe such a broad church – will go away. Any such turn might also collide with the state's preference for relevance. There is already a reaction to liberal ideas and a greater concern with structured inequality. But the state still continues to promote projects that purport to offer social engineering that 'solves' social problems. No doubt modernist empiricists and positivists will be more than happy to take the money and offer such advice. Arguably the prospects for an 'interpretive turn' will remain bleak for as long as this symbiotic relationship persists. We wrote this book in the hope that we can avoid this grim fate.

4 Westminster models

As we saw in the previous chapter, much of British political science remains modernist empiricist. It uses the modernist techniques of atomization, analysis, classification and correlation to explore objects of inquiry associated with Whig historiography. The combination of modernist techniques with a Whig historiography produces the Westminster model. For much of the twentieth century, the Westminster model acted as a lodestar for British political science. In this chapter, we offer a critical narrative of this model. We seek to denaturalize it. We reveal its partiality and contingency by decentring it, showing how it has been constructed differently from within various traditions and in response to various dilemmas.

If Britain is the 'mother of parliaments' bestowing largesse in the guise of the Westminster system on the dominions and colonies (De Smith 1961), then the governmental systems of those countries provide a sharp illustration of how traditions transmute transplanted beliefs and practices. Australian constitutional history is the history of their conceptions of the Westminster model. Even federalism is part of the Australian version of the Westminster model: whether it is seen as inimical, or as integral, it is indisputably part of Australian debates about the Westminster model. The two are inseparable. The simple point is that Australian concepts of the Westminster model have moved so far from British ones they are almost unrecognizable. In Britain, moreover, the family of ideas constituting the Westminster model approximates to a nuclear family, whereas in Australia it is an extended family. This chapter documents that variety, while showing both that these disparate ideas are linked over time and that elite actors cling to such shared Westminster notions as collective ministerial responsibility in part because they retain important legitimizing and symbolic roles. So, no matter how far removed sections of this chapter may seem from the original ideas of the Westminster model, they remain discussions of contemporary versions of that model. A tradition today may have little or nothing in common with its origins. We document the lineage to show that ostensibly disparate ideas are all part of continuing debates in local traditions about Westminster models.

In the first section, we identify two uses of the phrase 'Westminster model': as historical description and as normative guide to constitutional design. We prefer to treat the Westminster model as a tradition and ask what traditions shape Australian governance. In the second section, we decentre the Westminster model by exploring its roles in different Australian traditions. We argue that present-day Australian government is the heir to several traditions and each tradition constructs the structure of government differently. There are at least four traditions – the colonial heritage, responsible government, federalism and neoliberalism. The meaning of Westminster depends on the tradition, through which it is constructed. There is no single agreed definition of a Westminster system that it could be measured against. Westminster is a constructed notion. It does not have an essential core. It is contestable in all its features, the meaning of which varies from tradition to tradition.

The dilemmas posed by the initial combination of responsible government with federalism are recurring prompts to change. Often these dilemmas are seen as problems to be solved by constitutional reform. The stock response of the Commonwealth has been to centralize. The response of the states, minority interests and parties is to defend the existing system of checks and balances and argue that the everyday routines of government resolve all but the most difficult of intergovernmental issues. We conclude Westminster models are alive and well among the Australian political elite because they provide legitimating myths justifying the Commonwealth's search to centralize political power. Finally, and most, important, we show that an apparently common heritage, and shared appeals to a Westminster system, can come to mean dramatically different things.

Uses of the 'Westminster model'

In most of the literature on Australian government, the phrase 'Westminster model' has two uses: as a descriptive-historical account of Australian government, and as a normative guide to constitutional design. Perhaps the most comprehensive attempt to characterize Westminster systems is Arend Lijphart (1999: 3). He defines the Westminster model as a category in his modernist empiricist classification that has the following constitutive features: one party controls the power of cabinet; cabinet dominates parliament; two-party system; government is formed from the party with the majority in the lower house; interest groups exert pressure on government in a pluralist fashion; government is unitary and centralized; legislative power is concentrated in one house; conventions allow government to be flexible; judicial review is absent; and central banks determine monetary policy. In this classification, Australia does not qualify as a Westminster system! Indeed, Lijphart classifies only three countries as approximating to his version of the model – Barbados, Britain and New Zealand. Even these three are only approximations. For example, with devolved governments in Scotland and Wales and membership of the European Union, it is arguable that Britain is neither unitary or centralized let alone both. Even among Australian political scientists, there is a lack of agreement on how best to characterize their Westminster system.

There is also a confusion of descriptive and normative strands and an inappropriate use of foreign analogies (Jackson 1995: 5).

A great many uses of the Westminster model are prescriptions for reforming or preserving the constitution, even if they purport to be historical descriptions. L. R. Marchant (1999: 31–2) provides a wondrously eccentric version to justify his rejection of constitutional reform. He identifies Westminster with: a system based on freedom of the individual; separation of church and state; parliamentary sovereignty; the monarch is head of the state; all citizens must abide by the laws passed by parliament; an independent judiciary; separation of powers between legislature, executive and judiciary; and an independent public service. We have no idea why the separation of church and state is uniquely Westminster. But it is no matter. We want only to record the normative themes in the debate surrounding Westminster.[1]

Both the descriptive and the normative uses of the phrase 'Westminster model' are limiting and neither need detain us further. Rather, we will treat the Westminster model as a construct of various traditions and focus on two questions. What traditions shape Australian governance? How do these traditions shape our understanding of executive government in Australia? In answering these questions, we argue the Westminster model has many, contradictory variants. The theories held by observers influence how they conceive of things.

Traditions of Australian governance

Many political scientists highlight continuities from British to Australian government. Pat Weller and Jenny Fleming (2003: 14) write, for example, that 'the founders of the Commonwealth Constitution accepted, almost without dispute, the British system of parliamentary government for the new Commonwealth, a system which had already been adapted to the needs of Australians as the Australian colonies gained self-government after 1850'. In contrast, it is still rare for commentators to admit that federal theory has deep roots in Australian constitutional design. Yet, even before the Federal Conventions of the 1890s, there were debates about territorial decentralization and the Convention debates clearly show that the smaller states insisted on a system of checks and balances as a counterweight to responsible government. So, to go with its alleged Westminster system, Australia has a written constitution with judicial review and separation of powers. It has a separation of powers between head of state (governor-general) and head of government (prime minister); between Commonwealth and States (Federalism); and between House of Representatives and the Senate. Australia has both a British (responsible government) and an American (federal) heritage (Galligan 1995: 46–51), hence the appellation 'Washminster mutation' (Thompson 1980).

We can distinguish, however, between three responses to this inheritance. First, many commentators pass over federalism. Thus, David Butler (1973: 5) notes that Australia combines parliamentary government with federal government, and describes Australia as a pioneer, but then ignores federalism for rest of the book – for example, there are a mere three entries in the index and no chapter on the topic or even on the states. Second, others treat federalism as an unwelcome distortion of the Westminster model. Thus, Reid talks of the 'three *distorting* influences' (1981: 312–16, emphasis added) that federalism exerts on responsible government: namely, legalism, an elected senate and a formal division of powers. Finally, some treat the two government structures as incompatible. Lucy claims that 'Australian Federalism is incompatible with responsible party government' (1993: 292; see also Sharman 1990). When such commentators grapple with federalism, the result is usually a call for constitutional reform.

Here, we want to adopt a different tack. First, we make the simple point that federalism has been integral to Australian debates about its Westminster system from its inception. Second, we want to argue that present-day Australian government is the heir to several traditions and each tradition constructs the Westminster model and its associated structures of government differently. So, there is not one Westminster model but several, because each tradition constructs it differently. It is helpful to highlight at least four traditions in Australian government – the colonial heritage, responsible government, federalism and neoliberalism. The meaning of Westminster depends on the tradition through which people construct it (see Table 4.1). Of course, these are not the only traditions of relevance to Australian government. Others might include Benthamism, socialism and feminism. We cannot cover every tradition. We chose these traditions because they are the most relevant for our purposes.

Table 4.1 Traditions of governance in Australia

Traditions	Colonial	Responsible government	Federalism	Neoliberalism
Source of legitimacy	Governor-in-Council	Parliamentary sovereignty	Popular sovereignty	Liberal-market economy
Notion of executive government	States' rights	Party government	A federal republic	Centralization
Public service	Fragmentation – statutory bodies	Neutral, permanent bureaucracy	Concurrent federalism	Managerialism
Examples				
(i) Academic	Finn (1987)	Parker (1976, 1978, 1980a)	Galligan (1995)	Kelly (1994)
(ii) Practitioner	Brown (2003b)	Menzies (1967)	Official Record (1986)	Watson (2001)

Note
The table draws on Davis (1998), Wanna and Weller (2003) and the citations in this chapter.

The tradition of colonial self-government

It is not our intention, or within our capacity, to write a history of colonial Australia. For our limited purposes, we only need to trace the lineage of the Westminster model by identifying those aspects of nineteenth-century government that exert an influence today. For that exercise we rely on secondary sources (see, for example, Finn 1987; Hancock 1930; Wanna and Weller 2003). The neo-colonial tradition is no longer dominant because its main themes have been absorbed in the other traditions.

Australia was a settler society. As Paul Finn (1987: 2) shows, 'the colonies assumed their own character, had their own relatively isolated economies, had systems of administrative government which differed at least in their balances and emphases'. There was a 'blending of regional variations and British dependency'. He argues there was an important and distinctive 'indigenous contribution made to the development of Australian law and government'. There were two major differences with Britain. First, in the colonies the forces at work were '"centrifugal" so citizens looked to the central [colonial] governments for the satisfaction of needs'. Second, 'the raw conditions of the colonies . . . impelled governments into activities without counterpart in Britain' (*ibid.*: 3, 6). Finn uses the phrases 'imperfect imagining' and 'distorted local mirroring' to capture the differences between British and Australian versions of Westminster (*ibid.*: 81, 160, 165).

Even if the Westminster model was an imperfect image, it still operated so as to hand themes down to future generations. It is the source of six strands in present-day traditions.

Monarchy

The influence of the monarchy can be traced through the prominence of the Governor-in-Council to the continuing constitutional role of the governor-general (see Butler and Low 1991; Finn 1987; Low 1988). The head of state has three functions. First, in Anthony Low's (1988: 22) memorable phrase, constitutional heads of state are the 'chief ribbon bestowers and chief ribbon cutters'. Second, there is also the formal public role; for example, opening parliament, receiving foreign dignitaries. Finally, there is their contribution to the everyday working of the polity, which is frequently mundane. At times, however, the head of state can become embroiled in political controversy as in 1975 when the Governor-General, Sir John Kerr, dismissed Prime Minister, Gough Whitlam (see Low 1988, and Winterton 1983 for a bibliography on the crisis). The key point here is the continuing role of the head of state. As Butler (1991: 8) concludes in his survey of Governor-Generals, the simple fact is that 'each Governor-General operates under special rules or customs, developed in response to some special local situation or by mere chance'. Australia is no exception. Opaque is one possible summary of much British 'constitutional theory', but the importance of such ceremonial should not be underestimated; it burnishes Westminster as myth and legitimizes the government of the day.

States' rights

The belief in states' rights in the nineteenth century has been fully documented, especially in recent years (see Galligan 1995; Bach 2003: chapter 5; Sharman 1990; Uhr 1998: 77–81). A. J. Brown (2003a: 15) provides a recent contribution and an important challenge to conventional accounts of the origins of federal ideas, arguing British policymakers were 'thinking actively' about federal ideas and using them as a colonizing strategy. American ideas were current in Australia from 1822, long before the proposals for inter-colonial union in the 1840s and the federation debate of the 1880s and 1890s. He argues there are two federalisms. The first federalism dates from the 1820s and called for an active programme of territorial decentralization. The second federalism dates from the 1840s and is a pragmatic federalism associated with partial centralization. It may well be true that the authors of federation were not theorists but practical men defending their interests. Nonetheless, 'Australians seem always to have been in search of *both* a high level of national unity *and* serious political decentralization' (Brown 2003a: 31, emphases in original).[2]

Collective responsibility

Finn (1987: 45) argues that the 'two political principles of ministerial responsibility, the collective and the individual, coexist uneasily'. 'Local circumstances were to accentuate the importance of collective responsibility'. The effect was that 'coalition ministries called upon collective responsibility as a cement to their union' and faction leaders used it to control their administrations. This stress on collective responsibility devalued individual ministerial responsibility, suggesting 'an adherence to principles of political responsibility which to this day accord with Australian parliamentary practice' (*ibid.*: 53). 'Cabinet and ministerial government was the prize of the colonial constitutions. But lacking an environment of the country of its breeding, it evolved and was practiced in ways foreign to that of "Westminster"'. The consequences were 'heightened use of the Governor-in-Council' as 'public administration's supervisory body' (*ibid.*: 164), and collective rather than individual ministerial responsibility.

Pragmatism

There was a willingness to change institutions to fit local needs. The best example is the widespread use of statutory bodies. Administrative government was characterized by 'fragmentation' and 'a plethora of . . . administrative boards arose to mar the symmetry of the governmental landscape' (Finn 1987:

4, 14, 81, 161). Compared with Britain at the same time, there were weak moves toward a departmental system of administration, and a fashion for statutory boards, that eclipsed local government and individual MPs (paraphrased from *ibid.*: 161). It can be no surprise that the governors of Australia adopted familiar administrative forms such as functional boards with specific administrative remits. Responsible government 'was not accompanied by any immediate revolutionary change in administrative forms'; rather 'with typical Australian pragmatism, this had to await some good practical stimulus' (Wettenhall 1987: 1, 7, 12). However, as Finn (1987: 163) cautions, there is a temptation

> to emphasise the purely practical; to explain the evolving administrative systems in terms of the use of known forms in essentially practical ways, with inherited constitutional and administrative ideas and practices providing some constraints upon purely idiosyncratic action. One can likewise emphasize the urgent demands made upon the architects of government, the often reactive responses to immediate problems, the limited materials with which, the unprepared foundations upon which, to build. A loosely constrained pragmatism is thus given pre-eminence. Pragmatism doubtless played its part. But to emphasize pragmatism alone is to run the risk of using British assumptions to judge Australian actions.

Interventionism

Individualism was partnered with collectivist trends. Ward (1980: 244–5) notes the coexistence of individualism and collectivist tendencies. Thus, the bushman's dislike of authority goes with economic cooperation because the frontier settlers were wage earners. So, in sharp contrast to America, 'the conditions of the Australian frontier produced mateship, unions, a collectivist ethos' (Watson 2001: 28). The roots of this collectivism lie in the colonial governments. Finn (1987: 160) notes the varied responsibilities of colonial governments and argues that: 'Local exigencies, the rural economy, pragmatism, some would assert a Benthamite utilitarianism, contributed to this'. Keith Hancock (1930) famously argued that egalitarian and collectivist strands underpinned Australian state socialism. John Wanna and Pat Weller (2003: 68) talk of 'beliefs about state developmentalism . . . couched within a dirigist statism' that were shared 'across the party spectrum'. In short, Anthony Trollope (1967) was correct; Australia was liberal in thought and socialist in deed.

Two-party system

Australia's two-party system delivers majority party control of parliament and the government of the day. It lies at the heart of Australia's version of

Westminster-style responsible government.³ Labor parties existed in most of the colonies at federation and in 1899 Queensland had the first Labor government, though for a mere six days. The Australian Labor Party was founded in 1901, but its roots lie in earlier decades with members of the labour movement elected to state governments from 1859. It is the oldest Australian party. Competition between Labor and non-Labor parties dates from the first decade of federation. Although the modern Liberal Party was not created until 1944, its roots lie in the fusion of anti-Labor groups in 1910, originally calling themselves Liberal but changed to National in 1917 and then to the United Australia Party in 1931. The labyrinthine twists and turns of Labor and Liberal history matter not for present purposes. The simple, brute point is, 'it is appropriate to consider the political parties first amongst the institutions of Australian government, because they are the first bodies which occur to the Australian when he thinks of "politics", and they are inextricably woven into the fabric of government' (Miller 1959: 63).

In short, the colonial tradition bequeathed a set of constitutional beliefs, including monarchy, states' rights, collective responsibility, pragmatism, interventionism and a two-party system, that continue to inform the traditions and practices of present-day Australian politics.

The tradition of responsible party government

Both R. S. Davis (1995: chapter 4) and John Uhr (1998: 77–80) argue that the idea of responsible government was imprecise and had various meanings when the constitution was debated. Little has changed. Uhr (1998: chapter 3) usefully distinguishes between responsible parliamentary government (with its roots in the work of J. S. Mill) and responsible party government (with its roots in Dicey).

Robert Parker is perhaps the most influential recent apologist for the notion of responsible parliamentary government. Parker argues that Australia incorporated the 'essential elements of "the Westminster model"' (1980b: 118). One of his 'essential elements' is individual and collective ministerial accountability and it lies at the heart of his 'Westminster syndrome' (see Parker 1976, 1978, 1980a). There are four elements to the syndrome (see Parker 1978: 349–53, and summary diagram on 354). The first 'essential' part is the doctrine of individual and collective ministerial responsibility. The second part is the need for officialdom. The third part concerns 'the "proper" relations between ministers and officials'. Parker is not resurrecting the age-old distinction between policy and administration. He simply wants to insist that 'in all decisions ... the elected minister should *have the last word*' (emphasis in original). Finally, 'the lines of accountability of the whole administration run from the lowliest official up through the minister to the cabinet, the parliament and ultimately – and only by that circuitous route – to the elector'. This view of Westminster has achieved textbook status.

The idea of responsible party government is illustrated by the work of

Richard Lucy, for whom 'the term "responsible party government" is taken to mean the Cabinet is more responsible to the governing party than it is to the Lower House of parliament or, indeed, to any other group or institution' (1993: 3). For Lucy (*ibid.*: 325), the defining characteristic of Australian government is the struggle between responsible party government and the separation of powers – the 'twin eaglets model' of Australia's government.

The tradition of responsible government is not just a notion of academics. Politicians and public servants share it. As one example, Sir Robert Menzies is rightly described as more 'deeply imbued with the traditions of parliamentary responsible government than with federalism' (Galligan 1995: 49). Thus in his 1967 lectures, Menzies bemoans the limits imposed on the Commonwealth by federalism: 'how true it is that as the world grows, as the world becomes more complex . . . it is frequently ludicrous that the National Parliament, the National Government, should be without power to do things which are really needed for the national security and advancement' (Menzies 1967: 24). In effect, for believers in responsible government, federalism is a historical curio and potential encumbrance.

The federal tradition

As Brian Galligan (1995: viii) comments, federalism is both opposed as antidemocratic and neglected in the study of Australian government.[4] 'Party responsible government' is the 'conventional wisdom' and 'Westminster concepts and their variations' are 'taken for granted by Australian political scientists' (*ibid.*: 5–6). Yet from its birth Australia was a federal republic:

> The Australian people are sovereign and have constituted themselves in a federal polity under a constitution that controls the other institutions of government, including parliaments and executives with their monarchic form and responsible government practices. For this reason, Australia is properly a federal republic rather than a parliamentary democracy: the people rule through a constitution that is the basic law of the regime and incorporates the checks and balances of such a constitutional system with a federal division of governments and powers.
>
> (*ibid.*: viii, 1)

So, the framers of the constitution deliberately combined federalism with parliamentary democracy, knowing it would create tensions. The favourite quote is by John Winthrop Hackett from Western Australia, who warned of this unworkable construction: 'either responsible government will kill federation, or federation . . . will kill responsible government' (cited in Galligan 1995: 6; Davis 1995: 80–1, 83).

Galligan (1995: 7) argues, 'there is a 'hierarchy of institutional design [. . .] it is the federal Constitution that specifies a bicameral parliamentary legislature and, albeit obliquely, a responsible government executive as two of the three branches of the Commonwealth government'. The Constitution is primary – 'constituting and limiting the institutions of politics and shaping political processes'. The High Court can strike out Commonwealth and state laws. So, 'parliaments are not in any sense supreme' because the federation was *'the sovereign people of the colonies* constituting a federal system of national and State governments' (*ibid.*: 9, 13, 14, emphasis in original). Popular sovereignty is the cornerstone of the Australian constitution. Galligan adduces two key arguments to support this interpretation. First, delegates were elected to the federation convention. Second, the people voted to approve the draft in a series of referendums.

Federalism was copied from the American model and 'was designed specifically to prevent government, and in particular central government, from prescribing and promoting the common good' (*ibid.*: 45). It was a pragmatic merger of the incompatible. In Galligan's view, 'the purpose of responsible government is to unify and consolidate political power whereas that of federalism is to fragment and circumscribe its exercise'. Hence 'responsible government presupposes undivided sovereignty' since it 'derives from the English tradition of parliamentary sovereignty in which there were considered to be no legal limits on the sovereignty of parliament' (*ibid.*: 47).

The small states insisted on a strong Senate. Samuel Griffiths (Leader of the Convention) 'regarded a powerful federal Senate as a necessary condition of the smaller States' acceptance of federation and saw such an institution as being incompatible with traditional responsible government'. It was a check on the more populous states of New South Wales and Victoria (*ibid.*: 75, 78, 79, 68, 69).

However, the 'Senate is an integral and virtually coequal part of the national legislature'. It is not restricted to protecting states rights. Galligan denies that the Senate has only a states' rights function. It is 'a national parliamentary institution with multiple purposes of governance'. It is 'not at odds with parliamentary responsible government but can be seen as an institutional means of ensuring broader responsibility of governance' (*ibid.*: 69, 89). The Senate 'provides a powerful institutional check on the executive as well as the legislature in ways that are quite different from either the British or the American constitutions (*ibid.*: 87). For Galligan, federalism is not a hierarchy but a complex 'mixing and blending' of agencies from both levels of government. It is 'essentially untidy', with 'governments and parts of governments competing for a share of the action'. It is best understood as 'a policy matrix in which no government has a monopoly or complete authority' – as 'a communications network rather than a chain of command' (*ibid.*: 244).

The neoliberal tradition

The 1980s and the 1990s saw the ascendancy of neoliberal ideas in many advanced industrial democracies. Although commonly told as a story of economic change, the rise of neoliberalism is also the story of changing beliefs about government. Paul Kelly (1994) tells the economic story for Australia.[5] We add a brief account of the attendant changing beliefs about government.

Kelly documents the collapse of the 'Australian Settlement', which is defined as white Australia, protectionism, wage arbitration, state paternalism and imperial benevolence. Both parties supported this settlement and the real divide was not between Labor and Liberal but between 'internationalist rationalists' and the 'sentimentalist traditionalists'. Under the impact of the internationalization of the world economy, and weakened imperial ties with America and Britain, Australia underwent a 'decade of creative destruction', which saw the ascendancy of free market reforms. Competition was the new mantra (Brennan and Pincus 2002: 68–70).

Labor under Bob Hawke and Paul Keating juggled pragmatism with economic rationalism to create its new model of governance (Kelly 1994: 19). Although some compromises with Labor's factions and the unions were inevitable, Hawke and Keating were committed to financial deregulation, free market economics, a federal budget surplus, restraint on union claims, lower taxation, private sector restructuring, less protection and the reform of the public sector (*ibid.*: 31). An open economy, free markets and competition were now as much part of the Labor canon as equity or social justice. The Liberal Party renounced defence of the status quo for radical free market reforms and supported Labor. According to Kelly, 'by 1991 it was beyond question that the five ideas of the Australian Settlement were in irreversible stages of collapse or exhaustion' (*ibid.*: 661). The traditionalists were in retreat. Labor sought to balance market reform with a continuing but redefined role for state intervention. Not that Labor had come to the end of its reforms. As Don Watson (2002: 86) concedes, the Keating government was up for 'a push of one kind or another' on the labour market.

The Liberals were gung ho for more radical market reforms, and with their election in 1996 the neoliberalism agenda was pushed even further by the Howard government (Brennan and Pincus 2002: 68). Managed labour markets went the way of all the rest. The recognition that Australia now lived in a global free market economy drove the policy agenda of both parties. But the trick now was to internationalize the economy and protect the oldest Australian beliefs in social justice (Kelly 1994: 686). Or as Watson (2002: 675) comments, 'in Australia we might in ways unique in the world weld the good economy to the good society'. That was the dream of the 'bleeding hearts', but those hearts became harder and bled less under the Liberals. As Frank Castles (2002: 41, 49) concludes, the neoliberal agenda of Labor and Liberal governments in the 1980s and 1990s reshaped Australia's economic institutions, leaving Australians less protected from the exigencies of capitalism and reducing their welfare.

With neoliberal economics comes a distinctive set of beliefs about government, federalism and the public service. For Anna Yeatman (1996: 285), 'the new contractualism represents a neoliberal politicization of public management'. Citizens are no longer members of a political community but part of a chain of principal-agent contracts. Electors become individualized consumers of public services and the defining characteristics of this relationship are individual choice and competition (*ibid.*: 291). Yeatman continues, 'liberalism has always derived its power . . . by counter posing the integrity of individual rational choice against some form of paternalism which denies integrity to the individual'. Currently, this binary appears 'either as the paternalistic bureaucratic state, or governance as a cascading series of contracts' (*ibid.*: 292).

No neoliberal government worth its salt believes the public services do it better than the private sector. So, government services were outsourced. Of course, the neoliberal belief in efficiency and markets is not new. Similarly, anti-bureaucratic sentiments are as old as bureaucracy. But the neoliberal belief in the private sector, markets and efficiency mounted a concerted challenge to Australia's other traditions.

If government should do less, nonetheless it should be decisive in what it does. The neoliberal belief in strong leadership reinforces the centralized decision-making associated with the responsible government tradition; it goes with the neoliberal grain. As with Margaret Thatcher in Britain, so with John Howard in Australia, prime ministerial control is the order of the day. With its focus on efficiency, it is less than tolerant of the negotiative muddle that is federalism, stressing both the cost and the access problems of clients. With thanks to A. J. Brown (2003b) for the provocative phrase, neoliberals favour 'collaborative centralism', a notion espoused by no other tradition. Similarly, with its emphasis on central political control, it has little time for the 'frank and fearless advice' of the responsible government tradition and favours short-term contracts for top officials.

Traditions and the executive

What does this analysis tell us about the power of the executive in Australia? We answer this question under five headings: the concentration of political power in a collective and responsible cabinet; the accountability of minister to parliament; parliamentary sovereignty grounded in the unity of the executive and the legislature; a constitutional bureaucracy of non-partisan and expert civil servants; and an opposition acting as a recognized executive in waiting. Our comments are brief, focusing on the distinct interpretations of each tradition.

The concentration of political power in a collective and responsible cabinet

The power of the executive is a contested notion, varying over time and between traditions. Thus, Wanna and Weller (2003: 78–9) distinguish between the limited state (1901–1930s), the state triumphant (1940s–1970s) and the restructured state (1980s–2001). For believers in the responsible government tradition, this story of federal evolution is one of defensible centralization. So, Peter Wilenski (1983: 86) claims, 'those who seek great powers for central government do so . . . to try to overcome some of the limitations on reform through government action that are imposed by the conservative nature of federal constitutions'. On the Liberal side, Menzies (1967: 152) similarly defends centralization. He praises the 'liberal interpretations' of the constitution that make it a 'living instrument for generations and centuries to come'. He claims, 'the remarkable, and, we think, unanticipated growth of central power in Australia, illustrates the truth of these views'. More recently, this centralization led to the presidentialization thesis in which the prime minister is no longer first among equals (if he ever was), but a president in all but name. Weller (2003) cogently shows that the argument there has been a decline in cabinet government and a rise of an all-powerful prime minister fails to specify either the criteria for 'proper' cabinet government or the conditions under which it thrives. No matter, although the label may vary, the trend to dominant prime ministers is the new conventional wisdom for many Westminster systems (see Chapter 6; Elgie 1997; Foley 2002; Mughan 2000; Pryce 1997; Savoie 1999).[6]

Others acclaim the dilemmas posed by the separation of powers, seeing federalism as an important safeguard of democratic freedoms. As with the changing power of the Commonwealth, the relationship between the Commonwealth and the states evolved. Wanna and Weller (2003: 78–9) identify three stages in the evolution of federalism, from coordinate federalism with its separation of jurisdictions, to coercive federalism from the 1940s to the 1970s and on to today's collaborative federalism. For Galligan (1995: 244), collaborative federalism is a system of 'divided and diffused sovereignty'; of 'complex and diffuse power centres with an intermingling and overlapping of jurisdictional responsibilities and policy activity'. So, criticisms of the states are often misplaced. R. S. Davis (1995: 149) defends the states against charges of inefficiency, bloody-mindedness, failure to agree and costliness. He points out that the system should not be judged by the few, exceptional failures, but by the 'daily relationship of sharing and cooperation', by 'the commonplace, the usual and the normal'. On this interpretation of Australian government, the history of federalism is not a story of uniform centralization, and centralization is not defensible – it is an anathema.

The accountability of minister to parliament

To identify different traditions is not to deny there is also a shared heritage at a more abstract level. The colonial tradition bequeaths us, as Finn (1987) demonstrates, collective responsibility, with individual ministerial responsibility a poor second. As Elaine Thompson and G. Tillotsen (1999: 56) conclude: 'ministerial responsibility remains alive at the cabinet collective level' in that 'if ministers cannot publicly support a cabinet decision or the general direction of government policies, they resign', whereas 'if individual ministerial responsibility ever meant that ministers were expected to resign for major policy blunders or for serious errors of maladministration by a government department, it is dead'.

For adherents of the federal tradition, the key difference between it and the responsible government tradition lies in federal Australia's broader concept of accountability. It is not limited to collective cabinet responsibility to the lower house. It also encompasses government accountability under the constitution and through the High Court, the role of the Senate, and the division of powers with the states and consequent need to negotiate with them. For a federalist, the government is interdependent, not dependent, and called to account in various ways by many actors. R. S. Davis (1995: 103) provides a convenient summary of this take on responsible government:

> It is in many important respects [similar] to Westminster, Washington, and others, it is also unlike any of these systems. It is in a political and constitutional class of its own. The idea of responsible government is fundamental to our society, but to give a realistic idea of responsible government in Australia, it must be eased from its monogamous unicentric Westminster roots, and brought closer to the polycentric circumstances of Australian politics.

For exponents of the federalist tradition, responsibility is not offended because a government has to negotiate. Rather, they would argue that the accountability of the executive to the parliament (as distinct from the lower house) is strengthened, not weakened. The notion that shared responsibility is weakened responsibility is a responsible government notion that finds little resonance in the federalist tradition.[7]

Parliamentary sovereignty grounded in the unity of the executive and the legislature

Parliament, a term often confined to the House of Representatives, is not sovereign. It cannot amend the Constitution; that requires a referendum. The High Court adjudicates on legislation. The Senate divides the executive and legislature. Nonetheless, there are cries of outrage if the Senate, or the High Court or the states, frustrate the executive. The government will appeal to its electoral mandate, accuse the opposition of being 'unrepresentative swill' (Paul Keating, House of Representatives, 4 November 1992) and otherwise behave as if the lower house should have the decisive, indeed sole, voice. This view of the role of the lower house belongs to the responsible government tradition.

Those who hold dear the beliefs of the federalist tradition see the actions of the Senate, or the High Court or the states, as legitimate in a federal republic. Of course, there is a long-standing debate about the role of the Senate. As Gordon Reid (1981: 52) argues, prime ministers and other Commonwealth ministers use the Westminster notion of responsible government 'to reject the initiatives of political groups seeking to use the Senate's power to a government's disadvantage'. Conversely, the Senate appeals to the 'Australian adaptation of the doctrine' to strengthen its hand against ministers (*ibid.*: 55). For many the Senate is a problem. For Colin Sharman (1977: 73, 1999: 157), it has a continuing role as a house of states. For R. S. Davis (1995: 88), it became more an upper house of party. For Bach (2003: 354–5), it is not primarily an institution of responsibility (for creating and removing governments) but of accountability (for holding the government to account in a broader system of checks and balances). Governments hate it when the Senate interferes with legislation. Minority interests see it as an essential bulwark against over mighty government. When the party composition of the House and the Senate differs, it is hard to disagree with Richard Mulgan's (1996: 191) assessment that the Senate is 'subject to opposing interpretations and evaluations based on conflicting and irreconcilable political values'. We would simply add that those values are handed down to us through distinctive governmental traditions.

A constitutional bureaucracy of non-partisan and expert civil servants

Where the executive has the authority, it centralizes power. The clearest example of recent years is the reform of the Commonwealth public service. The Australian administrative tradition was characterized by state intervention, innovation and a non-partisan career public service. It was a world in which the notions of responsible government provided guidelines, on occasion camouflage, for relationships with ministers and parliament. This world has been challenged, first, by an era of corporate management concerned with greater efficiency through modern budget controls; and, second, by the contracting-out of services once performed in the public service.

Australia's neoliberal tradition embraced the 'managerialist' movement. Predictably, the response was spurred on by the perception of Australia's declining economic fortunes under the impact of globalization. Governmental traditions mediated these changes. In the Australian case, the Howard government's 'retreat' did not take the form of less government, but of government in a different form. It withdrew from established economic and social interventions: for example, to sustain full employment. The focus switched to improved efficiency and effectiveness for utilities and government-controlled commercial activities. It replaced ownership of institutions and policies with contracted out services subject to more regulation: hands-on control or direct management has given way to hands-off control or indirect management. It sought more control over less, but it was never reluctant to resort to direct management when the need arose, as in immigration policy (Marr and Wilkinson 2003).

Political control of the bureaucracy is the order of the day, irrespective of the party in power. Permanence and distance take a subsidiary place to contracts, a degree of personalization and greater responsiveness to the elected government. The statesmen in disguise of the ministerial responsibility tradition are now more explicitly servants of power and willingly so, as officials were the source of many of the initiatives. Such trends are abhorrent to adherents of responsible government. There are repeated claims that the public service has become politicized, that there has been a decline in the quality of advice and that fixed-term appointments have adverse consequences (Gourley 2003). But for exponents of the neoliberal tradition, the shift is long overdue.

An opposition acting as a recognized executive in waiting

The opposition has enjoyed formal status since federation in 1901, with the position of Leader of the Opposition established in the first national parliament. In the traditional two-party system of responsible government, the opposition party always presented itself as the alternative government or executive in waiting. Also, during the twentieth century, the status, legitimacy and political standing of the opposition increased. Arguably, the Australian opposition became cemented in the policy process.[8] Routinely, and without controversy, it has equal time in parliamentary debates, question time, media coverage of politics and publicly funded election broadcasts (and at most state functions and commemorations). It is briefed regularly by the public service; for example, before elections and on security matters. Oppositions can establish and chair Senate committees with support from other minor parties and independents. Oppositions also enjoy access to resources so they can perform their duties. These resources include: offices, staff, advisers, travel, cars, library and research facilities. In short, Australia's adversarial political culture may debate whether the opposition is fit to govern, but there is no debate about the legitimacy of its role in the governmental process, at least among proponents of the responsible government tradition.

However, it should be obvious by now that views of the role of the opposition will also vary across traditions. The legitimate opposition resides in the House of Representatives, not in the Senate. So, Prime Minister John Howard describes the Senate as 'obstructionist', and calls for constitutional reform, because the checks and balances of the constitution coalesce with the adversary politics of opposition to frustrate the majority party in the House of Representatives. More vividly, Paul Keating referred, in exasperation, to 'that little tin pot show you run over there' (*The Australian* 4 March 1994). It is all conceived differently from within the federal tradition. The Senate is both a house of party and a house of states. So, opposition is legitimate. The federal tradition has a broader notion of opposition, welcoming the many veto points, whether stemming from the constitution or party.

Conclusions

Parker suggested 'it is indeed arguable that Australia has moved a smaller distance from the original [Westminster syndrome] than has Britain' (1980b: 118; see also Butler 1973: 7 for the same phrase). In fact, both have moved a long way from the model. With membership of the European Union and the consequent derogation of parliamentary sovereignty, with devolution to Scotland and Wales and consequent creation of rival governments with tax powers; with evolving reforms of the upper house; and with a Bill of Rights that strengthens judicial review by British and European courts, maybe Britain is becoming more like Australia. But the point of our comparisons is to jar the reader out of easy conclusions.

Perhaps one might argue Australia is not now and has never been a Westminster system. Certainly there is no single agreed definition of a West-minster system that it could be measured against. Westminster is a con-structed notion without an essential core; it is contestable in all its features, the meaning of which varies from tradition to tradition. As our study of Australia shows, the notion of Westminster contains competing strands. Table 4.1 summarized the main traditions and their competing strands. Although each column bears a distinct label, each can be seen as a version of the Westminster model. At one time or another, someone – academic and practitioner – has described the Westminster model drawing on the distinc-tive beliefs of the responsible government, federal and neoliberal traditions. Each tradition stresses different features of the executive. The responsible government tradition stresses collective ministerial responsibility to the majority party in the House of Representatives. The federal tradition points to an executive dependent on, and accountable to, many actors. The neo-liberals counter bureaucracy and inefficiency with contracting and centralization: more control over less.

There are two wellsprings for this variety. First, the under-specified nature of the Westminster model means that key roles and relationships in govern-ment are governed by convention; for example, the role of the executive, and conflict resolution between the two houses of parliament. Second, dilemmas associated with the initial combination of responsible government with federalism are recurring prompts to change. Often these dilemmas are seen as problems to be solved by constitutional reform. The stock response of the Commonwealth has been to centralize. The response of the states, minority interests and parties is to defend the existing system of checks and balances and argue that the everyday routines of government – cooperation and negotiation – resolve all but the most difficult of intergovernmental issues.

The Westminster model as responsible government appears to be the dominant tradition, but it is only one among many. It is alive and well among the Australian political elite in part because it is a legitimating cloak, or if you prefer, a myth sustained by a long-standing tradition, that is useful to the governing elite as it confronts the dilemmas posed by federalism and seeks to centralize political power in the Commonwealth. Perhaps terms like 'responsible government' and 'federalism' are best seen as political rhetoric in ever-evolving contests across, but also sometimes about, intermingling and overlapping policy networks over which the Commonwealth typically seeks to exert both hands-off and hands-on controls.

5   Decentring governance

Modernist empiricists rewrote Whig historiography to construct an ahistorical Westminster model. This model defined the ways in which they approached British government in their classifications, correlations and case studies. However, the use of the modernist techniques of atomization and analysis also inspired new topics, including electoral behaviour and policy networks (for example, Rhodes 1988). Studies of these topics then fed into the governance narrative with which some modernist empiricists responded to dilemmas posed by Thatcherism, as we saw in Chapter 3. While the governance narrative continued to rely on modernist empiricist epistemology and techniques, it did challenge the Westminster model. It told a story of how British government had shifted from the government of a unitary state to governance in and by networks (Rhodes, 1997, 2000; Stoker 1999, 2000a, 2000b, 2004; and for discussion Marinetto 2003). Britain was a differentiated polity characterized by a hollowed-out state, a core executive fumbling to pull rubber levers of control, and a massive proliferation of networks. Of course, governance is variously defined, but typically such narratives appeal to inexorable, impersonal forces, such as the functional differentiation of the modern state or the marketization of the public sector, to explain the shift from a bureaucratic hierarchy to networks in a hollow state.

In this chapter, we denaturalize the governance narrative as told by modernist empiricists. We challenge the idea that inexorable, impersonal forces are driving a shift from government to governance. We show, instead, that governance is constructed differently in the Tory, Liberal, Whig and Socialist traditions. We provide an account of the diverse ways in which elite political and administrative actors understand the term. In effect, we replace the current accounts of British governance in and by networks, as told by modernist empiricists, with an analysis that focuses on the various British political traditions that have informed the diverse policies and practices by which elite actors have sought to remake the state.[1]

The Anglo-governance school

The Anglo-governance school provides an alternative to the Westminster model. They define governance as self-organizing, inter-organizational networks, and they explore the ways in which the informal authority of networks supplements and supplants the formal authority of government. Behind this definition, however, there lurks the idea that the emergence of governance reflects a logic of modernization; that is, of functional and institutional specialization and differentiation. Entrenched institutional patterns ensured that neoliberal reforms lead not to markets but to the further differentiation of policy networks in an increasingly hollow state.

The concept of differentiation is, however, ambiguous. Typically, political scientists understand it to evoke differences, or specialist parts of a whole, based on function. Whenever they use differentiation in this way, they offer positivist accounts of governance. They treat governance as a complex set of institutions and institutional linkages defined by their social role or function. They render any appeal to the contingent beliefs and preferences of agents largely irrelevant. On the other hand, differentiation can refer to differences of meaning, perhaps to differences of meaning in action. When we understand differentiation in this way, we will offer a decentred account of governance that accords with our interpretive approach. We will explore the institutions of governance by studying the contingent meanings that inform the actions of the individuals involved in all kinds of governing practices. Current positivist approaches to governance focus on the objective characteristics of policy networks and the oligopoly of the political market place. They stress topics such as power-dependence, the independence of networks, the relationship of the size of networks to policy outcomes and the strategies by which the centre might steer networks. To decentre governance is, in contrast, to focus on the social construction of policy networks through the ability of individuals to create meanings. A decentred approach changes our view of governance. It encourages us to examine the ways in which our social life, institutions and policies are created, sustained and modified by individuals. It also encourages us to recognize that the actions of these individuals are not fixed by institutional norms or some logic of modernization. To the contrary, they arise from the beliefs individuals adopt against the background of traditions and in response to dilemmas.

As we argued in Chapters 1 and 2, a decentred, interpretive approach will recognize the importance of beliefs, traditions and dilemmas for the study of governance. Any existing pattern of government will have some failings, although different people will have different views about these failings because they are not simply given by experience. Rather they are constructed from interpretations of experience infused with traditions. When people's perceptions of failings conflict with their existing beliefs, they pose dilemmas that push them to reconsider their beliefs and the intellectual tradition that informs those beliefs. Because people confront these dilemmas in diverse traditions, there arises a political contest over what constitutes the nature of the failings and what should be done about them. Exponents of rival political positions or traditions seek to promote their particular sets of theories and policies, and this political contest leads to a reform of government. So, any reform must be understood as the contingent product of a contest of meanings in action.

The reformed pattern of government established by this complex process will display new failings, pose new dilemmas and be the subject of competing proposals for reform. There will be a further contest over meanings, a contest in which the dilemmas are often significantly different and the traditions have been modified as a result of accommodating the previous dilemmas. All such contests take place in the context of laws and norms that prescribe how they should be conducted. Sometimes the relevant laws and norms have changed because of simultaneous political contests over their content and relevance. Yet while we can distinguish analytically between a pattern of government and a political contest over its reform, we rarely can do so temporally. Typically, the activity of governing continues during most political contests, and most contests occur partly within local practices of governing. What we have, therefore, is a complex and continuous process of interpretation, conflict and activity that produces an ever-changing pattern of governance.

A decentred account of governance represents a shift of topos from institutions to meaning in action. It begins with an acceptance of the broad narrative about British government of the Anglo-governance school; that is, a differentiated polity characterized by numerous and fragmented policy networks over which a core executive struggles to retain any control or impose any co-ordination. This governance narrative helpfully corrects the exaggerated emphases of the Westminster model – a unitary state, parliamentary sovereignty, cabinet government, executive authority and a neutral civil service. It shifts attention to limits of political integration and administrative standardization. It describes how governance takes place through a maze of networks at the boundary of state and civil society. It reminds us that central government is just one of the several public, voluntary and private bodies involved in the policy process, and that it does not always achieve its intentions.

However, the Anglo-governance school often restrain the centrifugal impulse of this account of a differentiated polity by approaching it through modernist empiricism. They reduce the diversity of governance to a logic of modernization, institutional norms, or a set of classifications or correlations across networks. They thereby tame an otherwise chaotic picture of multiple actors creating a contingent pattern of rule through their conflicting actions. In contrast, a decentred approach implies governance arises from the bottom-up. Governance is a product of diverse practices that are themselves composed of multiple individuals acting on all sorts of conflicting beliefs which they have reached against the background of a range of traditions and in response to varied dilemmas. A decentred approach leads us, then, to replace aggregate concepts that refer to objectified social laws or institutions with ones that we craft to explain the particular beliefs and actions of interest to us. It inspires narratives of traditions and dilemmas.

Narratives of governance

There are four main narratives of British governance: intermediate institutions, networks of communities, reinventing the constitution and joined-up government (see Table 5.1). For each narrative we outline the relevant tradition and give examples. Our choice of traditions is conventional (see, for example, Barker 1994). Here we provide the briefest of summaries and focus on how elite actors in each tradition understand and make governance. Equally, the table and our examples are not comprehensive. We are illustrating an argument, not documenting all those webs of beliefs that played a part in the construction of British governance.

As we argued in Chapter 1, our approach calls for thick descriptions of governance using the accounts or texts of participants, not academic commentaries. However, there is often no clear-cut distinction between academic commentators and elite actors. So, for example, Lord Crowther Hunt was both a member of the Fulton Committee on Civil Service Reform and a Fellow of Exeter College, Oxford University. Subsequently, he became a political adviser to Prime Minister Harold Wilson, whom he advised on implementing the recommendations of the Fulton Committee (Cmnd 3638 1968). Individuals can be academics, authors of official documents and political actors all at once or at different times in their lives. Also, academics and practitioners share a language about 'the system'. Tivey (1988: 3) deploys the concept of 'the image' to denote 'a set of assumptions about '"the system" . . . and how it works'. Each image contains 'operative concepts' or 'operative ideals': 'the views of the authors are taken', moreover, 'to be of some influence; what they have said has to some extent become operative'. Indeed, his images 'have gained currency among those who study politics, and diluted and distorted they have reached the practitioners' (*ibid.*: 1; see also Beer 1965: xiii, 404). In

Table 5.1 Narratives of governance

Traditions	Tory	Liberal	Whig	Socialist
Narrative of reform	Preserving traditional authority	Restoring markets and combating state overload	Evolutionary change	The bureaucratic state
Narrative of governance	Wrecked intermediate institutions	Building networks of communities	Reinventing the constitution	Joining-up government
Examples				
(a) Practitioner	Gilmour (1992)	Willetts (1992)	Bancroft (1983)	Mandelson and Liddle (1996)
(b) Official report	Anderson (1946)	Efficiency Unit (1988)	Cm 2627 (1994)	Cm 4310 (1999)

this chapter, all our narratives, the shared images if you will, are drawn from politicians and senior civil servants in this broad sense and from official sources. In ensuing chapters, we will provide more detailed accounts of the beliefs and traditions that inform the actions of other actors in the dramas of British governance.

The Tory tradition

Some strands recur in the Tory tradition. For example, Michael Oakeshott (1962, 1975) provides the philosophical underpinnings for several raconteurs of Tory narratives. So, Gilmour (1978: 92–100, 1992: 272–3), a former Cabinet Minister (1979–81), underpins his version of the Tory tradition with Oakeshott's distinction between the state as a civil and an enterprise association (see Chapter 3: p. 47). He argues for a civil association on the grounds that a free society has 'no preconceived purpose, but finds its guide in a principle of continuity ... and in a principle of consensus' (Gilmour 1978: 97). For Gilmour, 'the fundamental concern of Toryism is the preservation of the nation's unity, of the national institutions, of political and civil liberty' (*ibid.*: 143). The Tory tradition favours civil association and only accepts the state as an enterprise association 'when individuals are able to contract out of it when it suits them' (Gilmour 1992: 272). Nonetheless, Gilmour (1978: 236) accepts that some state intervention will often be expedient, practical politics, essential to preserving the legitimacy of the state. For all its hedging about the role of the state, the Tory tradition upholds its authority. People are driven by their passions and hierarchy is necessary to keep order. Scruton (1984: 11) makes the point forcefully: 'the state has the authority, the responsibility, and the despotism of parenthood (see also Gamble 1988: 170). Strong leaders wield that authority to uphold national unity, to correct social and economic ills and to build popular consent.

Gilmour (1992: 198–224) portrays the public sector reforms of the 1980s as a 'series of tactical battles' that wrecked Britain's intermediate institutions, such as the monarchy, the church, the civil service, the judiciary, the British Broadcasting Corporation (BBC) and local government. These 'barriers between state and citizen', he argues, were torn down in the drive to create an enterprise culture and a free market state. Gilmour values the pluralism of intermediate institutions and wants to return to moderation in the exercise of power. Similarly, on civil service reform, Gilmour (1992: 185) regrets that civil servants abandoned their principal function of drawing 'attention from long experience to the flaws of instant panaceas' and decided that 'the way to live with ideology was to appear to share it'. So they 'executed ordained error without demur'. They neither retarded nor palliated. They did not resist reforms with a vigour nourished by a proper confidence in the old values of the British constitution.

There was never a neat divide in the Conservative party between the paternal statism of the High Tories and economic liberalism, but during the

1980s and 1990s the former was a submerged tradition. Official reports did not articulate the High Tory reverence for the old values. Of course there are many examples from earlier in the post-war period. A favourite example is the Anderson Committee because its truths were so self-evident, it was never deemed necessary to publish the committee's report. It began work in November 1942 as a cabinet committee enquiring into the fitness of the machinery of government for the extended role of the state after the war. Its status as a cabinet committee ensured that the review lay in the hands of ministers and civil servants rather than outsiders. In effect, the committee carried out a 'survey for practitioners by practitioners' (Lee 1977: 18). Anderson submitted his report to the prime minister in May 1945. It was never published (but see Anderson 1946). The following passage captures the tone of the exercise:

> The Ministerial Committee was paralleled by a small official committee of three senior civil servants chosen by Anderson himself for their special qualities of judgement. This collated the views of people who were referred to as 'great and wise men' and gave ministers the benefit of their advice in confidence.
>
> (PRO/T222/71:OM 290/01 cited by Chapman and Greenaway
> 1980: 129)

The following passage similarly captures the tone and scope of the review's conclusions:

> While I emphasise the departmental responsibility of ministers as a necessary and vital principle, I at the same time stress the importance, as a practical matter, of adequate machinery for making a reality of collective responsibility. As a means to this end, I would rely on the institution . . . of a permanent but flexible system of cabinet committees.
>
> (Anderson 1946: 156)

As Lee (1977: 151) concludes, the Anderson Committee was a 'special mixture of ambiguity in definition and ambivalence in discussion'. Turbulent times produced not a radical review, but a return to the eternal verities of the insiders of British government. The Committee sought to perpetuate such Tory themes and symbols as the generalist civil servant acting as Platonic guardian of an imagined, national good.

The Liberal tradition

'New Conservatism' revived the liberal tradition by stressing freedom, applying the principles of freedom to the economy and accepting the welfare state on sound Conservative grounds. Thus, David Willetts (1992), Conservative MP and junior minister under both Margaret Thatcher and John Major, finds the roots of the New Conservatism in the One Nation Group's (1954) arguments against government intervention and in such philosophers as Friedrich Hayek and Michael Oakeshott. For Willetts (1992: chapter 6) Adam Smith's 'system of natural liberty' provides the intellectual justification for free markets. Markets tap 'two fundamental human instincts'; the instinct to better oneself and the instinct to exchange. These instincts, when 'protected by a legal order which ensures contracts are kept and property is respected' are 'the source of the wealth of nations'. Big government cannot deliver prosperity, undermines markets and erodes communities. But 'rampant individualism without the ties of duty, loyalty and affiliation is only checked by powerful and intrusive government'. So, Conservatism stands between collectivism and individualism and 'Conservative thought at its best conveys the mutual dependence between the community and the free market' – 'each is enriched by the other' (Willetts 1992: 182). The Conservative Party's achievement is to reconcile Toryism and individualism. This achievement also belongs to Thatcher. Thatcherism is not the antithesis of conservatism because it too recognizes there is more to life than free markets; it too sought to reconcile 'economic calculation with our moral obligations to our fellow citizens'. It restores markets to their allegedly rightful place in Conservatism: it 'is within the mainstream of conservative philosophy' (*ibid.*: 47, 54).

State intervention stultifies. Competition improves performance: 'free markets are . . . the route to prosperity' (*ibid.*: 136). Bureaucracy is the problem. Marketization is the solution to bureaucratic inefficiency (Thatcher 1993: 45–9). Sir John Hoskyns (1983) was one of several business leaders seconded to Whitehall. On leaving, he reflected in writing on his experiences. In doing so, he criticized the failure of government to agree and define objectives. He complained about the small world of Westminster and Whitehall, and especially about a civil service closed to outsiders, lacking in confidence and energy, and serving political masters with whom it does not agree. He challenged the convention of political neutrality as leading to passionless detachment instead of radically minded officials, and to the low quality of much policy work. His main proposal for change was to break the civil service monopoly of top jobs and to appoint business outsiders on seven-year contracts. In a similar vein, Leslie Chapman (1978), a former regional director in the (then) Ministry of Public Building and Works, castigated the civil service for waste, inefficiency and inadequate management. His solutions included a new investigative audit department and better, accountable management. During the 1979 election campaign, he advised Thatcher on efficiency within the civil service (Metcalfe and Richards 1991: 5–6). Although Chapman was widely tipped to become Thatcher's adviser on efficiency in government, that mantle eventually fell on Sir Derek Rayner, joint managing director of Marks & Spencer.[2]

The recurrent liberal concerns with business-like efficiency, setting clear policy objectives and recruiting better managers, pervade various official reports of the last two decades. The Efficiency Unit (1988: 3–5) argues, for example, that 'senior management is dominated by people whose skills are in policy formation and who have relatively little experience of managing or working where services are actually delivered'. It strongly believes that 'developments towards more clearly defined and budgeted management are positive and helpful'. It accepts that senior civil servants must respond to ministerial priorities but argues the civil service is 'too big and too diverse to manage as a single entity'. So, it recommends setting up agencies 'to carry out the executive functions of government within a policy and resources framework set by a department'. Senior management will have the freedom to manage. So, there will now be 'a quite different way of conducting the business of government'; a central civil service consisting of core departments servicing ministers and agencies at arm's length with clearly defined responsibilities for service delivery.

Not all liberals focus on reforming public management. Willetts (1992: 71) wants to claim community as a core principle in the liberal tradition. He rejects the idea of community embodied in the nation-state for the notion of an 'overlapping network of communities'. He denies that free markets destroy community. On the contrary, liberalism reconciles markets and community with the idea of 'micro-conservatism' or 'the particular network of communities which gives each individual life meaning'. The role of the state is to sustain 'a political order in which this multiplicity of communities can survive' (*ibid.*: 105). Micro-communities populate the boundary between state and civil society, an image with a close affinity to nineteenth-century notions of governance as private collectivism.

The Whig tradition

As we have seen, the Whig tradition now emphasizes the Westminster model, and the study of institutions or the rules, procedures and formal organizations of government (see Chapter 3). It upholds the value of organic change of the British constitution to preserve old virtues while also responding appropriately to new times.

There was a time in the early 1980s when it seemed as if the Conservative maelstrom would sweep aside the traditional civil service. Lord Bancroft (1983: 8), a former head of the home civil service, reflected on these changes in true Whig style:

I am reminded that Abbot Bower of Inchcolm, commenting on the legislative enthusiasm of James I of Scotland in the Parliament of 1426, applied what he thought an apt quotation: 'to enact new laws with facility, and to change the old with facility, is marvellous damaging to good order'. He was quoting Aristotle. We are heirs to a long inheritance.

Lord Bancroft, again like a true Whig, contrasts his argument 'for organic institutional change, planned at a digestible rate' with a defence of the status quo. Indeed, he explicitly criticizes 'the overnight fever of a new department here and a new agency there, in order to accommodate a transient personal whim or political tantrum' (see also Bancroft 1984; the concluding remarks in Dale 1941: Appendix C; Sisson 1959: 153). He wants gradual evolution through sympathetic reforms that work with, and so perpetuate, all that is salutary in Britain's constitution and political practice.

The White Paper, *The Civil Service: Continuity and Change* (Cm 2627 1994) reflects on a decade of change and, in true Whig fashion, seeks to consolidate the changes in the broader heritage and pattern of historical development. The White Paper's summary of the role and functions of the civil service claims that the civil service has 'a high reputation, nationally and internationally, for its standards of integrity, impartiality and loyal service to the Government of the day' (*ibid.*: 6). It suggests, 'the particular standards that bind the civil service together are integrity, impartiality, objectivity, selection and promotion on merit and accountability through Ministers to Parliament' (*ibid.*: 8). Although recent reforms delegated management responsibility to agencies, the government acknowledges 'the need to ensure that the defining principles and standards of the civil service are not relaxed'. The White Paper instances the new, unified Management Code, which lays down the relevant standards, and promises a statutory code or a New Civil Service Act. The proposed reforms are meagre. The White Paper even phrases its proposals for open competition for top jobs cautiously:

> Departments and agencies will always consider advertising openly at these (senior management) levels when a vacancy occurs, and then will use open competition wherever it is necessary and justifiable in the interests of providing a strong field or introducing new blood.

Such words hardly herald an open season on top posts in the civil service. The White Paper's title is an accurate reflection of its contents. The Whig tradition's response to public sector reform is 'wherever possible' to use 'traditional and familiar institutions for new purposes' and so to 'go with the grain of Westminster and Whitehall and their traditions' (Hennessy 1989: 734, see also 1995). Empathy with the Whig interpretation of the British constitution leads to an organic reinvention of that constitution.

The Socialist tradition

Here, because our concern is governance and recent public sector reforms, we focus on the New Labour strand in the Socialist tradition. New Labour reinterpreted the concerns highlighted by the New Right from within the Socialist tradition (Bevir 2005). The Old Labour model built on the Fabians' faith in experts and resembled a top-down, command-style bureaucracy based on centralized rules. The Party became associated with hierarchic patterns of organization in which co-ordination is secured by administrative orders. The New Right rejected this model, arguing it was inefficient and it eroded individual freedom. The Thatcher governments tried to make public services more efficient through privatization, marketization and the new public management. Citizens became consumers able to choose between arrays of public services. Although command bureaucracy remains a major way of delivering public services, privatization, the purchaser–provider split and management techniques from the private sector have become an integral part of British governance.

New Labour does not defend the command bureaucracy associated with Old Labour. There has been a shift in the Socialist tradition inspired in part by the New Right's concerns with market efficiency and choice. For example, Peter Mandelson, former Secretary of State for Northern Ireland, and Roger Liddle explicitly reject the 'municipal socialism' and 'centralized nationalization' of the past (Mandelson and Liddle 1996: 27). New Labour 'does not seek to provide centralized "statist" solutions to every social and economic problem'. Instead New Labour promotes the idea of networks of institutions and individuals acting in partnerships held together by relations of trust. New Labour's concern with networks based on relations of trust does not exclude either command bureaucracy or quasi-market competition. Rather, New Labour proposes a mix of hierarchies, markets and networks, with choices depending on the particular nature of the service under consideration. Government policy is that services should be provided by the best-placed sector and this can be the public, private or voluntary sector, or partnerships between them (Cm 4011 1998). Even a simple service is liable to display a mix of structures, strategies and relationships.

Equally, New Labour embodies a critique of the New Right's model of public service delivery. It suggests the New Right has an exaggerated faith in markets. New Labour believes individuals are not just competitive and self-interested, but also co-operative and concerned for the welfare of others. So, public services should encourage co-operation while continuing to use market mechanisms when suitable. For example, David Clark (1997), then the Minister for Public Services, explained that policies such as market testing 'will not be pursued blindly as an article of faith' but they 'will continue where they offer best value for money'. New Labour insists markets are not always the best way to deliver public services. They can go against the public interest, reinforce inequalities and entrench privilege. Besides, much of the public sector simply is not amenable to market competition. Indeed trust and partnerships are essential. Without the conditions for effective markets, one has to rely on either honest co-operation or specify standards in absurd detail. Far from promoting efficiency, therefore, marketization can undermine standards of service quality.

New Labour's emphasis on individual choice and involvement overlaps with several themes found in the New Right. In promoting customer-focused services, New Labour adopts features of the new public management when it considers them suitable. Yet New Labour's model of service delivery does not follow the New Right's vision of the new public management. On the contrary, New Labour argues that many features of this new public management, such as quasi-markets and contracting-out, maintained an unhealthy dichotomy between the public and private sectors: public bodies did not work with private companies but merely contracted services out to them. This argument is used, for example, to justify abolishing the internal market within the National Health Service. The Third Way, in contrast to the vision of the New Right, is supposed to develop networks that enable public and private organizations to collaborate. Examples of such collaboration appear in the partnerships between the public and private sector that are so important to the delivery of the New Deal for the unemployed.

New Labour's networks for public service delivery are supposed to be based on trust. Tony Blair describes such trust as 'the recognition of a mutual purpose for which we work together and in which we all benefit' (Blair 1996: 292). Trust matters because we are interdependent social beings who achieve more by working together than by competing. Quality public services are best achieved through stable, co-operative relationships. Blair talks of building relationships of trust between all actors in society. Trust is promoted between organizations through the Quality Networks programme: organizations should exchange information about their practices to facilitate co-operation. Trust is promoted inside organizations through forms of management that allow individual responsibility and discretion increasingly to replace rigid hierarchies: individuals should be trusted to make decisions and implement policies without the constraint of strict procedures. Trust is promoted between organizations and individuals through the Service First programme: citizens should trust organizations to provide appropriate services, and organizations should trust citizens to use services appropriately.

So, the Labour government uses networks based on trust to institutionalize its ideals of partnership and an enabling state. Blair stated the aims succinctly: 'joined-up problems need joined-up solutions' (*The Observer*, 31 May 1998). This theme runs through the *Modernising Government* White Paper, with its frequent references to 'joined-up' government and 'holistic governance' (Cm 4310 1999; see also Cabinet Office 2000). The term covers both horizontal joining-up between central departments and vertical joining-up between all the agencies involved in delivering services. So, services must be effective and co-ordinated and the principles of joined-up government apply across the public sector and to voluntary and private sector organizations. The state is an enabling partner that joins and steers flexible networks. The task is to build bridges between the various organizations involved in designing policies and delivering services. Civil servants will manage packages of services, packages of organizations and packages of governments.

Conclusions

In brief, governance arises only as the differing constructions of several traditions. There is no necessary logical or structural process determining the form governance takes, neither a process based on the intrinsic rationality of markets nor one on the path dependency of institutions. Rather, governance is the diverse actions and practices inspired by the varied beliefs and traditions we have discussed. Patterns of governance arise as the contingent products of diverse actions and political struggles informed by the beliefs of agents as they arise in the context of traditions. These conclusions apply, moreover, whether we are talking about the civil service, public sector reform, governing structures, or state–civil society relations. There may be some agreement that the boundary between state and civil society is being redrawn, and that the form and extent of state intervention is changing, but there is little agreement on how, why or whether it is desirable. If we adopt a broad concept of governance as the relation of the state to civil society, governance as private collectivism can appear to have been eroded by successive periods of centralization fuelled by the two world wars. The reinvention of the minimal state by the New Right and the discovery of networks by New Labour are attempts to find a substitute for the voluntary bonds diminished by state intervention and the erosion of intermediate institutions such as local government. We are witnessing, in this view, the search for an extended role for civil society in an era of large organizations.

Appeals to networks can be seen not only as a counterweight to the centralization of the 1960s and 1970s, but also as an example of how governing in late modern society involves engaging individuals in governance in their everyday life (as employees, users, citizens). It has come to do so because of the contingent ways in which politicians from within the various traditions responded to the dilemma of overload by introducing reforms that ask individuals to get involved. So, politicians in the liberal tradition sought to involve individuals in markets, while New Labour seeks their involvement in networks. Again, such citizen involvement is not the result of any necessary structural process but a contingent outcome of political actions and beliefs.

Our account of British governance provides a valuable corrective to both the traditional Westminster model of British government (see Chapter 4) and more positivist accounts of governance itself. We use the notion of governance to develop a more diverse view of state authority in its relationship to civil society. And we seek to explain patterns of governance in terms of contingent traditions and dilemmas cast at various levels of aggregation

We had no expectation that we could provide a true account of an objective process unaffected by the mentalities of particular individuals. Rather, we have related governance to the actions of many individuals; described the conflicting but overlapping stories that inform the actions of these individuals; and we have used the concept of tradition to explain why these actors construct their worlds as they do. Individuals inherit traditions and they enact and remake these traditions in their everyday lives. We argue governing structures can only be understood through the beliefs and actions of individuals located in traditions. Historical analysis is the way to uncover the traditions that shape these stories. Political ethnography enables us to tell the stories of different individuals and we turn to this task in Part II.

Part II

Reading practices

6 The Blair presidency

In Part II, we provide a series of ethnographic and historical studies that help to decentre British governance. In Chapter 1, we argued that people in identical situations could hold different beliefs, so an interpretive approach must explore the ways in which social practices are created, sustained and transformed. Ethnographers reconstruct the meanings of social actors by recovering other people's stories (see, for example, Geertz 1973: chapter 1; 1983; Taylor 1971: 32–3). Thus, we follow Hammersley and Atkinson in making the basic claim for ethnography that 'it captures the meaning of everyday human activities' (1983: 2). Fenno argues, 'the aim is to see the world as they see it, to adopt their vantage point on politics' (1990: 2). Ethnography encompasses many ways of collecting qualitative data about beliefs and practices. For example, Cris Shore's (2000: 7–11) cultural analysis of how EU elites sought to build Europe uses participant observation, historical archives, textual analysis of official documents, biographies, oral histories, recorded interviews and informal conversations as well as statistical and survey techniques. We use a similar battery of methods.[1]

In Chapter 1, we also argued that people adopted beliefs and performed actions against the background of an inherited tradition that influenced them. So, historical accounts of traditions provide the principle form of explanation for the beliefs and actions recovered as ethnographic data. In Part I, we offered critiques of modernist empiricism and the Westminster model with their Whiggish inheritances. Although the governance narrative has challenged complacent accounts of Westminster, we suggested it remained indebted to modernist empiricism. It embodied assumptions about the stability or even naturalness of institutions and networks, and about the possibility of explaining them through correlations and classifications that ignored beliefs. We concluded by highlighting the importance of decentring governance. Political scientists might explore the contingent and competing beliefs and traditions by which governance is made and remade not only by politicians but also by civil servants, street-level bureaucrats and citizens. Part II provides such decentred studies of the Blair presidency, life in a government department, the National Health Service (NHS) and the police. We begin in this chapter by looking at arguments about the 'Blair presidency'.

In this chapter, we begin by asking the deceptively simple question, 'how do we understand the relationship between the prime minister, ministers and the rest of Westminster and Whitehall?' We document briefly the long-standing claim that post-war Britain witnessed expanding prime ministerial power and the growth of the UK presidency. We then turn to its most recent manifestation – the story of a Blair presidency. This story makes three main claims: that there has been a centralization of coordination, a pluralization of advice and the personalization of party leadership and elections.[2] Obviously, we draw on the work of our academic colleagues, especially where they cite interviews, but we concentrate on the views of practitioners.[3] We rely on the obvious sources of prime ministerial, ministerial and civil servant auto-biographies, diaries and memoirs as well as official publications.[4] We compare these several narratives and show there is much inconsistency and contradiction.

A paradox recurs – even as people tell tales of a Blair presidency, they recount also stories of British governance that portray it as fragmented and multipolar. In particular, we argue New Labour appears to accept key tenets of the governance narrative. Innovations like joining-up and the reforms at No. 10 recognize the weakness of the centre and fuel claims of a Blair presi-dency. But New Labour ignores the other half of the governance narrative that stresses interdependence and cooperation, not command and control. So, claims of a Blair presidency founder on policymaking and implementation deficits. We argue this paradox reveals the distorting influence the West-minster Model still exerts on many accounts of British politics. Also, the simple nostrums of the Westminster Model serve to mask the contingency of political life. The prime minister wins, loses and draws as one might expect given the volatile nature of high politics. There is no simple phrase, no single theory, which captures this contingency. The preoccupation of British political science with analysing institutions and how they constrain political actors obscures the capacity of actors to define and redefine their practices. We point not just to the volatility of political life but also to the variety of prime ministerial practices.

The view from practitioners

Many claim there are problems with the evidence of practitioners.[5] As Anthony Mughan (2000, 134) remarks 'for every "insider" . . . assertion that prime ministerial government has arrived in Britain, it is possible to find the counter-assertion that cabinet government remains the order of the day'. For us such inconsistencies are the puzzle. We focus on divergent evidence because it highlights the paradox between presidential claims and the governance narrative. Also, presidential tales are not told of all prime ministers. Sweeping judgements about the standing of prime ministers invite disagreement but many would agree with most of Peter Hennessy's (2000b: chapter 19) judge-ments on post-war prime ministers. He treats Clement Attlee and Margaret Thatcher as the two great 'weather makers'. Edward Heath and Tony Blair are seen as 'system-shifters'. Winston Churchill and James Callaghan are seen as 'seasoned copers'. Harold Macmillan and Harold Wilson fall into the 'promise unfulfilled' category, although post-Iraq many might move Blair to this box (Riddell 2001: 40). Alec Douglas-Home is a 'punctuation mark', John Major was 'overwhelmed' and Anthony Eden was a 'catastrophe'. So, of the twelve post-war prime ministers, only three have attracted the epithet 'presidential' – Harold Wilson (1964–70), Margaret Thatcher (1979–90) and Tony Blair (1997 to date) – and with all of these three, judgements about their presidentialism varied while they were in office. Our survey focuses on these three prime ministers.

When George Brown, Foreign Secretary, resigned from Wilson's government on 15 March 1968, he claimed that he 'resigned as a matter of fundamental principle, because it seemed to me that the Prime Minister . . . was introducing a "presidential" system in to the running of the government that is wholly alien to the British constitutional system' (Brown 1972: 161). Later memoirs and diaries lend support to Brown's view.[6] For example, Richard Neustadt thought that Wilson 'means to take all decisions into his own hands'; he said Wilson 'wants not only to make ultimate decisions but to pass issues through his own mind, sitting at the centre of a brains trust . . . on the model, he says, of JFK' (cited in Healey 1990: 330). Denis Healey, who was Wilson's long-serving Minister of Defence and then Chancellor of the Exchequer, comments 'this was all true', and 'no Prime Minister ever interfered so much in the work of his colleagues' (Healey 1990: 332) – a judgement confirmed by Wilson's best biographer (Pimlott 1992: 563; see also Benn 1989: 2, 1985: 290).

Of course, there were differing views about Wilson. On 7 October 1969 Tony Benn[7] was invited to join Wilson's inner cabinet (Benn 1989: 206). By 1 November 1974, Wilson was demanding written assurances that Benn accept collective responsibility – 'the whole thing got very bitter and unpleasant' (Benn 1990: 254–5). By 1 October 1976, Benn was writing 'thank god that man has gone' (1990: 617). His view in 1979 was that 'the centralization of power into the hands of one man . . . amounts to a system of personal rule' (Benn 1985: 222).

If George Brown and Tony Benn complained about presidential tendencies, then Barbara Castle and Richard Crossman were criticizing Wilson's style for lacking clear strategic direction – he was not presidential enough (Castle 1984: 640; Crossman 1975: 582). Wilson (1977: 12–24) refused to entertain the ideas of prime ministerial government. When he became prime minister for a second time in 1974, he claimed 'there would this time be no "presidential nonsense"' (cited in Donoughue 1987: 47; see also Castle 1993: 452; Walker 1970: 96). Even Susan Pryce, a convinced advocate of the presidentialization thesis, concedes that Wilson 'remained constitutionally a prime minister' (1997: 137), and there were no cries of presidentialism during Wilson's second term. As his biographer Ben Pimlott (1992: 347) concludes:

'He was in many ways a civil servants' Prime Minister,' says Peter Shore. 'He liked advice coming to him from different angles,' says an ex-official. Both were true. He was not, as Marcia [Williams] and other members of the political staff complained, swamped by Whitehall advice; neither was he, as some officials and politicians, and hence many journalists, often alleged, the creature of the kitchen cabinet, cut off from the wider world. Playing one off against another, he often frustrated both: and remained his own man.

In short, opinions on Wilson's presidentialism varied between individuals, over time and with the personal standing of the minister with the prime minister.

The record is just as varied for Margaret Thatcher. Reg Prentice[8] concluded that 'the old idea that the Prime Minister was the first among equals has given way, step by step, towards a more presidential situation' (cited in Young and Sloman 1986: 45–6). As Kenneth Baker (1993: 270), Secretary of State for Education, observed, she relished the soubriquet 'The Iron Lady'. Three of her senior colleagues resigned ostensibly because of the way she ran cabinet. Michael Heseltine (2000: 312), Secretary of State for Defence, resigned over the Westland Affair, claiming he had been denied the opportunity to put his case to cabinet. Sir Geoffrey Howe, Foreign Secretary, criticized the way she ran her government, especially her 'roman intemperance' on European Monetary Union, which led her to criticize publicly her own government's policy. His cricket analogy has passed into parliamentary folklore: 'it is rather like sending in your opening batsman to the crease only for them to find, the moment the first balls are bowled, that their bats have been broken before the game by the team captain' (Howe 1994: 641, 666).

Nigel Lawson, Chancellor of the Exchequer, was no more impressed. He complained vigorously and often that there were two government economic policies, that of the chancellor and that of the prime minister and her personal economic adviser. Publicly expressed disagreements over the exchange rate were undermining both him and the government's policy (Lawson 1992: 955–6, 960–61), so he resigned. Perhaps Francis Pym, Foreign Secretary during the Falklands war, was most trenchant: 'I object to a system that deliberately pits Downing Street against individual Departments, breeds resentment amongst Ministers and Civil Servants and turns the Prime Minister into a President' (1984: 17).

Other ministers disagreed. Peter Walker (1991: 202–3) reports how Thatcher appointed him as Secretary of State for Wales knowing he favoured economic intervention and higher public spending. She thought he was 'awkward', and she knew he would not tackle the Welsh economy as she would tackle it, but she backed him fully. Peter Carrington (1988: 276) admired the way she allowed her 'highly intelligent head' to rule her 'natural impulses'. Nicholas Ridley (1991: 30) held several cabinet posts. While acknowledging that Heseltine, Lawson and Howe all resigned because of the way she conducted cabinet, he professed 'I . . . have no complaints to make about the way Margaret Thatcher ran her Cabinet'. He also observes that, in 1979, 'in many respects it was Willie Whitelaw's Cabinet which she first appointed'. Only after the Falkland's conflict and the 1983 election victory was the cabinet truly hers. Again, in her later years, she lost the cabinet to dramatic effect because, when she needed their support in the leadership contest of November 1990, it was not forthcoming. Her pre-eminence was contingent on the support of the public, the parliamentary party, and the cabinet. She lost all three and the cabinet delivered the final blow (Jones 1995: 107). So, again, beliefs about prime ministerial power varied between individuals, over time, and with the personal standing of the minister with the prime minister.

Hennessy (1998: 19) reports a conversation with one of Heseltine, Lawson or Howe: 'We talked about the coming Blair premiership . . . and agreed it would be on the command model. "This would only store up trouble for him", I said, "Yes," replied X, adding ruefully, "but you can get away with it for a very long time"'.

Given the chequered history of his presidential predecessors, we now turn to the questions of whether, and for how long Blair 'can get away with it'.

Presidential tales

Journalists have repeatedly described Tony Blair as presidential from the moment of his election as prime minister. In Britain, *The Independent* ran an article by Anthony Bevins entitled 'Blair Goes Presidential' on 6 May 1997. In the US, *The Washington Post* ran one by Dan Balz entitled 'Britain's Prime Minister Assumes Presidential Air' on 2 October 1997 (see also Rawnsley 2001: 292–4, 379). The notion of a Blair presidency, of a Bonapartist order, fuses several issues. It suggests that he is the most powerful prime minister in living memory. It highlights the institutional reforms that his government uses to strengthen the control of Number 10 over policy and its presentation. And it suggests that Blair personally combines the charisma and ease of a rock star with a remarkable tactical and strategic reach.

Political scientists too have paid attention to these issues, arguing Blair has manipulated his personal resources and expanded his institutional power to achieve a degree of predominance unmatched in British history.[9] For our purposes the key point is that insiders share such views. At the start, Jonathan Powell (No. 10 chief of staff) had famously warned senior civil servants to expect 'a change from a feudal system of barons to a more Napoleonic system' (*Daily Telegraph* 8 December 2001 cited in Seldon 2004: 437). Blair's No. 10 aides claim:

> Cabinet died years ago. It hardly works anywhere else in the world today. It is now a matter of strong leadership at the centre and creating structures and having people do it. I suppose we want to replace the Department barons with a Bonapartist system.
>
> (Quoted in Kavanagh and Seldon 2000: 291)

Blair's ministerial critics do not demur. Mo Mowlam (2002: 356, 361), former Secretary of State for Northern Ireland, claims 'more and more decisions were being taken at No. 10 without consultation with the relevant Minister or Secretary of State'. She criticizes 'the centralising tendency and arrogance of No. 10', especially 'their lack of inclusiveness of the cabinet, MPs, party members and the unions leads to bad decisions. Try as I might, I got no indication that their views or behaviour would change'. Similarly, Clare Short (2004: 272, 278) talks of 'the concentration of power in No. 10' criticizing Blair's 'informal decision making style' with 'his personal entourage of advisers' because it 'enhances the personal power of the Prime Minister and reduces the quality of decision-making'.

While 'President Blair' asserts:

> To my certain knowledge that has been said about virtually every administration in history that had a sense of direction. I remember that people said that back in the Eighties about Thatcher. Of course you have to have Cabinet Government.
>
> (*The Observer* 23 November 1997; see also the citations in Hennessy 2000c: 11, n.70)

So, we assess the three main claims made to support the contention that Blair has transformed his role as prime minister into that of a president; namely, that there has been a centralization of coordination, a pluralization of advice and a personalization of party leadership and elections.

Centralization

Structural changes at No. 10 and the Cabinet Office are the way in which Blair has strengthened the centre of government (Holliday 2000). The Policy Unit mutated into the Policy Directorate when it merged with the Prime Minister's Private Office. From day one Blair surrounded himself with a network of special advisers. Their numbers rose from eight under John Major to twenty-seven under Tony Blair (Blick 2004: Appendix; on the growth of advisers see next section). Total staff employed at No. 10 rose from 71 in 1970 under Heath, to 107 under Major to over 200 under Blair (Kavanagh and Seldon 2000: 306), creating 'the department that-will-not-speak-its-name' (Hennessy 2002d: 20). Initially the focus was on improving communications with Alistair Campbell heading the Strategic Communications Unit (SCU). Latterly the emphasis fell on policy advice. The Cabinet Office was reformed to improve central coordination. Several new units were created: for example, initially, the Social Exclusion Unit and the Performance and Innovation Unit, latterly the Strategy Unit, the Office of Public Services Reform and the Delivery Unit. As Hennessy (1998: 15) observes, 'Number 10 is omnipresent'. The Cabinet Office has always been a ragbag of functions bequeathed by former prime ministers. Now it groans under its own proliferating units posing the question of 'who will coordinate the would-be coordinator?' Blair seeks to control government functions without bothering himself with too many operational details.

In presidential tales, the prime minister's department in all but name allows Blair to remain on top of several projects if not in detailed touch. It checks the problem of prime ministerial overload. As Anthony Seldon (2004: 630) observes, 'however distracted Blair might be by other events, domestic and international, the work of monitoring . . . went on regardless ("The [Delivery] Unit never sleeps", Blair was told)' (see also Hennessy 2000a: 390).

Pluralization

In the Westminster model, the civil service has a monopoly of advice and this advice is collated and coordinated by the cabinet through its ministerial and official committees and the Cabinet Office. This neat and tidy picture has given way to one of competing centres of advice and coordination for which, allegedly, Blair is the only nodal point. The Cabinet Office has been 'gradually brought into the orbit of Downing Street . . . serving as a part of a prime ministerial centre, rather than the cabinet collectively'. Blair cut back on collegial decision making, 'reducing most meetings of the Cabinet to just forty minutes of approving decisions already taken elsewhere, parish notices and short speeches either delivered by the Prime Minister or vetted by him in advance' (Rentoul 2001: 540; see also Hennessy 1998: 11; Kavanagh and Seldon 2000: 278; Rawnsley 2001: 33; Seldon 2004: 437). Blair rarely chairs cabinet committees. There are fewer committees, meeting less often and not always reporting to full cabinet. Most decisions take place in 'bilaterals' – agreements struck in ad hoc meetings between Blair and ministers directly – a style favoured by both the prime minister and the chancellor (Rawnsley 2001: 53). In his first three years of office, Blair held 783 meetings with individual ministers compared with John Major's 272 for the same period (Kavanagh and Seldon 2000: 279). As Blair said, 'I think most Prime Ministers who have got a strong programme end up expecting their Secretaries of State to put it through; and you've always got a pretty direct personal relationship'. Also, he would not expect ministers to raise matters in cabinet: 'look I would be pretty shocked if the first time I knew a Cabinet Minister felt strongly about something was if they raised it at the cabinet table [. . .] I would expect them to come and knock on my door' (cited in Hennessy 2000c: 12).

The list of decisions never even reported to cabinet includes: Independence for the Bank of England, postponement of joining the Euro, cuts in lone-parent benefit and the future of hereditary peers (Rentoul 2001: 540). Robin Butler, former Cabinet Secretary and Head of the Home Civil Service, has reported that 'during the late 1940s, cabinet met for an average of 87 times a year, with 340 papers being circulated; in the 1970s, 60 times a year, with 140 papers; and by the late 1990s, no more than 40 times a year, with only 20 papers' (cited in Hennessy 2000b: 5) We might add, also, that Thatcher massively expanded the use of bilaterals as the primary means of decision-making: Lawson recalled laconically, 'I used to look forward to Cabinet meetings as the most restful and relaxing event of the week' (Rentoul 2001: 540). Nevertheless, both the frequency and content of Cabinet meetings are said to have diminished significantly under Blair, 'although a lot of the business of government continued to be done in cabinet committees' (*ibid.*: 540). Bilateral agreements have replaced collective government, and Blair is the coordinating nodal point. According to Rentoul (*ibid.*: 542), there is no 'trusted group of inner courtiers'. Blair is the only person able to see all government functioning.

Blair is supported in this role by the new machinery of the centre and by sources of advice other than the civil service. Each cabinet minister can have two special advisers but the total number remains small compared with 3,429 members of the senior civil service. The civil service monopoly of information and advice was broken under Thatcher. The trend to more varied sources of advice has deep roots. Thatcher accelerated the trend. Blair took it further. He knows the general direction in which he would like government to move, but not how to get there.

> They say, in effect, "Tell me what *you* want and *we'll* do it. But he keeps saying different things. Richard Wilson [Cabinet Secretary and Head of the Home Civil Service] finds it very difficult the way the Prime Minister jumps around. It's a succession of knee jerks.
>
> (Cited in Hennessy 2000c: 9)

The result is a frustrated civil service and special advisers. Derek Scott was Blair's economics adviser at No. 10 and he was clearly frustrated by what he saw as Blair's limited grasp of economics (Scott 2004. 14, 17, 206). He argues that Blair paid less attention to his policy advisers and civil servants than to 'the occasional outsider or those members of his inner circle who had little grasp or real interest in policy'. Moreover, Blair's circle was not the only, or even the most important, source of advice on social and economic policy. Gordon Brown had his own coterie, and his pre-eminent consigliore was Ed Balls, Chief Economic Adviser to the Treasury and a key Brown supporter. So, pluralization of advice also meant competing centres of advice and the competition between Blair and Brown's teams was intense.

Personalization

Yet another theme in tales of a Blair presidency is the 'professionalization of New Labour's relationships with the media through the use of spin doctors and public relations consultants' (Foley 2000: 4).[10] This professionalization is harnessed to two bigger purposes – continuous electioneering and personalizing that campaign, and indeed the government, by an almost exclusive focus on Tony Blair. Andrew Rawnsley amusingly illustrates the point: 'when Blair was asked why the manifesto contained seven pictures of himself and not one of the Cabinet mutes sat behind him, Brown's features were a study in granite

... the Deputy Prime Minister [John Prescott], wearing what his mother called his "ugly face", looked like a man one provocation away from a detonation' (2001: 488).

Blair did not invent media management as a way of sustaining the pre-eminence of the prime minister. However, his 'public communications, from the designer leisure wear to the designer accent and the designer press conferences probably attracted more public interest than those of any previous British government' (Seymour-Ure 2003: 7). Managing the media, or 'spin', is a game of chance and Blair's gambler-in-chief, his 'spin doctor' managing the media, was Alastair Campbell, Director of Communications and Strategy. The key organization was the Strategic Communications Unit, created in 1997. Its job was to monitor the news and provide a rapid response, expounding the government's position and, where necessary, rebutting any criticisms of government policy. Campbell was the prime minister's voice. His job was to ensure that the prime minister's voice was also that of the government. He was the spin doctor who used his daily lobby briefings to control government links with the media. Also, this prime ministerial centre extended its role to commanding the press relations of all ministers. Early in 1997 he even 'informed all departmental press chiefs that media bids for interviews with their ministers must be cleared first with him' (*The Independent*, 6 May 1997). In this way, Blair allegedly got an advanced news management service akin to that of an American president (see also Scott 2004: 15–18; Seldon 2004: chapter 22). Managing the media was also a central element in policy formulation. The strategy is called 'triangulation'. It involves packaging policies so they conflict with the left-wing of the Labour Party, thus winning support from the right-wing press.

Blair's premiership is also said to have been marked by a significant increase in the personalization of power. Contemporary media create an environment in which a politician's ability to attract publicity is crucial to electoral success. Indeed, Blair's office contributed to creating this environment by including 'personal convictions and experiences of the premier ... in the launch of policy initiatives and reviews' (Foley 2000: 256). For example, when Blair spoke of a rise in the rates of cancer, he publicly mentioned the death of both his own mother to throat cancer and his wife's aunt to breast cancer. In this way, Blair personalized politics both by adding his own sincere concern to issues and by making those matters public information. As Seldon (2004: 432–6) documents, whenever Blair thought he was not getting the results he wanted, he took personal charge. He identified himself personally with policy initiatives in, for example, crime, education, health, immigration and transport. In the pungent phrase of the leader of the opposition, Michael Howard, when he takes charge he has 'more summits than the Himalayas'.

Governance stories

Even as journalists, political scientists and practitioners tell tales of a Blair presidency, so they continue to recognize many limitations to Blair's ability to get his own way. Andrew Rawnsley (2001: 292–4) initially subscribed to 'the command and control' view of Blair. But by June 2003 he wrote of 'a prime minister who is not looking in the least bit presidential' at the head of 'a government displaying signs of drift' (*The Observer* 15 June 2003). In similar vein, Riddell commented 'If Mr. Blair has been a Napoleonic figure, he has been a frustrated rather than a commanding one' (2001: 40). So, there is a second story that focuses on the problems of governance and sees Blair as perpetually involved in negotiations and diplomacy with a host of other politicians, officials and citizens. He is cast as just one actor among many interdependent ones in the networks that criss-cross Whitehall, Westminster and beyond. So, now we tell the story of the Blair government from the standpoint of Whitehall governance and governance beyond Whitehall.

Whitehall governance: Blair and Brown

Even political scientists who support the notion of a Blair presidency typically mention the Treasury, under Gordon Brown as Chancellor of Exchequer, as 'a great crag standing in the way of a thoroughly monocratic government' (Hennessy 2002: 21). Brown and the Treasury have come to influence an ever-growing range of activities. In particular, Brown implemented a new system of Public Service Agreements (PSAs) that define and direct the activities of government departments by setting agreed targets and then monitoring them. This control of public expenditure shows Brown's reach throughout government. Blair helped to increase the scope of Brown's authority by appointing him to chair the main economic committee of the cabinet – a post historically occupied by the prime minister.

Recognition of Brown's authority requires us to shift from tales of a Blair presidency to stories of at least a dual monarchy: 'Brown conceived of the new government as a dual monarchy, each with its own court' (Rawnsley 2001: 20). This notion has its roots in the 'infamous' Granita restaurant story – a meeting between Blair and Brown in Islington on 31 May 1994.[11] 'Brown believed that he had his wish granted to be the central figure over economic and social policy in the future Labour government'. There is much disagreement about, and little documentary evidence on, the degree of control ceded to Brown, 'But there is no doubt that substantial if imprecise control was granted to Brown' (Seldon 2004: 193–4). James Naughtie (2002: 71) believes command over economic policy and 'significant chunks' of social policy were conceded (as do Keegan 2003: 124; Peston 2005: 58; Rawnsley 2001: 20, 111). While there is no documentary evidence to support a deal on handing over the prime ministership to Brown,[12] there is some evidence on the policy deal (*Guardian* 6 June 2003). Michael White, Political Editor of the *Guardian*, concludes, 'Blair had effectively ceded sovereignty to Brown in the economics sphere' (cited in Seldon 2004: 669; see also Peston 2005: 67). Rawnsley describes Blair as 'the chairman and Brown the chief executive' (2001: 143; see also Wheatcroft 2004: 68).

There have been several occasions on which Blair has found his authority checked by Brown. Such checks have occurred most often and dramatically over Blair's European ambitions and the budget. For example, Brown frustrated Blair's wish to join the Euro (Peston 2005: chapter 6; Keegan 2003: chapter 12; Seldon 2004: 682–3). Brown also controlled the budget by withholding information. As Scott comments 'getting information about the contents of Gordon Brown's budget was like drawing teeth' (2004: 24; see also Peston 2005: 99, 226–7; Seldon 2004: 674). And it mattered because 'Brown always put his "poverty" agenda above Blair's "choice" agenda' (Seldon 2004: 688; on the choice agenda see Blair 2004: chapter 43). Thus, Brown 'viewed the big increases he achieved in NHS spending as a huge moral victory against Blair', while he thought Blair's policy on hospitals was a 'distraction from his achievement in increasing expenditure'. Blair's policy on tuition fees for universities was also deemed a distraction from the real achievement of Brown increasing education expenditure (Seldon 2004: 682–3).

It may be accurate that in the second term 'while Blair aimed . . . to limit Brown's authority over domestic policy, Brown fought to increase it' (Seldon 2004: 627). But the result was two men presiding over territory ever more jealously guarded. Brown was 'immovable', 'dominating his own territory' with 'jagged defences designed to repel any invader, including the Prime Minister'. Not only was Downing Street left 'wondering on the latest thinking about the Euro', but 'unthrifty ministers' found him 'unrelenting in his pursuit of his own strategy'. Brown's role was that of 'social engineer who was redistributing wealth'. So, Blair and Brown 'were not interested in submerging their differences in outlook, but in making an exhibition of them' (Naughtie 2002: 352).

Seldon speculates on 'how much more Blair would have accomplished since 1997 had not so much time, emotional energy and goodwill been consumed' by their deteriorating relationship. He opines, 'Brown's achievements were almost undimmed by the shadow the relationship cast, while Blair felt hemmed in and often unable to realise his ambitions' (2004: 689). By 2005, their relationship had deteriorated to an all-time low. Their 'TeeBee-GeeBees' are a long-running soap opera in the media.[13] By the general election in 2005, Brown believed that Blair had torn up their deal (see Peston 2005: chapter 10). Brown was reported as saying to Blair, 'there is nothing you could ever say to me now that I could ever believe' (Peston 2005: 349). Brown was now 'the official opposition to Blair within the very heart of the Cabinet' (Peston 2005: 13, also 353).

A key characteristic of the past eight years is this shifting of fortunes, the contingency, of the court politics and the duumvirate.[14] Hennessy (2000b: 493–500) has conscientiously mapped Blair's inner circle and its changing membership. Many commentators discuss its influence (see, for example, Rawnsley 2001: 292; Rentoul 2001: 542–3; Seldon 2004: 407).[15] Beckett and Hencke (2004: chapter 14) describe the 'oestrogen-fuelled', '*Girl's Own*', comic book' view of life at the No. 10 court (see also Oborne and Walter 2004). We do not need to accept any account of life at No. 10 to make the observation that court politics are an important feature of the British executive.

Moreover, court politics are not confined to Blair and Brown. The barons still compete:

> Ministers are like medieval barons in that they preside over their own, sometimes vast, policy territory. Within that territory they are largely supreme. . . . The ministers have their own policy space, their own castles – even some of the architecture of departments . . . reinforces the perception – and their own courtiers. The ministers fight – or form alliances – with other barons in order to get what they want. They resent interference in their territory by other barons and will fight to defend it.
>
> (Norton 2000: 116–17)

The rivalry between Brown and Mandelson is a constant: 'one of the great laws of British politics . . . is that any action by Mandelson causes an equal and opposite reaction by Brown' (Peston 2005: 223; see also Rawnsley 2001: 20; Seldon 2004: 162). There have been other major, running conflicts; for example, between Brown and Alan Milburn, Secretary of State for Health, over Foundation Hospitals. Other ministers struggle to become heavy hitters. David Blunkett's frank if injudicious comments on the abilities and progress of his cabinet colleagues are a public example of a conversation that Westminster and Whitehall conducts all the time in private.[16] Such gossip is the currency of court politics and the judgments are markers in the endless ministerial jockeying for position and recognition.

Amid this jostling, cabinet, and its infrastructure of committees, continues. As Rentoul observes 'a lot of the business of government continued to be done in cabinet committees' (2001: 544). Also ministers play their traditional roles. David Blunkett rationed his contributions to key issues and not interfering in the affairs of other departments. Also highly political issues such as introducing identity cards were fully ventilated in cabinet and run through cabinet and interdepartmental committees (Pollard 2005: 26, 305–6). Desuetude is not yet cabinet's fate. The story of Blair and Brown, and their ubiquitous court politics, shows how misleading it is to focus only on the prime minister and cabinet. Political power is not concentrated in either prime minister or cabinet, but more widely dispersed. It is contested, so the standing of any individual, prime minister or chancellor, is contingent.

Governance beyond Westminster and Whitehall

The governance narrative recognizes the interdependence of prime minister and chancellor. It stresses the horizontal and vertical networks of interdependence in which the core executive is embedded. As the story of the rival courts of Brown and Blair demonstrates, the core executive can itself be seen as a set of overlapping networks. In this section we focus not on the horizontal networks of Westminster and Whitehall, but the networks beyond Westminster and Whitehall. Government policymaking is all too often confounded by central fragmentation and the Blair reforms of the centre seek to impose the desired degree of co-ordination. Add the simple fact that service delivery is disaggregated to a multiplicity of networks and the explanation of the gap between hopeful rhetoric and unwieldy reality is obvious. The implementation gap is ubiquitous. Unintended consequences are inevitable. This argument is illustrated by several studies of policy under Blair (Toynbee and Walker 2001; Seldon 2001b; Savage and Atkinson 2001). Of course, there are policy successes; for example, devolution to Scotland. Polly Toynbee and David Walker (2001: 40) confess that a 'deep-dyed cynic' would be impressed by Labour's commitment to a fairer society and conclude they have improved the lot of the poor. Nonetheless, in many other policy areas there has been little change or the results are unclear.

During the first term, changes in social security were incremental and they often recalled Conservative policy. It is the same story in housing policy. Health is a more complex tale, and it differs across the four nations of the British Isles (see Chapter 8). In England, there has been a clear shift to mixed public-private provision, but it is too early to assess the effects of these changes. Clearly, there has been a massive injection of public spending, although by international standards the UK is still well down the league table of spending on health. There has been a similar injection of cash in education, but again the long-term outcome is uncertain (for a preliminary balance sheet see Seldon 2001a: 593–600). There is a major emphasis on improving service delivery with ever more demanding performance measurement and evaluation. However, Tony Wright, Labour Chair of the Select Committee on Public Administration, summed it up succinctly: 'it is just not technically feasible, never mind desirable, to have that much centralization. If everything is a target, nothing is a target' (cited in Rawnsley 2001: 292). The emphasis on greater choice for users of public services is welcome but, as Clare Short (2004: 279) points out 'public sector reform cannot succeed on the basis of headline-grabbing slogans'.

Then there are the known domestic problem areas – higher education, immigration and transport – that still wait for their 'solutions'. There are the cock-ups – for example, privatizing air traffic control, the railways, tax credit payments, reform of the House of Lords, passports. There are the disasters that discredit governments. The examples include: the millennium dome, the Hutton Inquiry into Iraq and weapons of mass destruction, the Joe Moore affair over her claim that 9/11 was a 'good day to bury bad news' and the proposed referendum on the Euro.

Finally, there is the rest of the world. Events such as 9/11, Northern Ireland, Kosovo, the Afghan war and Iraq divert prime ministerial attention from domestic policy. Over Iraq, for example, not only did Blair have to persuade international leaders on the case for war, which he conspicuously failed to do, he also had to maintain support at home, which he did but at the price of eroding his authority in the party and with the electorate. The war presented Blair with the embarrassing resignations of two of his cabinet colleagues, Robin Cook (formerly Foreign Secretary, at the time Leader of the House of Commons) and Clare Short (Minister for International Development). The resignation of Cook and the ensuing fallout increased Blair's dependence on his cabinet colleagues. John Kampfner (2003: 161–2, 225–6, 272, 277, 315) describes the extent of the opposition to the invasion of Iraq in the Parliamentary Labour Party. The rebellion by 139 Labour MPs was the largest ever and the public demonstration in London was the biggest in decades. Even the cabinet was uncertain, verging on divided. In the understated phrases that are employed at times of stress and conflict, cabinet support moved from 'rock solid' to 'broad' and 'fears were being expressed with uncharacteristic candour' (Kampfner 2003: 294, 255). Although a prominent critic of government policy, Robin Cook's (2003: 271–2) assessment is judicious:

> Part of the political cost of Iraq was that it created in the public mind an image of their prime minister as preoccupied with fixing the world rather than running Britain. The irony is that this political damage to the Labour government was a self-inflicted wound. It could have been avoided by listening to the majority who were opposed to the war.

All governments fail some of the time. All governments are constrained by world events (Rose 2001). All prime ministers intervene. Few control and then only for some policies, some of the time. There is little evidence, for example, that James Callaghan's efforts to promote new policy initiatives in, for example, housing and education had much success (Donoughue 1987: 124). The test of success in politics is elusive and shifting. Maybe, as Enoch Powell said, all political careers end in failure. Maybe, as George Orwell said, 'every life is a defeat seen from the inside' (cited in Wheatcroft 2004: 69). But Blair's failures stand in stark relief to the early promise, making the disappointment of his supporters more acute. The problems the Blair government shares with all others have been compounded by two problems of his making: conflicts at the centre and his management style.

Blair's initiatives have depended on Brown's support – for example, top-up fees for students where Brown called off the dogs at the last moment (Peston 2005: 55; Seldon 2004: 648; Stothard 2003: 83). Although improving public services lies at the heart of the modernizing agenda, 'there were few signs that Blair was winning over his critics on public service reform' (Seldon 2004: 634, 636). Blair's weaknesses included 'a tendency to embroider, to persuade, and then to forget' (Wheatcroft 2004: 64) and 'his lack of policy making and management skills' (Seldon 2004: 692).

> What he wants is results. He has a feel for policies but not how the results come. He finds it hard to understand why things can't happen immediately.

There is a frustration in waiting for the pay-off and he doesn't have time. He comes back to this when one or other of the policy areas gets hot: education, then transport and now health.

(Official cited in Hennessy 2000c: 10)

However, although 'the machinery of government was in a state of permanent revolution at the centre after 1997 . . . he never succeeded in finding a structure that suited him'. In effect, the reforms were a sign of weakness not strength (Seldon 2004: 694). So Riddell (2001: 38–9) talks of a 'beleaguered centre' and a prime minister weak on detailed policies.[17]

Westminster smokescreens

We have told stories about the dependence of the prime minister on the court politics of the core executive and on the networks of service delivery. We have heard about the importance of party support, and the impact of political adventures in the international arena on domestic politics. To compare Blair before and after Iraq is to see that prime ministerial pre-eminence comes and goes; to witness the transition from President Blair to the 'unfulfilled prime minister' (Riddell 2001), who is 'in office but not in power' (Wheatcroft 2004: 68). The Blair presidency exists at most, therefore, in the interstices between political rhetoric and reality.

Some of the claims about the changing pattern of political leadership in Britain are accurate. It helps to distinguish between the electoral, policymaking and implementation arenas. First, personalization is a prominent feature of media management and electioneering in Britain. If we must use presidential language, it is here in the electoral and party arena that it is most apt, although the court politics of the duumvirate fits uncomfortably with the notion of monocratic leadership as does Brown's pre-eminent role on the 2001 election (Seldon 2004: chapter 31).[18] In the policymaking arena, there is some truth to the claim that Blair centralized policymaking on No. 10 and the Cabinet Office and eschewed cabinet government. However, this claim applies to selected policy areas only, with the equally important proviso that the prime minister's attention was also selective. The continuous reform of the centre speaks of the failure of co-ordination, not its success. The prime minister's influence is most constrained in the policy implementation arena, so it is conspicuous for its absence in most accounts of presidentialism. Here, other senior government figures, ministers and their departments, and other agencies are key actors. Similarly, although personalization can affect implementation, that effect is intermittent. Too often, the presidential thesis treats intervention as control. There is much that goes on in British government about which the prime minister knows little and affects even less. And all these arenas are embedded in dependence on domestic and international agencies and governments, making command and control strategies counterproductive.

So, we have a paradox. On the one hand, journalists, political scientists and

practitioners are telling tales of a Blair presidency characterized by centralization, personalization and pluralization. On the other, the same people
recount governance stories in which British politics consists of fragmented
policymaking and policy implementation networks over which a core
executive maintains a fragile – and increasingly fraught – influence. We want
to draw attention to two ways of interpreting this paradox.

First, all the chatter about a Blair presidency is a counter both in the court
politics of the duumvirate and in wider party politics. So, it matters not that
the presidential analogy is misleading because the game is not about empirical
accuracy but about expressing personal hostility to Blair in particular and the
Labour government in general. The critics have several specific targets. Foley
(2004) argues the epithet can refer to Blair's personal characteristics, to claims
that he is too powerful, to the consequences of Blair's command and control
style of government, to his international adventures and attendant disregard
of domestic politics, to his flouting of constitutional conventions, to the
influence of the USA on British politics, and to the failure to understand the
shift from government to governance. So the term is somewhat rhetorical – a
smoke screen behind which lurk several criticisms of Blair and the Labour
government.

Conversely, when critics bemoan the demise of cabinet government, what
exactly has been lost? Weller (2003: 74–8) distinguishes between the cabinet
as the constitutional theory of ministerial and collective responsibility, as a
set of rules and routines, as the forum for policymaking and coordination, as
a political bargaining arena between central actors, and as a component of the
core executive. Blair's critics single out cabinet's policymaking and coordination functions, yet it has been clear for over a quarter of a century that these
functions have been carried out by several central agencies, including but not
limited to the cabinet. To suggest that Blair has abandoned the doctrine of
collective responsibility is nonsense. Leaks are abhorrent. Unity is important
to electoral success. Dissenters go. To suggest that any prime minister in the
post-war period has adhered to anything but a pragmatic view of individual
ministerial responsibility is equally foolish. Ministers go when the prime
minister judges it is expedient, not before and not for departmental errors. In
short, and again, key terms about British government act as smoke screens.
But what are they acting as a smoke screen for?

Why do so many people who describe British governance as multipolar
nonetheless constantly talk about a Blair presidency? We argue the paradox
arises because of the misleading faith so many people have in the Westminster
model of British politics. The tales of presidentialism are a smoke screen that
upholds Westminster fictions but behind which we find a widespread acceptance of the governance story. If a commentator accepts any version of the
governance narrative, with its stress on interdependence, then any tale of a
Blair presidency will be undermined. Command and control mix with interdependence and cooperation like oil and water.

The interweaving of the two tales is obvious if we revisit briefly the accounts of Foley and Weller. Thus Foley's review of the uses of presidentialism encompasses the consequences of Blair's command and control style of government and the failure to understand the shift from government to governance. Both are core themes in the governance narrative. In a similar vein, Weller's account of the varieties of cabinet government includes cabinet as a political bargaining arena between central actors, and as a component of the core executive. Again both are key notions in the governance narrative.

So how does the Westminster model infuse talk of a Blair presidency? As we saw in Chapter 4, the effect will vary because people understand the Westminster model differently. There is no one version of that model. We will discuss three versions – Tory, Whig and Socialist.

Philip Norton is a Tory and a combative defender of the UK constitution against all comers (see, for example, Norton 1982). He believes the Blair presidency is 'dangerous' because it centralizes power in No. 10, adopts a principal-agent relationship with departments 'that is likely to be difficult to sustain', relies on goodwill for implementation 'that may not be forthcoming' and 'ignores parliament'. These problems are compounded by 'the lack of experience and, indeed, understanding of government by the prime minister and many of those around him' coupled with a 'leadership . . . obsessed with power' and 'no understanding . . . of relationships within the system' (Norton 2003: 277). Underpinning this critique is a governance interpretation of British government.

> Interdependency is a necessary feature of government in the United Kingdom. This interdependency has enabled government to cohere and deliver programmes of public policy because each part of the political system has recognised its distinct role within the system. It has been an interdependency of defined parts . . . The more the prime minister and senior ministers have sought to centralize power in their own hands then perhaps paradoxically, the more fragmented British government has become. The glue of government has started coming unstuck.
>
> *(Ibid.*: 276)

What to do? We need to end the 'institutionalization of fragmentation' by returning to the 'party-in-government' as the body 'responsible for public policy' that 'can be held accountable by electors at a subsequent general election' (*ibid.*: 278). In our preferred terminology, Norton uses the governance narrative to urge a return to the eternal verities of the Westminster model. He criticizes the notion of the Blair presidency to resurrect the Westminster model.

Hennessy (2000b: 535) is a Whig: 'history is a discipline that sobers up its practitioners'. He rejects the command and control model of the prime minister as chief executive for two reasons. First, 'command models sit ill with open societies'. Second, 'British political culture reflects the compost in which it is grown'. It is a parliamentary not a presidential compost. So he defends the 'deep continuities' of the constitutional side of the job – relations with the monarchy, accountability to parliament, collective government and a career civil service (Hennessy 2000b: 539). However, he too recognizes that Britain must change to meet the challenges of an interdependent world. He foresees prime ministers ever more entangled in international affairs, an expanding 'hybrid arena' where international and domestic mingle, relentless media pressure, 'the avalanche of information' and a reconfigured British state because of, for example, devolution (Hennessy 2000b: 538). In sum, he describes a world of complex interdependencies.

To meet these demands, he envisages, for example, No. 10 distancing itself from the hurly burley and developing both a plurality of analytical capacities and a greater capacity to provide risk and strategic assessments. All such changes would be within the context of collective government. Or to rephrase, to meet the challenges posed by the governance narrative, Hennessy envisages a return to cabinet government with reinforced analytical and strategic support. His notion of the British presidency is less that it is dangerous, although it may well be, but that to institutionalize it is to plant an alien invention in British soil.

The Socialist tradition in the guise of New Labour has its own conception of how British government should be run. In Peter Mandelson and Roger Liddle's (1996: chapter 10) 'shadow' manifesto they argued that, to succeed, Blair needed 'personal control of the central-government'. They describe with approval Mrs Thatcher's 'focus on a clear set of goals' and 'strength of will', claiming it 'says a lot about leadership in government'. Tony Blair should follow her example 'in getting control of the centre of government'. In particular there should be a 'more formalised strengthening of the centre of government' so it can 'give much-needed support to the prime minister' and 'provide a means for formulating and driving forward strategy for the government as a whole'. So, the No. 10 Policy Unit should be 'beefed-up', and the Cabinet Office needs to be more 'pro-active'. When New Labour came to power, therefore, it should have been no surprise that 'there was never any intention of having collective Cabinet government'. Blair was 'going to run a centralized government, with a commanding Policy Unit which was solidly New Labour' (insider cited in Seldon 2004: 437).

There are two features of New Labour's approach worth noting. First, it is strongly influenced by the example of Margaret Thatcher's leadership style. Second, it consigned Labour traditions, many of which are more democratic, to the dustbins of history. The contrast with Jim Callaghan or Harold Wilson is marked:

> From time to time there is discussion about the need for a formal Prime Minister's Department . . . such talk frequently overlooks the instruments he already has. He is able to provide himself with his own sources of information, he can send up a trial balloon or fire a siting shot across a Ministerial bow without directly involving his own authority or publicly

undermining that of the Minister; and has the necessary facilities to take a decisive hand in policy-making at any moment he chooses to intervene. (Callaghan 1987: 408; on Attlee see Morrison 1959: chapter 1; on Wilson, see Wilson 1977: chapter 1).

Deserting Labour traditions for Thatcherite dynamism had its costs. It provoked criticism for eroding the

> traditional norms of democracy and administration in favour of a model that rested more on central diktat. His three predecessors as Prime Ministers, Attlee, Wilson and Callaghan, had governed collectively: no previous Labour leader, from Keir Hardie to John Smith, had adopted such a personal style of control, and in this respect, as in others [Blair] showed himself to be a leader lacking empathy with the traditions of his party.
>
> (Seldon 2004: 694)

Yet Blair and his entourage consistently deny they have abandoned collective government, arguing their reforms are consistent with present-day constitutional conventions. In part, such a defence is mere convenience. If policymaking is presidential, then only the president is to blame when things go wrong. However, when the government faced its many policymaking and implementation problems, it blamed those long-standing whipping boys of the Westminster constitution – the civil service – said to lack both ideas and drive (Seldon 2004: 436). Others saw a problem with Blair's policymaking and management style and the mistaken belief that running the government was like running the Labour Party writ large. Such auto-critique was not on the central agenda.

Of course the government could see that policy success depended on others co-operating – hence the drive to 'joined-up' government (see, for example, Cm 4310 1999; Cabinet Office 2000; Mulgan 2001). The ubiquity of networks was drawn to the government's attention by its own think tanks (see, for example, Perri 6 1997; for comment, Bevir 2005: 29–53). They did not translate this recognition of dependence into a new leadership style. The governance narrative conflicted with their view of a strong centre. Command and control remained in vogue for running services built around many governments and organizations. But whatever the attractions of command and control, it did not work. New Labour's beliefs about the best way to run government positioned Blair between the rock of presidential critiques and the hard place of governance. Only the Westminster Model obscured the dangers of such a position.

Finally, there is one characteristic of the Westminster model that is present in every tradition – it is inward looking. Once we look at the role of the prime minister beyond the confines of Westminster and Whitehall, any assessment of his or her presidentialism must be tempered. Writing before 9/11 and Iraq, Richard Rose (2001: 3) commented: 'At Westminster and Whitehall, the Prime

Minister's power has increased greatly, but in the world beyond Dover it has greatly diminished'. 9/11 and Iraq rubbed salt in to the wounds of dependence. But, as Rose also comments, the spirit of Dicey, of parliamentary sovereignty and the Westminster model, lives on, with Britain's leaders 'living in denial' (*ibid.*: 244). The debate about presidentialism is a false debate, a smoke screen obscuring the frailty of the eternal verities of a tattered constitution.

Conclusion

When commentators focus on Westminster and Whitehall, the prime minister is indeed the first minister. When their focus shifts beyond Westminster and Whitehall, to the rest of the UK and beyond, then any presidential pretensions are a hollow crown. The inescapable fact is that Blair has to work in, with and through a complex of organizations, governments and networks with his power constrained by ever more pervasive and complex patterns of dependence. The more we look outside the Westminster Model, the more we find that centralization, pluralization and personalization represent not a concentration of power, but an endless search for effective levers of control by a core executive less powerful than many commentators and insiders claim.

We have contrasted the Westminster and the governance narratives to show that recent trends in British government do not provide certain evidence of prime ministerial power. Tales of the Blair presidency can be retold as tales of the unfulfilled prime minister. There are two major limitations to the focus on presidentialism. First, when used as a smoke screen for attacks on the prime minister and government, the term is but a flag of convenience. It is better by far to focus on the specific criticisms. If used as an analogy to identify leadership changes, it is potentially misleading because the differences between a parliamentary and a presidential system far outweigh the likenesses by some margin (see Rose 2001: 236–44). Better to talk of changing patterns of leadership. Second, a focus on presidentialism is too narrow, excessively preoccupied with Westminster and Whitehall. If there are important changes in the British executive, we can explore them adequately only through decentred studies of the beliefs and practices of politicians, civil servants, health practitioners, police officers, citizens and others. Such an approach will necessarily lead us to look at the contingencies of political life and the ways in which individuals modify traditions in response to dilemmas. If one conclusion is clear, it is that prime ministers vary in beliefs and practices. The office does not dictate their practices. We believe the analysis of changing patterns of leadership should start here and not with misleading analogies with polities categorized as presidential. The aphorism that 'the prime minister is first among equals' only needs the addition of 'but often he is more equal than others' to capture life at the top.

7   Everyday life in a ministry

A decentred approach to governance prompts us to explore patterns of rule as they emerge from the diverse actions of politicians, civil servants, street-level bureaucrats and citizens. In Chapter 5, we provided a broad-brush account of the dominant traditions that had inspired elite attempts to remake British governance. In the last chapter, we argued that we can only explore changes in the British core executive through decentred studies of the beliefs and practices of politicians and by looking at the contingencies of political life and the ways in which individuals modify traditions in response to dilemmas. We pointed to the volatility of political life, but also to the variety of prime ministerial practices. In this chapter, we turn our attention to permanent secretaries and ministers. We use ethnography to provide us with evidence of the actions and beliefs of key actors, and historical narratives to provide explanations of why they hold these beliefs and so perform these actions. We continue our theme that to understand change in the public sector, we must analyse the beliefs and practices of the people involved. The relationship between ministers and civil servants may be shaped by, for example, the traditions of the department, but it is not determined by that history. There is always scope for situated agency and it is only through the micro-level analysis of minister and public servants at work that we can understand how governance changes.

It should be a commonplace that to understand British governance we need to look inside government departments. Yet, as David Marsh *et al.* note, 'there is an absence of research into government departments' (2001: 1), and as Simon James comments, public administration 'has neglected ministers and their departments' (1999: 251; for a full review of the literature see Smith *et al.* 1995). There are many ministerial biographies, autobiographies, memoirs and diaries but, as James again notes, 'ministerial memoirs proliferate, but are often not much use to a student of Whitehall' (1992: 254). Even the 'veritable blizzard' of memoirs since the 1980s led to little of quality (James 1999: 252). Philip Norton comments there has been 'a dearth of scholarly literature on senior ministers' (2000: 101). We found few studies based on non-participant

observation (see, for example, Silverman and Jones 1976). The few quantitative studies that exist are arid (Blondel 1985; Rose 1987; for a critical
assessment see Dogan and Pelassy 1990: 116; Chabal 2003). Barberis is
surprised 'there has never been a book specifically devoted to permanent
secretaries' (1996: xvi) and argues we know little about these officeholders
beyond the popular television programmes, *Yes Minister* and *Yes Prime Minister*.
There are few memoirs by senior civil servants and all too often they are
'unintentionally revealing of the more tortuous cast of mandarin mind' (James
1992: 255; and see, for example, Bridges 1950; Dale 1941; Denham 2002;
Part 1980). There were exceptions to these judgements when they were
written. There are some useful novels (see, for example, Clark 1966; Edelman
1961; Snow 1964). There have been some valuable additions to the literature
in recent years. But the general point remains valid. We have few non-fiction
accounts of life at the top of British government.[1]

Everyday life at the top – scope and methods

We aim to describe the changing world of permanent secretaries and ministers.
We seek to recover their beliefs about the world. We rely on ethnography to
postulate the beliefs on which they act. Our methods included: diary analysis,
shadowing, elite interviewing and non-participant observation with extensive field notes. The fieldwork was conducted between January 2002 and
April 2004. It generated seven sets of primary data. The first set includes
transcribed repeat interviews with nine permanent secretaries. The second
consists of transcribed interviews with three secretaries of state and three
ministers. Third, we taped and transcribed interviews with nineteen other
officials. Fourth, we acquired copies of curriculum vitae, speeches and public
lectures. Fifth, we had field notes from two days of non-participant observation in each private office (two ministers and three permanent secretaries).
Sixth, we had field notes based on five working days spent shadowing each of
two ministers and three permanent secretaries. Seventh, we had copies of the
committee and other papers relevant for meetings during the non-participant
observation and shadowing.

The original selection of interviewees sought to combine male and female;
recent with long-standing appointments; central agencies and other departments; and London-based with devolved and Brussels-based appointments.
Once the project was underway, we 'snowballed' interviews, asking each
interviewee who else we could usefully talk to. We took whatever interviews
we could get. The interviews covered nine broad topics: personal information,
career, relationship between ministers and permanent secretaries, departmental management, external relations, transition to a Labour government
and changes since 1997, the future of the senior civil service, effects on private
life, and likes and dislikes.

To protect the identities of the departments and their staff, we have not used names, referring only to the minister, the department and the permanent secretary (PS). Civil servants and ministers provided the information 'for citation but not for attribution without express permission'. We illustrate the methods used and show how they help us to identify the beliefs and practices of the permanent secretaries and ministers. We also essay some generalizations about the behaviour of officials and politicians.

The cast of characters

The scene is London and the hurly-burly of the square mile around the Palace of Westminster (or Parliament) and Whitehall (or the central departments of the national government also known as ministries). The specific sets are three middle-ranking domestic service ministries, all within ten minutes' walk of Parliament. The main characters are the appointed public or civil servants and the elected secretary of state or minister. The top official in the department is known as the permanent secretary. Most are middle-aged, white, university-educated men who have spent their working life in the senior civil service. They are a small elite group who work closely with elected politicians. Their job is to advise the minister, manage the department and represent both to the outside world. The project covers the second term of the UK's Labour Government, which began on 8 June 2001. Tony Blair, prime minister and head of the government, appoints all ministers, both secretaries of state and junior ministers, who are drawn mainly from the majority party in the elected House of Commons, but some junior ministers will be from the non-elected House of Lords. The secretaries of state are members of cabinet, the fulcrum committee of British government, although its role and importance varies with the whims and wishes of each prime minister. The other key coordinating central bodies are the Treasury, which holds sway on all matters financial, and the Cabinet Office, which is home to a rag bag of central functions, unkindly referred to as the rest home for the pet projects of past prime ministers.

Private offices support both ministers and permanent secretaries. Civil servants staff both offices. A principal private secretary (PPS), who will be a young, fast stream civil servant with a bright future, heads each office. The chief difference is that the minister's private office contains ministerial advisers. They are political appointments, not career civil servants. They are on tap but not on top. The private offices vary in size from four to sixteen, although ministerial offices were always larger. Most ministries are divided into functional directorates, headed by a Director-General (DG), although the terminology varies. Few departments directly run services. They have hands-off service responsibilities. They work with and through agencies, headed by a chief executive. Broadly speaking, the department is responsible for policy and the agency for implementation.

Methods

Diary analysis and workload

Commentary

At the outset, we must comment on the limitations of the data drawn from the diaries. The diary secretary in the permanent secretaries' private office keeps the diary. There is no standard method of recording appointments. So, a meeting with a named individual in one department will be recorded as a 1:1 (one-to-one) in another diary. While we coded all meetings with the minister as policy, that meeting could be about anything. Similarly, a meeting with an official colleague could have much policy content and nothing in the diary would show that. Each diary secretary went through their permanent secretary's diary with us, but obviously could not remember the topic of every meeting. The diary is an incomplete record in other ways too. There are many meetings on the spur of the moment – colleagues pop in for a quick chat, the minister wants a minute. The differences in the total hours worked by each permanent secretary are more likely to reflect the incompleteness of the diary record than real differences in workload. We did not always agree with the civil service on how to code some activities. For example, we thought trips to agencies located outside London should be coded as representational, while the permanent secretary thought it should be coded as internal management. As we aim primarily to reveal how ministers and permanent secretaries see their world, their views prevailed. Finally, the list of specific activities is less diverse than the diaries reveal simply because we had to limit the categories to get a degree of comparability. In brief, the portrait is a broad-brush approximation of their workload.

The work of a permanent secretary is conventionally divided into the policy, management and representational roles. Figure 7.1 shows how much time is spent on the representational role (26–30 per cent) and how little on policy (7–13 per cent). Although we have no time series data, we are confident the time spent on management is a substantial increase on twenty years ago. The increase reflects a shift of time and effort from policy-related work to managing the department. However, and perhaps more significant, it reflects the longer hours worked. All our interviewees knew they worked longer now than at any other period in their career. Most were reluctant to compare their workloads with that of their predecessors but, when pressed, thought life in early times was less pressured. Some thought a five-year stint was enough given the demands of the job. The 'Other' category refers to a miscellany of indecipherable entries.

Table 7.1 shows the diversity of the permanent secretaries' workloads. To

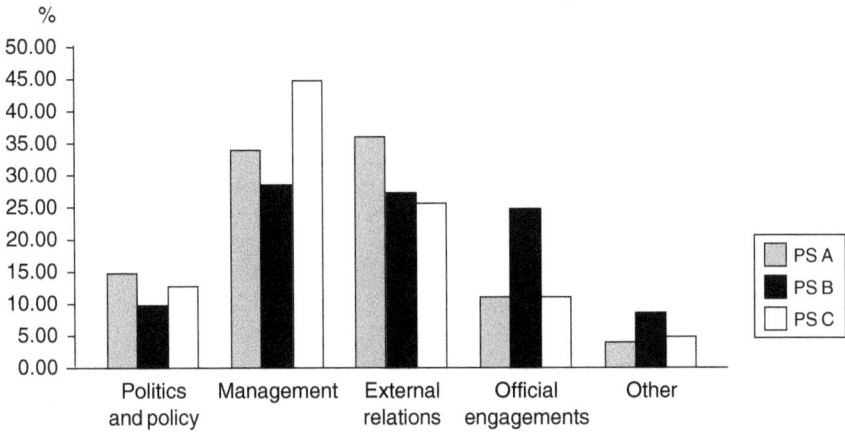

	%
	50.00
	45.00
	40.00
	35.00
	30.00
	25.00
	20.00
	15.00
	10.00
	5.00
	0.00

Politics and policy   Management   External relations   Official engagements   Other

PS A
PS B
PS C

Activity groupings	PS A Hours	%	PS B Hours	%	PS C Hours	%
Politics and policy	232:40	14.80	147:40	10.36	223:25	12.59
Management	538:05	34.22	410:00	28.75	800:55	45.14
External relations	565:10	35.94	399:00	27.98	455:15	25.66
Official engagements	179:30	11.41	352:15	24.70	204:45	11.54
Other	57:10	3.64	117:05	8.21	90:05	5.08

Figure 7.1 Comparing permanent secretaries' workloads

some extent it is seasonal – the budget comes but once a year. Accountability to parliament is a core doctrine of the Westminster model, but it accounts for precious little of a permanent secretary's time, although appearances before the Public Accounts Committee involve intensive dress rehearsals. Here, however, the diary is misleading. The departments all have elaborate procedures for processing parliamentary questions, but they rarely involve the permanent secretaries. Perhaps most dramatic is the finding that only 6 per cent of the permanent secretaries' time is spent working alone, reading and preparing papers, although this figure is slightly misleading. Our figures refer only to time allocated in the diary. They exclude, for example, reading the files. It is not just the minister who has to consume endless towers of paper. It is the lot of permanent secretaries also. Much reading and writing is done in the early evening when the diary is empty and outside office hours, travelling to and from work.

In sum, as with senior managers in the private sector, permanent secretaries spend their time communicating, not thinking, meeting people, not writing papers or developing strategy. It should also be borne in mind that meetings are not only about decisions but also about departmental memory. They are the mechanism for the permanent secretary to get an update on where the department is with a particular topic.

Table 7.1 A comparison of three Secretaries: a full year's activities by hours and per cent

Activities	PS A Hours	%	PS B Hours	%	PS C Hours	%
Policy and politics						
Secretary of State	84:45	5.39	72:50	5.11	96:05	5.41
Other ministers	56:55	3.62	34:20	2.41	59:35	3.36
Parliament	31:30	2.00	17:45	1.24	22:30	1.27
Media	8:45	0.56	21:00	1.47	30:00	1.69
Substantive policy	50:45	3.23	1:45	0.12	15:15	0.86
Sub-total	232:40	14.80	147:40	10.36	223:25	12.59
Management						
Strategy	24:15	1.54	42:45	3.00	53:45	3.03
Thinking time	6:45	0.43	1:30	0.11	133:15	7.51
Board	90:30	5.75	53:05	3.72	118:15	6.66
Budget	14:00	0.89	6:15	0.44	14:15	0.80
Management general	272:10	17.31	208:05	14.59	327:50	18.48
Management KITs	95:15	6.06	42:25	2.97	33:00	1.86
Mentoring	5:30	0.35	7:00	0.49	14:00	0.79
One-to-one	28:40	1.82	46:10	3.24	106:35	6.01
Accounts officer	1:00	0.06	2:45	0.19	0:00	0.00
Sub-total	538:05	34.22	410:00	28.75	800:55	45.14
External relations						
Whitehall	163:35	10.40	145:10	10.18	149:10	8.41
Wed am meeting	33:00	2.10	29:00	2.03	37:15	2.10
Other UK organization	181:30	11.54	96:20	6.76	188:30	10.62
Centre of Govt	27:05	1.72	8:00	0.56	36:20	2.05
Agencies	65:00	4.13	27:05	1.90	0:00	0.00
EU	91:30	5.82	36:40	2.57	0:00	0.00
Other Govts	3:30	0.22	56:45	3.98	44:00	2.48
Sub-total	565:10	35.94	399:00	27.98	455:15	25.66
Official engagements						
Conferences etc.	47:30	3.02	56:40	3.97	80:30	4.54
Working lunches	13:30	0.86	125:15	8.78	12:00	0.68
Evenings	118:30	7.54	171:20	12.01	112:15	6.33
Sub-total	179:30	11.41	352:15	24.70	204:45	11.54
Other						
Hello meetings	0:00	0.00	20:45	1.46	36:15	2.04
Cancellations	0:00	0.00	0:00	0.00	0:00	0.00
Phone calls	1:15	0.08	0:00	0.00	6:40	0.38
Private	27:00	1.72	67:50	4.76	1:30	0.08
Miscellaneous	13:40	0.87	19:45	1.38	25:40	1.45
Don't know	15:15	0.97	8:45	0.61	20:00	1.13
Sub-total	57:10	3.64	117:05	8.21	90:05	5.08
Total	1572:35		1426:00		1774:25	

There is also a culture of long hours. Most work a 40–50 hour week as a matter of routine and often much more. Official engagements in the evening consume large chunks of time. They can lead to behaviour akin to a bear with a sore head, not because they have drunk too much, but because they have been bored too often for too long.

Long hours are the fate of the private office. It is staffed as long as the permanent secretary (or minister) is there and often longer, getting ready for the following day. They are young and the expense of London housing drives them to the outer ring. Journey times of over an hour are not unusual. Bluntly, join the private office and lose your private life. The expression 'I'll never forget what's his name' applies to spouses rarely seen in daylight hours. Permanent secretaries can also live a long way out, but they are older and better paid, so they can afford a small flat in central London as well as a comfortable house in Cambridge or Hertfordshire.

On a more personal note, it is worth stressing the unrelenting pace of work. If the phrase 'lonely at the top' is a cliché, it is not without meaning. Permanent secretaries and ministers live in a small, even claustrophobic, world. There are few people they can talk to other than one another. Secrecy may be an obsession, but there are some good reasons for it – for example, we sat in on discussions that we could have used for personal profit through insider trading – and being circumspect is unavoidable.

Notebook

Below we give an extract from our field notes made during a crisis about training. It covers 40 minutes in the life of the permanent secretary (PS). We sat in his room throughout, taking notes as if we were his private secretary. Every PS always has a private secretary taking notes at any meeting unless he specifically decrees otherwise. We draw mainly on interviews with nine PSs (one female) and six ministers (three female). To protect individual identities, we use the male pronoun throughout.

Day 3. Wednesday, Permanent Secretary's Office.
The day before the events described here, several newspapers reported that a national Agency had made important mistakes and the papers dramatized the mistakes with heartbreaking human-interest stories.

PS arrives 09.07 and starts talking about last night. He had had a glass of wine with the Minister before he left. The Minister was in a state. The Minister thinks there will be accusations of not being in control.

Private Office pops in and inquires what the PS has done about the efficiency memo. He has done nothing, so he tells the Private Office, 'Harass me about it'. But he is doing nothing because he doesn't like it. 'Too complex, calls for too much information and will be a burden on the Director Generals [DGs].'

There is tension in the air. The responsible DG, Press Office and Principal Private Secretary (PPS to the Minister) arrive for an unscheduled meeting. They've just left the Minister who was in the loading bay waiting for the official car – off to a meeting. The Minister is having a strop, wanting dramatic action NOW. Off the top of the Minister's head, he wants an independent inquiry, with Chief Executive (designate) to chair it. PS and DG must talk to Chief Executive (designate) NOW. The Minister insists, 'we must be seen to address the issue'. The Minister knew he was being over-the-top. The Minister is back at 13.00 and wants a meeting.

The meeting rehearses where they are. The officials in the Agency are seen as too hands on. The press is bad. It's a lead story in all the main newspapers (and that's the sensationalist tabloids as much as the serious broadsheets). The story is spreading, as is public concern.

PS: 'Let's pause. I'll discuss with the Chief Executive and come back for 13.00'. He has to be at Cabinet Office for the usual Wednesday morning meeting of all PSs. It's a strategy meeting. (He makes it obvious that strategy comes second to the crisis but he has to go).

Press Officer: 'The Minister will only get one shot at it. We can't go for a drip, drip response.'

DG: 'And we can't wait.'

They leave.

PS muses aloud as he gets ready to go to Cabinet Office: The Minister is worried. It's important for a minister to have success. It doesn't help when you have to deal with crises. We have had too many crises – in recent months the department has had three. It gives the impression we are not in control. 'The Minister is not a big hitter' (in the cabinet or the government) and so the Minister is worried about the future. It's also true for the junior minister if he wants a promotion. It doesn't directly affect me but I want the department to be a success. And nowadays we move on after 3 to 5 years.

DG returns briefly. He is unhappy about one of his senior managers. 'He should be here on a day like this' (that is, cancel pre-existing appointments because protecting the Minister is the over-riding priority) . . . The Minister is already unhappy with him. You (PS) should be aware of this. He's not proactive enough. DG then reports on yesterday's events. The meeting with the Agency officials 'went fine'. 'The worry is we still don't know what it's all about'. The Minister wants a report and wants advance notice of what it will say. The Minister wants to see the 'alternative scenarios'. We need to respond quickly and the Minister's not sure all officials are 'on the ball'. The Minister is 'unnerved' by press reports. The Agency's press briefing was factually accurate but the presentation was 'appalling'. DG repeats the Minister's call for an inquiry headed by the Chief Executive.

PS: 'Barmy idea. Don't suggest the idea to the Chief Executive' . . . Just tell him the Minister is alarmed and wants decisive action. We must have the facts. It's a big issue. What more can be done?

Neither PS nor DG knows exactly what happened or why. A letter from the Agency has been made public and it can bear several interpretations. The Press have seen the letter and they have put the worst possible construction on it.

PS: 'Yes, I know and I've told the Minister that, but it isn't what the Agency meant'.

DG leaves and PS tells Diary Secretary to rearrange his diary. He schedules a 13.00 meeting with the Minister and cancels an honours meeting (to discuss who will get a gong). 'It's more important than giving the "Rock Star" a knighthood'. He digresses. 'I was there for that. Those of us who remembered the 60s grimaced at that. The "Cultural Icon" speaks for popular culture. I speak up for my world.'

PS: 'I'll have to explain what's going on at perm secs. There'll be some amusement that it's me not them! No. They're more supportive than that . . . but only slightly' {laughs}. First time he's done that this morning. The PS is a relaxed individual but the tension is manifested in his businesslike manner minus the usual social niceties of humour.

Press Office rings. He briefs them about contacting the Chief Executive and he stresses that we must build the Chief Executive up. Press Office wants to see PS. They want five minutes on what we know.

PS: 'No. I know there's an issue but I don't want my mind cluttered up with the detail.' The need to 'get the story straight' becomes a recurrent motif.

09.48 PS goes to perm secs. On the way down to the car – it's about 400 metres to the Cabinet Office – his Private Office briefs him on a meeting with another PS at the end of the Wednesday morning meeting.

Commentary

This short extract may cover only 41 minutes, but it encourages several reflections on life at the top. First, the PS's schedule is hectic. His life is a continuous series of meetings, planned and unplanned. The pace is fast and unrelenting. In all three private offices, the Private Office told us the PS wanted to avoid back-to-back meetings, and in every office the PS had them most days of most weeks. Thus, at 4.00 pm, the permanent secretary arrives at his fifth meeting that day and cannot remember why he is there. He confesses to his lapse of memory, asks a junior colleague 'to get him up to speed', then takes over the meeting after a few minutes when he remembers. And most meetings are not about making decisions. They are about refreshing the department's memory, updating everyone on how things stand. Thinking time, writing time and reading time, were all at a premium.

Top civil servants and ministers learn through the stories they hear and tell one another. Such stories are a source of institutional memory, the repositories of the traditions through which practitioners filter current events. The basis for much advice is the collective memory of the department – its traditions if you will. It is an organized, selective retelling of the past to make sense of the present. Permanent secretaries explain past practice and events to justify recommendations for the future. Most if not all civil servants will accept that the art of storytelling is an integral part of their work. Such phrases as 'Are we telling a consistent story?' and 'What is our story?' abound. They do not use the phrase 'story telling' but talk of 'getting the story straight'. Throughout the crisis, the emphasis fell on getting the facts, finding out what happened. Lying is a worse sin than error, accident, even incompetence.

In telling the story, they are also rehearsing lines and explanations to see what they sound like. Is it plausible? They want the reactions of their colleagues so they can anticipate the reaction of a larger, external audience. They are also risk averse, so they are careful about facts in case they are shown to be in error later. A simple illustration will suffice. On his desk, the PPS had a red phone dedicated to monitoring telephone conversations by the PS. He kept a handwritten note of any potentially delicate matter or decision made or agreed to by the PS. Everyone called this phone the 'Bat phone', after the instrument used by the mayor of Gotham City to summon the redoubted caped crusader. Regrettably there was no spotlight projecting the departmental logo on low-lying cloud. Even more regrettable, the Bat phone has now been replaced by a modern phone. But still calls are monitored. The world of the department is a world where even a casual remark in a phone call can have important repercussions. Such care and caution may seem exaggerated, but it is nothing compared to the maelstrom the media can unleash on the unwary. Ministers may call for the civil service to be less risk averse. They don't mean it!

Interviews

Below we give an extract from an interview that took place before the crisis. We edited the transcript to correct the English, no more. The PS is talking about his Minister.

RR   What do you expect from your Minister?
PS   Well I expect [long pause]
RR   Presumably you have got expectations about what you are supposed to do out there
PS   Yes
RR   and therefore you expect the Minister to support you.

PS   Yes I expect that. You said something earlier about holding civil servants to account for delivery but I expect the Minister to take ultimate responsibility for the success of our operations.

RR   That's for the public presumably? In private they are going to hold you to account.

PS   Yes they are but I expect us to share that responsibility, which my Minister has done. I expect the Minister to give very clear leadership about what they want. I expect an engagement with us on the really difficult issues, the willingness to listen to us, and then clarity of decision. And I have certainly got that from my Minister. But you also get a willingness to listen, which is legendary really. So I want that. I want my Ministers to be very influential with their colleagues because I need them to go out there and argue for resources and so on, of course. And because in our world the ability to persuade and communicate is so important to getting everybody to go along with you, I need Ministers who are very good publicly and very good at connecting with their audiences and communicating. I don't know what else I need from them.

RR   It's not quite the same question but it is going to sound like it. What do you like in your Ministers?

PS   Do you mean what do I like in them, what do I actually like, or what would I like them to be?

RR   Obviously you would like them to meet all those expectations but you might like certain kinds of personalities, you might like certain characteristics in the Minister, personality characteristics. If you look at the textbooks, people use phrases like 'married' because they get so close to one another, you almost know what the other one is going to think before they say it.

PS   I am completely devoted to the Minister, I am, I don't mind being on the record. Why? Well because, and I think this is stroke of luck, we spent three, more than three years, working together on policy and we therefore had developed a relationship of trust which we were able to transfer immediately, on that first day after the election, to Permanent Secretary and Secretary of State. I don't suppose that will be replicated ever, will it?

    We share a lot of understandings and share a lot of values really, about the policy system. I completely understand how the Minister is going to react. If I am there at 9:00 on the morning or earlier it's because I know that I just need to say something to the Minister about what is going on that day because I know that will be an issue. We have learned how to read one another, how we react to certain situations. We have also been through some difficult things together and we have stood together.

    What do I like about the Minister? The Minister has an almost unique ability to connect with the audience. That is something quite special about the Minister, which people don't see on these big occasions but the Minister has that ability. The Minister is somebody who listens intently to others and to civil servants and respects the advisers, all of them. And the Minister is someone who trusts people and enters genuinely into a debate. The best debates I have had about policy, in my entire career, are around the Minister's table because the Minister is in an equal position where, you know, together we are exploring the solution.

RR   Yes okay.

PS   And of course eventually, the Minister then takes the decision but the Minister is able to create a sense of a team working towards the Minister's achievements.

RR   You've worked with several Ministers over the years.

PS   Yes and I've liked a lot of them.

RR   What do you dislike about Ministers?

PS   [very long pause] *{sound of drinking}*

RR   You can always edit it out.

PS   I know that. It's difficult. I was trying to think of the ones I didn't like and then trying to generalize what I didn't like about them. What I most dislike is when all they are interested in is themselves. That is the moment which I have disliked most and when it seems that everything that they do is not for the public good but for their own position, career and self-advancement. That is what I have most disliked and occasionally that has been so. There is something of that in a lot of Ministers. It is in all of us isn't it – in civil servants too? But just occasionally there have been people who have put that a long way ahead of anything else and I disliked that.

   I dislike it when you can't get them to think straight. Oh, I have some civil servants like that as well. You know, I think Ministers are just human beings like all the rest of us. They share exactly the same range of strengths and weaknesses as the rest of us. Sometimes, because of the position they occupy, myths develop about them that magnify their strengths and weaknesses. There aren't a lot of things I don't like about Ministers.

RR   Short-termism?

PS   I am very tolerant of that because it is sort of in the nature of the beast. Of course, I mean the changes, the chopping and changing and the short-termism. I'm afraid I accept that as part of the political process and maybe I am too tolerant of it but I just accept it goes with the territory. I am sometimes amazed that governments are as long-term as they are. The Prime Minister said the other day about something which will remain nameless, 'It's amazing isn't it that we are investing in this, the benefits are probably coming in about 25 years time.' [PS laughs]. Some of the benefits of policy now are the result of decisions taken a long time ago.

Commentary

For many academics, the Westminster model is an outmoded account of British government. But it isn't for top civil servants. When Sir Robert Armstrong (1985) restates the constitutional position that 'the duty of the individual civil servant is first and foremost to the Minister of the Crown who is in charge of the department in which he is serving', he states a belief widely shared by top civil servants. What place does the Westminster model occupy? The short answer is that it legitimates the role of the civil servant. In classic Weberian fashion, the doctrine of ministerial responsibility means that the role of civil servants is to follow orders, and that of politicians is to give them. A belief in the Westminster model is integral to the anonymity and political impartiality of civil servants.

Similarly, there is a belief in a public service ethos. Sir Richard Wilson (2003) defines the character of the civil service as integrity, political impartiality, merit, ability to work for successive governments and public service. On public service he comments: 'What attracts people to the Civil Service is the wish to make a contribution to the community. We have some of the best, most challenging jobs in the economy at every level. This gives us a deeply committed workforce.'

They may live in the era of new public management, but long established beliefs, actions and practices persist. They are captured by the term 'generalist', who is clever, loyal, reasonable and able to synthesize complex arguments quickly and clearly for the lay minister.

What shines out of our interview extract is the PS's loyalty to his minister. Perhaps the greatest crime in the civil service canon is to betray one's minister. Loyalty is a core belief and practice socialized into the newest recruit to the senior civil service. That loyalty can spill over into, literally, devotion. He was 'very upset' when the minister had to resign. Loyalty is extended not only to ministers but also to other colleagues. The corollary of trusting ministers and civil servant colleagues is that they trust you. And trust is not just a matter of personal loyalty. It is also about being trusted to get on with the job, to be kept in the loop and to be respected for one's judgement.

A process of socialization sustains these beliefs and practices. A new fast stream recruit will have a mentor to guide them through the early years. They will have patrons as they progress through its ranks. They will work in a private office and have a stint in either the Cabinet Office or the Treasury, perhaps both. They are taught the norms and values of the higher civil service and learn about personal behaviour, the job and its values and 'the framework of the acceptable'. They are 'socialized into the idea of a profession'. Now that civil service appointments are increasingly made by open competition, there are fears the newcomers will not be socialized in the service's traditions. They will not have sat across the desk from a mentor learning the rules of the Whitehall village game. They will not have had a patron to advise them on career development. They will not have worked the rites of passage through a private office, the Treasury and the Cabinet Office. Thus, the public service ethos could be eroded. Loyalty might become conditional and contingent and formal mechanisms of co-ordination may replace the glue of trust and shared codes.

The minister

Missing from our three commentaries is the minister. While ministers share many of the beliefs and practices of their top civil servants, there are significant differences. The most obvious is their concern with publicly visible performance and being seen to make a difference. 'Making a difference' has several distinct if related meanings. Obviously it refers to legislation and policy that changes the lives of citizens. It also refers to the minister's standing in the pecking order of the governing party. Ministers seek to be 'onside' with the prime minister and the chancellor and look, first, to survive in the cabinet and, second, to move to one of the great departments of state such as the Treasury or the Home Office.

Of course, such behaviour can be dismissed as an egotistical search for a place in history books. Such a judgement may be true of some. Others believe they can make life better; for children, for the elderly, for whichever section of society they govern. It places them in the media eye, to a frightening extent. We saw one minister, who to the best of our knowledge had made no mistake, hounded by the press. They were not interested in the facts of the case. They did not know, and did not want to know, the accurate story. They wanted a headline. They wanted blood in the guise of a resignation. We saw a minister taut with worry trying to fend off the pack. The voice gave facts. The body spoke tension. The minister's hands were clasped together on the tabletop, as taught in the media classes they all take. But the legs were twined and twisted under the table and the breathing was shallow and rapid. The journalists did not listen. They talked among themselves. The press treated the minister as an object, not a person.

It is hard to overestimate the impact of the media (press, radio and television). The Private Offices religiously scan the newspapers for any story affecting their departments. There is a daily cuttings service for the scurrilous tabloids, the serious broadsheets, regional newspapers and professional journals. Surprisingly, there is no daily summary for the minister or the PS of the stories on radio and television. The office television is only switched on for big events, which includes the budget, but is just as likely to be England's key qualifying match in the European Championship. Of course, there is a section of the department dedicated to managing the media and it has close relations with radio and television, setting up interviews, events and official announcements. The Labour government has achieved some notoriety for its emphasis on spin and every department seeks to stay onside with the government's communications strategy. But the printed word remains the preferred medium of communication in the everyday life of the permanent secretary and the private office.

Ministers not only live in a fishbowl, they also have to be adaptable. They move from meeting-to-meeting, engagement-to-engagement, topic-to-topic, with barely time to read, let alone digest, their briefing. The diversity can be breathtaking. One moment it is the daughter of a civil servant on a school project, the next it is a party of overseas visitors bringing comradely greetings from their political party, a meeting of business people on new legislation followed by the unions, then the Private Office wants to sort out the diary and related papers before the minister is taken to a public speaking engagement. Lunch is a sandwich, bought by the Private Office, eaten while signing various letters and replying to e-mails. So it goes – endlessly.

Both ministers and permanent secretaries have Private Offices to help them cope with their daily routines and the literature describes them as forcing grounds for rising civil servants. They may be, some of the time, for some high flyers. But much of the work is administrative routine and boring. A Private Office works long hours. The minister is never unattended. But most of the work is mail, papers and appointments. It is exciting because it is working at the top of the organization for the top people, but it is routine because the aim is to make sure everything runs as smoothly as possible. The maxim is 'no surprises'. The minister and permanent secretary have to be in the right place at the right time and with the right papers. Keeping them happy is the cardinal virtue.

Diary secretaries are key players in keeping everyone happy. They regulate access to the minister and the protocol is strict and covers all Whitehall. There is a hierarchy of ministers. So, the more junior minister rings and waits to be put through to the senior minister. Senior ministers wait for no one on the phone. Some diary secretaries had been in post for twenty years. They moved with their minister and permanent secretary. They know what he wants before he wants it. The young fast stream civil servant sitting opposite on an eighteen-month posting will be eaten for breakfast, if the diary secretary can be bothered. It is rarely necessary. To remain fast stream, you learn fast.

What is striking about the worlds of politician and administrator is their similarities. Both confront unrelenting events, which they struggle to grasp with the help of a private office that exists only to serve. Distinctions between policy and management, politician and civil servant, are meaningless when confronted with the imperative to cope and survive. But coping is not a dramatic activity. It is surprisingly ordinary. Private offices exist to domesticate trouble, to defuse problems, to take the emotion out of a crisis. The style of the permanent secretaries is low key. There are rituals aimed at relaxing new arrivals and making them feel at home. Tea and coffee are served at virtually every meeting. Stothard refers to 'coffee sipping amity' and to the messengers who deliver it as 'a source of continuity and a kind of comfort' (2003: 34, 61). In our departments, it was tea more often than coffee, but the quality of ritual comfort remained. Stories are built up through successive meetings with colleagues. KITs – Keeping in Touch – and 1:1s are the mechanisms for managing everyday life, sharing experience, arriving at stories and building loyalty. They are crucial to domesticating a hectic life. And its ordinariness should not mislead. These everyday routines are unquestioned, to a degree unrecognized. They make the exceptional ordinary. They can also make the unacceptable acceptable.

Conclusions: prospects and problems

After reading a draft of this chapter, one colleague commented, 'fun stuff, but at the end of the day, so what?' 'What do we know from this project that we don't from *Yes Minister* or from our own experience of working in any organization?' What practices that puzzle outsiders make perfect sense when viewed against the backdrop of the beliefs and traditions described in our story? We find it odd that we were asked this question. It reflects the mainstream bias to ostensibly 'hard' evidence, especially as the answers are obvious. Knowledge of one's own organization is not the same as evidence about the beliefs and practices of another organization. No one would dream of mistaking one's own organization for the universe of organizations. We study organizations to identify both the common and the unique. Similarly, *Yes Minister* was fiction. Our story is not.

Each of our illustrations provides distinctive observations on the characteristics of everyday life at the top. It may try the reader's patience, but we repeat some of the key observations.

First, the workload for both permanent secretaries and ministers is heavy and diverse. The pace of events is relentless and endless. They live in a goldfish bowl. Our experience of universities and other organizations leads us to describe the workload of permanent secretaries and ministers as punishing. The idea popularized by Anthony Trollope that departments are rest homes for the idle and incompetent has been embraced by political parties and tabloid newspapers ever since. It is palpable nonsense. Indeed, the fieldwork prompted the opposite reflections. It made us acutely aware of the limits to human ability; of the fragility of the webs of meaning and action that we weave. As crises unfolded, it was tiring simply watching people cope, and we were not emotionally engaged with the events. We are not medical doctors but, over several months, we saw one permanent secretary display obvious signs of stress – white pallor, a greyness of flesh tone, taut skin around the eyes, and an absence of humour previously ever-present. Decision-making under stress becomes a source of stress. It is an 'adrenalin high'. They miss the action acutely when they leave office. But they pay a price in health and in their personal lives. It prompts doubts about the quality of advice and decision-making under such conditions.

On reading this paragraph all three top civil servants insisted they were 'not in a permanent state of crisis' and 'the punishing schedule is manageable because one is able to control and shape the timetable and the decision making processes'. They preferred to dismiss their several crises as 'a one off'. While shadowing, every department had a crisis. Everyone told us of other, recent crises. Everyone told us it was exceptional – 'it's not like this normally'. Maybe, but compared to universities or local government – two other types of organizations with which we are also familiar – life in a government department is more demanding because they live in a media goldfish bowl which can take any problem and make it a crisis. So, the interesting observation is about the capacity of senior officials and politicians to absorb crises and treat them as if they are one-offs.

Second, civil servants and ministers learn through the stories they hear and tell one another. Such stories are a source of institutional memory, the repositories of the traditions through which practitioners filter current events. Also, in the corporate world, the wish to get the story straight might perhaps translate into 'find a story that won't come unstuck, further down the track'. But the civil service emphatically did not do that. They did not look for a reliable, defensible story; they wanted to know what had happened. They wanted to present an accurate account of events. It seems obvious that the roots of this belief lie in the public service ethos of integrity and impartiality and the risk-averse tradition that seeks to protect the minister.

Third, civil servants believe in the Westminster model, which is integral to their anonymity and political impartiality, in a public service ethos and in loyalty to the minister. For example, they stick fast to the Westminster model's constitutional conventions. Ministerial responsibility may be a fiction in that ministers do not resign when their departments are at fault. But civil servants act as if ministerial responsibility is a brute fact of life (see also Marsh *et al.* 2001).

Fourth, a key maxim is 'no surprises'. This can refer to the private office making sure the minister and permanent secretary are in the right place at the right time and with the right papers. It can also refer to the frightening extent to which they live in the media eye and need to be adaptable, to cope with the many uncertainties. Private offices exist to domesticate trouble. Permanent secretaries exist to point out the hole to the minister before he falls in, to pull him out of the hole afterwards and then to argue that he never fell in.

Fifth, distinctions between policy and management, politician and civil servant, are meaningless when confronted with this imperative to cope and survive. Heclo and Wildavsky (1974) coined the phrase 'political administrator' to cover both permanent secretary and minister. They were so dependent on one another in carrying out their respective roles each was one side of the same coin. While reforms have emphasized their different roles, every crisis has continued to demonstrate their mutual dependence. The distinction between permanent secretary and minister can seem almost as arbitrary as that between politics and management and policy and implementation.

Sixth, rituals are the key to managing this pressurized existence. Everyday routines are unquestioned, unrecognized and surprisingly ordinary. Crisis management may be about the press conference, questions in parliament and the television interview. It is also about chats, meetings, tea, a drink after work and the everyday routines that domesticate the unexpected. To our earlier example of the tea ritual, we can add the conventions of polite behaviour. People do not run, they do not shout and they do not express overt emotion. Points are made politely. There are few if any cries of 'rubbish', and even expostulations are expressed mildly. All defer to the chair. Remarks are addressed to others through the chair. Indeed, the committee remains the mechanism for bringing together people and information within and between departments. E-communication has not replaced the committee; it just means the minutes are produced more quickly. Even to an Englishman it all can seem 'very English', and that is an observation not a criticism.

Or, to move down the organizational hierarchy, what will be lost when messengers go? Originally, as their name implies, they delivered mail. But e-mail has decimated that task and the coffee machine, the out-sourced delivery of food and the microwave oven eat at their remaining overt tasks. Their covert role as office glue will be lost. Every cup of tea signals the meeting of a London accent with middle class vowels to discuss the weather, TV, a new baby or how you are – to which the answer is 'well, thank you', any itemizing of complaints would be well out of order. It breaks tension. Perhaps it is the music of our cribs, but the clatter of cups and saucer, the sound of a teaspoon on china, is wondrously reassuring. Few see the demise of the messenger as an example of work being depersonalized, of a weakening of organizational glue, but that is one consequence.

Of course, the obvious retort to these comments is that we knew it already. That is an ever-present danger for all who are doing political research. But the portrait of a story-telling administrative and political elite with beliefs and practices rooted in the Westminster model that uses rituals to domesticate crises is not the conventional portrait.

8   National Health Service reform

A decentred approach to governance explores the diverse beliefs and actions through which individuals collectively construct various patterns of rule. It encourages us to go beyond formal institutions and official policies to examine the ways these are transformed as they are enacted in the interactions of senior civil servants, street-level bureaucrats and citizens. In the last chapter, we described how government departments draw on Whiggism, the Westminster model and rituals to domesticate crises and calls for radical change. In this chapter and the next, we want to travel outside the elite world of Westminster and Whitehall. We ask how the public sector's middle-level managers construct and enact governance. And we answer by appeals to ethnography and history.

The UK National Health Service (NHS) offers a classic case study of the role of beliefs in institutional change. First, it might be regarded as the canonical welfare state institution among advanced industrial societies. Second, from its birth, it was founded on strong, explicit beliefs. Third, throughout its development it has been characterized by conflicting beliefs. Fourth, as with all other public sector institutions, it changed significantly in the 1980s and 1990s under successive Conservative governments – notably those of Margaret Thatcher. Fifth, it changed during the first Blair government from 1997 to 2001; there was a purportedly radical shift in its mode of governance, and it was fragmented geographically following devolution to Scotland, Wales and Northern Ireland. Finally, it has always been a unique public sector institution because it commands great esteem among the public.

Obviously any analysis structured around discrete periods is arbitrary and can accentuate continuities in and discontinuities between periods. Nonetheless this chapter examines beliefs about institutional change in three periods: from the establishment of the NHS in 1948 until the first Thatcher government in 1979; from 1979 until the election of the first Blair government in 1997; and from 1997 to the end of the first Blair term of office. We have chosen these periods because they help us to answer the question: what beliefs about the NHS changed and why?

We provide a historical account that emphasizes the expressed beliefs of practitioners – doctors, managers and politicians. We seek to provide a historical account of the beliefs about both modes of governance and policy. To do so, we rely on textual analysis of official documents, supplemented with the written accounts of participants and interviews. We also focus on a key dilemma: the conflict between the belief of doctors in medical autonomy and the belief of managers and politicians in responsible financial or corporate management. The conflict between these beliefs strongly influenced institutional formation and change throughout the history of the NHS.

The NHS 1948–79: Laying the foundations

Shared beliefs

To identify the main beliefs underpinning the NHS, we need to look back to the seminal report written by the principal architect of the welfare state – Sir William Beveridge. In his *Report on Social Insurance and Allied Services* (1942) he set out the foundations of the welfare state, not just as an expression of political, economic or organizational principles, but also as social and moral duties. He referred to the 'Restoration of a sick person to health' as being 'a duty of the State and the sick person, prior to any other consideration' (1942: 14). He set out a plan for attacking what he described as the five Giant Evils – want, disease, ignorance, squalor and idleness. The two core beliefs underlying Beveridge's plans were collectivism (the responsibility of the state for its citizens, exercised through collective action) and universalism (all citizens having access to the services provided by such collective action).

The wartime coalition government's 1944 White Paper spelt out the priorities: health care available 'irrespective of means, age, sex or occupation', free at the point of use and operated both as a publicly sponsored' and a 'publicly organized' service (Cmd 6502 1944: 6). The White Paper expressed two other founding principles – comprehensiveness and equality – and echoed Beveridge's view that prevention of ill health was as important as treatment and cure.

According to Rudolf Klein (1983: 1), the NHS, when created, 'was a unique example of the collectivist provision of health care in a market society'. It was this collectivist principle that so offended the New Right three decades later (see Thatcher 1993: 6). Yet, at its creation, and for much of the period 1948–79, these beliefs were the source of a broad social and political consensus. The expressed opposition of most Conservative MPs at the time the NHS Bill was going through Parliament (in 1946) was not directed mainly at these beliefs, but at the proposed organizational arrangements – notably to nationalizing the hospitals and to the prospect of General Practitioners (GPs) becoming full-time salaried employees. This opposition was to have long and significant ripples. The message 'that the Tories could not be trusted with the NHS went deep into the British psyche' (Timmins 1995: 130).

There are two other important points to make about the NHS at its inception. First, as negotiated by Aneurin Bevan – its principal political architect –

it was an overwhelmingly publicly funded and publicly provided service. There is an important qualification. Bevan conceded the right to private practice, even for hospital consultants employed in the state scheme in NHS hospitals. Second, the NHS Act enshrined the principle of clinical autonomy. Also, for primary care, the Act conceded that collectivist provision would be through independent (privately employed) contractors – the GPs. The legal requirement that doctors secure for their patients whatever they judged to be clinically required was to be the source of important later tensions. The recurrent motif in the post-war history of the NHS is the conflict between public beliefs in collectivism (and judgements about aggregate needs and allocating aggregate resources) and professional beliefs in clinical autonomy and assessed individual need. The Act also sowed the seeds of enduring conflict between the beliefs of universalism and selectivity, and between clinical autonomy and clinical governance: about the need for rationing in a context of limited resources but potentially unlimited demand.

In many respects the period 1948–79 was one of institutional stability. The broad collectivist consensus spanned ten governments between 1948 and 1979, six Labour and four Conservative. It developed within, and was dependent on, post-war economic growth throughout the 1950s and early 1960s. With such sustained growth there was little concern for rising social expenditure (as a percentage of GDP) and consequently rising public spending. According to Michael Hill (1993: 46), it was a remarkable period for social policy because of policy continuity and lack of institutional change. The main concern of all governments was to be good managers of the welfare state and the NHS.

The shared belief in collectivism did not extend to universalism. In contrast to the Labour party's emphasis on egalitarianism and redistribution, the Conservative party saw the welfare state as providing a minimum standard only; it wanted much greater selectivity. There were early concerns (from 1951) about inexorably rising NHS costs leading the Conservative government elected in 1952 to introduce charges for prescriptions and dental treatment. In fact, the previous Labour government drafted the legislation on charges – made necessary only by 'overriding economic necessities' imposed by the defence programme (McNeil 1951 quoted in Webster 1988: 181). The proposal led to Bevan's resignation because he regarded it as a betrayal of the basic principle of an NHS free at the point of delivery.

Six years later a Conservative Chancellor of the Exchequer (Thorneycroft) resigned because the cabinet refused to introduce hotel charges for NHS in-patients. In part, this change illustrated the broad – if pragmatic – commitment to a limited universalism by Conservative governments of the 1950s and early 1960s. It also illustrated their 'nervousness about the electoral effects of being seen as hostile to strengthening the NHS' (Hill 1993: 62). The Labour government elected in 1964 took only a year to implement its manifesto commitment to universalism by abolishing prescription charges. But faced with growing economic problems – including a large balance of payments deficit – it reintroduced them (though with many exemptions) in 1968 as part of the large spending cuts associated with the 1967 devaluation of the pound. Allied to the reality of economic constraint and rapidly expanding demand, even the Labour government accepted there were practical limits to universalism.

The Conservative government of 1970–4 took the same view. It was determined 'to adopt a more selective approach to the social services'; 'instead of the present indiscriminate subsidies, help will go where it is most needed' (Chancellor of the Exchequer Anthony Barber, quoted in Timmins 1995: 281). The rationale for such selectivity appeared to be underlined in 1973, when the OPEC oil price rises (following the Arab–Israeli war) effectively spelt the end of the post-war economic boom. The result was severe public spending cuts to which welfare services were no exception.

Early governance

The main concern of successive governments from the mid-1960s was to reorganize the NHS, if not to unify, then at least to integrate the tripartite structure of hospital, general practice and local authority services created in 1948. From 1964 to 1974 there was a concerted attempt by both Labour and Conservative governments to increase managerial efficiency within the public sector, but not to erode that sector. It was the heyday of planning and rational policy analysis that culminated in the Conservative government's 1972 White Paper and 1973 NHS Act. Keith Joseph (the Secretary of State) introduced his White Paper (on NHS reorganization in England) as being 'about administration, not about treatment and care'. Given the NHS's size – 'one of the largest civilian organizations in the world' – the growing complexity of treatments and techniques, and the growing cost, the White Paper stipulated that:

> Real needs must be identified. . . . Plans must be worked out to meet these needs and management and drive must be continually applied to put the plans into action, assess their effectiveness and modify them as needs change or as ways are found to make the plans more effective . . . more systematic and comprehensive analysis of needs and priorities . . . will lie behind the planning and operations of each area.
>
> (Cmnd 5055 1972: v–vii)

The changes, which came into effect on 1 April 1974, represented the first major structural reorganization of the NHS in its twenty-six-year history. For the first time, they also introduced different arrangements in each of the four constituent parts of the UK. The three main aims of the reorganization were: better horizontal integration across hospital, local authority and general practice (though GPs remained as independent contractors); better coordination between health authorities (reduced in England to 90 area health authorities) and local authorities by introducing coterminous boundaries and a requirement to plan services jointly; and more efficient management. The latter was put into practice by giving hospital doctors an explicit role in multi-disciplinary teams working with consensus management rules. At a time of concern about rising NHS costs, the reorganization sought: 'to promote managerial efficiency [and] create an effective hierarchy for transmitting national policy' (Klein 1989: 99). Beliefs in management had reared their heads and the twin doctrines of cost containment and corporate decision-making were on a collision course with clinical autonomy.

In effect, consensus management at local level and an effective hierarchy replaced the administrative bureaucracy that had characterized the NHS from its birth. The ostensibly principal–agent relationship between centre and periphery in practice involved negotiation and considerable local discretion in policy implementation. One Secretary of State for Health rued his limited 'command' and 'control' over the fourteen regions, claiming their chairs behaved like 'semi-autonomous satraps' towards a 'weak Persian emperor' (Crossman 1972a: 10). Compounding this relative 'top-down' weakness, health and hospital administrators typically behaved like 'diplomats' when dealing with their medical colleagues (Harrison 1994). The 1974 reorganization 'was completed by the introduction in 1976 of a planning system [which] can be seen as a variety of classic chain-of-command management' (Harrison 1994: 18). However, the main problem in securing management efficiency down this chain lay in confronting the spenders of the resource – the doctors.

Here, it is important to recognize not only the beliefs of different stakeholders, but also the power and special position of the medical profession from the inception of the NHS. Their position was set out clearly both by the profession and by the government. For the former, a Negotiating Committee of the British Medical Association (BMA) and Royal Colleges set out, in 1946, the seven 'Essential Principles' to be considered in discussions about the establishment of a national health service. The second of these principles stated that:

> The medical profession should remain free to exercise the art and science of medicine according to its traditions, standards and knowledge, the individual doctor retaining full responsibility for the care of the patient, freedom of judgement, action, speed and publication, without interference in his professional work.
>
> (*British Medical Journal* 30 March 1946: 468)

Successive governments readily acknowledged this position. The 1944 White Paper was clear on the point: 'whatever the organization, the doctors taking part must remain free to direct their clinical knowledge and personal skill for the benefit of their patients in the way in which they feel to be best' (Cmd 6502 1944: 26). Nearly thirty years later, in his White Paper spelling out the framework for the first major reorganization of the NHS, Keith Joseph (Secretary of State) wrote similarly that:

> The professional workers will retain their clinical freedom – governed as it is by the bounds of professional knowledge and ethics and by the resources that are available – to do as they think best for their patients. This freedom is cherished by the professions and accepted by the government.
>
> (Cmnd 5055 1972: vii)

The implications of such power for any 'external' managerial control are obvious. The implications for health policymaking and service delivery of the professional (or medical tradition) in which doctors typically exercised clinical autonomy are less clear, mainly because a second core theme of this tradition has been the dominance of a particular model of care. This so-called 'medical model' stresses: individual rather than collective health; functional fitness rather than welfare; and cure rather than prevention. The central beliefs of this model saw physiological factors ('genes and germs') not psychosocial factors as the main causes of illness. It is a model, which, in policy terms, translates into a prime concern with the treatment and cure of individuals' ill health, especially in acute sector settings. The relative lack of attention to the effects of psychosocial, economic and environmental causes of ill-health led to policies that downplayed prevention, rehabilitation and the promotion of a broader, social conception of health.

The enduring power of the medical profession is a key issue in any analysis of practices of governance in the NHS. The concerns of these 'professional monopolists' (Alford 1975) have long held sway against the 'corporate rationalizers' charged with health planning and management. Also politicians, managers and public alike have long deferred to the medical profession (see, for example, Hill 1993: 35). There had been no 'major frontal criticism of the medical model of ill health by successive governments and NHS managers since 1948' (Harrison *et al*. 1990: 7). For most of the period 1948–79, there was another enduring set of beliefs – about the primacy of clinical autonomy. But it, too, was challenged, from 1982 especially, as rising demand and rising costs fuelled government interest in securing cost-efficiency.

The NHS 1979–97: Attacking the foundations?

New ideologies

The election of Thatcher's Conservative government in 1979 marked the beginning of a significant challenge to the medical tradition and its twin tenets of the medical model and clinical autonomy. The mode of governance of the NHS was set to change. The NHS has been described as the 'jewel in the crown' of the welfare state (Hill 1993: 31). It is an institution that 'ranked next to the monarchy as an unchallenged landmark in the political landscape of Britain' (Klein 1989: 32). So what did Margaret Thatcher do to this jewel? She didn't leave it unchallenged, but she was aware of its widely perceived jewel-like status and of the equally widespread perception that it had been crafted and polished principally by successive Labour governments. Her policies had four aims. First, they aimed to strengthen hierarchical control of the service – and of the medical profession – by introducing general management and annual performance review. Second, they aimed to improve cost-efficiency and cost-effectiveness by introducing private sector manage-ment techniques. Third, they sought to expand the range of alternative provision by fiscal and other means. Finally, they introduced the competitive discipline of the internal market: 'competition between hospitals – both within the NHS and between the public and private sectors – would increase efficiency and benefit patients' (Thatcher 1993: 611). Thatcher and her colleagues also did something else less tangible, but in the long run no less important: her government frequently denigrated public sector provision and the public service ethos.

In opposition, Thatcher and her colleagues became convinced that the collectivism and intervention of the welfare state were wrong, both in principle and in practice. Thatcherism responded to the dilemmas of inflation and state overload. The overload thesis, so popular in the 1970s (King 1975), drew attention to the limits to state authority. The Thatcher response from within the liberal-market tradition was to attack intermediate institutions such as local government and professional groups such as doctors and to reassert central authority through the strong state (Gamble 1988). So, the government rejected intervention and corporatism. Instead, it was committed to marketization and managerial rationality – planning became strategic policymaking, targets became clear objectives and performance measures. The Thatcher reforms challenged the socialist belief in bureaucracy and endorsed beliefs in greater efficiency by emulating private sector management. Its notion of governance evoked a reduced role for the state, greater scope for markets and a return to self-help (see Chapter 3: 47 and Chapter 5: 79–81).

Thatcherites believed in an individualist economic liberalism. They wanted services returned to the market and the role of the state kept to a minimum. Only a free, competitive market would guarantee economic growth and individual rights and freedoms. In practice, too, the welfare state was not affordable. They believed it was, as Robert Bacon and Walter Eltis (1976) argued, a non-productive drain on the wealth-creating sectors of society. The central tenets of this New Right Conservatism were a residual role for the state and selective rather than universal provision: that is, the state acted as a safety net for only the most disadvantaged and vulnerable. This determined attack on collectivism marked a clear rejection of the social democratic consensus and the beliefs that had underpinned the NHS since 1948.

Initially, Thatcher was not concerned with or about social policy. In her words, it was not until 1982 (when preparing the election manifesto) that 'we really started to turn our attention to social policy' (Thatcher 1993: 284). Her priorities were privatizing the main utilities, such as gas and water. Also she was well aware of the public's regard for the NHS. Even as late as 1987, she 'was reluctant to add the Health Service to the list of areas in which [the government] were proposing fundamental reform', since the NHS was seen by many as 'a touchstone for our commitment to the welfare state' (Thatcher 1993: 571).

Indeed, throughout her term as prime minister, Thatcher remained cautious of too radical change to the NHS, always aware of the political costs. Nevertheless, according to her health policy advisor Roy Griffiths, 'the NHS was an easy dislike for Mrs Thatcher', something which if it had been politically possible – which she knew it wasn't – 'she would have got rid of' (Griffiths quoted in Timmins 1995: 374).

Changes in governance

Strengthened hierarchy

During the period 1979–89 the Thatcher governments concentrated on: improving management efficiency and accountability within the NHS; and encouraging private provision and private insurance. The decisive date for strengthening management was 1982 with the appointment of Sir Roy Griffiths. As managing director of a successful private sector company (the supermarket chain Sainsbury's), Griffiths was expected to shine the penetrating light of commercial practice on the dingy public sector inefficiencies of the NHS. He did his job memorably, noting that 'if Florence Nightingale were carrying her lamp through the corridors of the NHS today she would almost certainly be searching for the people in charge' (Griffiths 1983). He recommended appointing general managers (replacing administrators) with clearly defined remits and taking personal responsibility at all levels in the service from the Department of Health downwards. He was also clear that doctors 'must accept the management responsibility that goes with clinical freedom' (*ibid.*: 18). The government readily accepted and implemented his proposals. With this strengthening of a clear, hierarchical chain of management, the government introduced in 1982–3 a system of annual performance review down this chain as well as short-term contracts and performance-related pay. According to Sir Kenneth Stowe (1989: 52), the (then) Permanent Secretary at the Department of Health and Social Security:

> Taken together with the establishment of 'accountability review'; i.e. a review by the next higher level of authority of the year's performance measured against agreed objectives, and with the development of performance indicators . . . the Griffiths recommendations were intended to establish a more rational framework for the relationship between Ministers and their Departments on the one hand and the Health authorities on the other.

Thatcher's governments are wrongly remembered solely as the architects of the NHS internal market. In the decade before its creation, her governments introduced the clearest hierarchical mode of governance in the NHS's forty-year history. As the Secretary of State, Norman Fowler, remarked in 1982 when introducing the accountability reviews and performance indicators:

> With these arrangements I shall be able to hold Regional Health Authorities to account for the ways in which resources are used in their regions and for the efficiency with which services are delivered. In turn, the regional health authorities will hold their constituent health authorities to account. . . . The object of these new arrangements is to ensure that the health service obtains the maximum amount of direct patient care and the greatest value for money from the resources which the government have made available to the NHS.
>
> (UK House of Commons *Hansard* 12 January 1982)

Accordingly, the major concerns of managers in the 1980s were to keep the service within budget and demonstrate value for money. Following Griffiths, they operated systems of management budgeting and, from 1986, resource management. They were also subject to a plethora of other initiatives. These included: the requirement for health authorities to put their cleaning, catering and laundry services out to competitive tender (most subsequently won by in-house tenders); the requirement to make annual efficiency savings from their cash limited budgets by cost improvement programmes; and the encouragement (though not requirement) to purchase services from the private sector.

There was also a continuing tension between professional and managerial beliefs. From 1982, there was a serious attempt to assert the legitimacy of managerial beliefs (of value for money in allocating public money) in the face of professional beliefs. The 'introduction of general management was the first major and systematic threat to clinical freedom' (Harrison 1994: 41) since the start of the NHS. It represented the promotion of the managerial beliefs of the corporate rationalizers as a counterweight to the beliefs of clinical autonomy.

Health (and social care) markets

The markets introduced after the 1989 White Papers, *Working for Patients* (Secretaries of State 1989a) and *Caring for People* (Secretaries of State 1989b) were distinctive in several ways. These proposals were enshrined in the *NHS and Community Care Act* 1990. The main organizational principle was the purchaser/provider split. In health care, health authorities (and in certain circumstances GP practices) were to become the purchasers of services from hospitals, which, as competing providers, would be semi-autonomous trusts. These markets were, however, managed ones. The government required managers to ensure, initially, minimal disruption and 'smooth transition'. We should note too that the markets in health and social care differed from one another. Although both markets were quasi-markets in which the public sector acted as proxy consumers, in health it was essentially an internal (intra-NHS) market, whereas the social care market was (and remains) an external market.

What were the beliefs underpinning the market changes that the Thatcher government sought to institutionalize? Boiled down to their essence they were beliefs in competitive self-interest, managerial efficiency and entrepreneurship, all in the context of economic individualism. There was, after all, as Thatcher once famously asserted, 'no such thing as society'. The Thatcher governments were thus largely contemptuous of the 'old fashioned' public sector and beliefs in a public service ethos.

The effects of such a shift in beliefs are well illustrated by what came to be known as the 'Yorkshiregate' scandal. These events covered a five-year period from 1989 to 1994. It involved senior managers in the Yorkshire Regional Health Authority (RHA). Investigations into alleged misconduct culminated in a report by the senior committee of the UK House of Commons – the Public Accounts Committee. The committee considered it 'unacceptable' that the authority made irregular relocation expenses totalling nearly half a million pounds. They were 'appalled' that the Director of Personnel had been switched from a general manager's to a senior manager's contract 'simply to enhance her redundancy terms'. They considered it unacceptable that this same individual awarded contracts to a company owned by her husband without declaring an interest. Finally, they were 'appalled'

> That the former authority spent some £695,000 on functions and dinners at hotels between April 1992 and March 1994. These included events which clearly should not have been paid for from public funds, such as two 'supersleuth' weekends at a cost of £10,000 and excessive hospitality in top quality hotels, including expensive wine.
>
> (UK House of Commons Committee of Public Accounts 1997: xii)

The committee's report notes deep concern about 'failures of governance of the most serious kind that have resulted in the loss to public funds of millions of pounds which should have been spent on treating patients' (*ibid.*: xvii). There are other noteworthy comments by the committee. It poured scorn on the laxity and impropriety of management and of the culture that allowed, even fostered it.

> While we recognise that this was a period of unprecedented change in the NHS and managers were being encouraged to adopt a more businesslike approach, we cannot accept that this entitled senior managers . . . to put the former authorities and public funds at risk . . . there is no reason why a proper concern for the sensible conduct of public business and care for the honest handling of public money should not be combined with effective programmes for promoting economy and efficiency.
>
> (*ibid.*: xxix)

It would be a distortion to suggest that what happened here typified behaviour throughout the NHS at the time. There were other managers, however, who also thought they had been encouraged to adopt a more businesslike approach and that such an approach – more entrepreneurial, more competitive – involved some shedding of traditional public sector constraints and beliefs. According to one senior manager, in the NHS internal market a 'really acquisitive, selfish, self-centred, destructive, adversarial system was created' (interview transcript). And for the wider health and social care system, the market 'totally switched off the evolving relationships between health and local authority including the embryonic development of whole systems, integrated care'. 'In that culture', he said, 'you got a more aggressive, adversarial kind of management culture that was not about partnerships, it was about competition'. In the view of this senior manager, he and his colleagues 'were judged to be successful because they got their own organization strongly badged'. Since 1997, by contrast, there has been recognition of the need 'to get people to badge the service rather than badge the organization'. It is to this change that we now turn.

The NHS 1997–2001: Re-laying the foundations?

A third way?

Distinctively, New Labour's programme of reform assumes it is possible to make the state work. New Labour constructed the dilemma of state overload differently from the New Right, which has a vested interest in state failure. It rejected not only Old Labour's top-down, command-style bureaucracy based on centralized rules, but also the New Right's commitment to rolling back the state by using markets. New Labour's Third Way seeks to transform the state into an enabling partner by promoting the idea of networks of institutions and individuals acting in partnership and held together by relations of trust (Bevir 2005: 83–105).

New Labour reinterpreted the concerns highlighted by the New Right. On one hand, the Party adopted a more positive view of markets; quasi-market mechanisms as well as privatization are entrenched on its agenda. Similarly, Old Labour's faith in experts and top-down, command-style bureaucracy based on centralized rules was eroded. Mandelson and Liddle (1996: 27, 151) explicitly reject the 'municipal socialism' and 'centralized nationalization' of the past. Yet, on the other hand, New Labour is critical of the New Right for having had an exaggerated faith in markets. New Labour emphasizes that economic prosperity depends not only on a commitment to macroeconomic stability, but also on supply-side policies to boost innovation and industry (Bevir 2005: 106–27). New Labour also embodies a critique of the New Right's model of public service delivery for being too reliant on markets. It insists markets are not always the best way to deliver public services. Markets can go against the public interest, reinforce inequalities and entrench privilege. Besides, much of the public sector simply is not amenable to market competition. Indeed, trust and partnership are essential. Without the conditions for effective markets, one has either to rely on honest cooperation or specify standards in absurd detail. Far from promoting efficiency, therefore, marketization can undermine standards of service quality. Public services should encourage co-operation while continuing to use market mechanisms when suitable.

So, New Labour's model of service delivery does not follow the New Right's vision of the new public management. To the contrary, New Labour argues that many features of this new public management, such as quasi-markets and contracting-out, maintained an unhealthy dichotomy between the public and private sectors. Public bodies did not work with private companies but merely contracted services out to them. This argument is used, for example, to justify abolishing the internal market in the National Health Service. The Third Way, in contrast to the vision of the New Right, is supposed to develop networks that enable public and private organizations to collaborate. Examples of such collaboration appear in the partnerships between the public and private sector to build new hospitals.

For New Labour, quality public services are best achieved through stable, co-operative relationships. This theme runs through the *Modernising Government* White Paper with its frequent references to 'joined-up' government and 'holistic governance' (Cm 4310 1999; see also Cabinet Office 2000). The term covers both horizontal joining-up between central departments and vertical joining-up between all the agencies involved in delivering services. Services must be effective and co-ordinated and the principles of joined-up government apply across the public sector and to voluntary and private sector organizations.

The NHS is no exception. In its 1997 White Paper *The New NHS. Modern. Dependable* (Cm 3807 1997) the newly elected Labour government set out what was described as a 'third way' of running the NHS, that of partnership. Adopting this 'third way' constituted an explicit rejection of the 'old centralized command and control systems of the 1970s' and of the 'divisive internal market system of the 1990s' (*ibid.*: 7 para. 2.1). The new government was withering in its criticism of the latter: 'it has been an obstacle to the necessary modernization of the health service. It created more problems than it solved. That is why the government is abolishing it' (*ibid.*: 8 para. 2.9).

In his foreword to the White Paper, Tony Blair described it as 'a turning point for the NHS. It replaces the internal market with integrated care'. Rhetorically, his government was signalling the shift from hierarchies and markets to networks. However, it is important to recognize that, whatever the rhetoric, and even if it is a significant shift, it is not the complete replacement of one form of service delivery by another. It is increasingly recognized that we are seeing the continued development of different modes of service delivery simultaneously (see, for example, Exworthy *et al*. 1999; Flynn *et al*. 1997). It is not a question of one form replacing or superseding another, but of the three – hierarchies, markets (or quasi-markets) and networks – coexisting.

In its more recent *NHS Plan* (for England), the government is anxious to foster local partnerships widely in and beyond the statutory sector (Cm 4818-I 2000). It speaks of rectifying long-standing 'fault lines' – introduced at the inception of the NHS in 1948 – between health care and social care, and between public sector health care (in the NHS) and private and voluntary sector health care. 'For decades there has been a standoff between the NHS and private sector providers of health care. This has to end. Ideological boundaries or institutional boundaries should not stand in the way of better care for NHS patients' (*ibid.*: 96 para. 11.2).

The Plan refers to the intention to formalize an agreement with the private for-profit and voluntary sectors. It was published three months later in the form of a *Concordat* between the government (for patients in England) and the Independent Health Care Association (Department of Health 2000).

'Modernization' and 'partnership' are the leitmotifs running throughout the policy pronouncements of New Labour – across all service areas and sectors of the economy. In pursuit of its modernization agenda, the Blair government repeatedly stressed getting the best people for the job irrespective of whether they come from the public, private or voluntary sector; and its belief in the public sector and public services. In the *Modernising Government* White Paper (Cm 4310 1999), the prime minister wrote an open letter to public servants. 'This', he said, straightforwardly 'is a government that believes in public service' and 'we will value public service, not disparage it'. The 2001 Labour Party election manifesto repeated the theme and talked of the challenge of reversing decades of denigration and under investment (Labour Party 2001: 17).

The main organizational change set out in *The New NHS* was (in England) that of primary care groups (PCGs). The intention was to develop a primary care-led NHS and the PCGs became primary care trusts (PCTs) in April 2002. The latter will replace health authorities as the commissioners of health care: but, in a conflation of the internal market's purchaser–provider split, they will also be the providers of primary care. Partnership between health and social care – the absence of which was one of the principal NHS 'fault lines' identified in the *NHS Plan* – is a reinforced statutory duty. It will be facilitated by the 'flexibilities' built into the 1999 *Health Act* (section 31). These powers – for example, to pool (to unify) budgets – are intended to remove not only the barriers to joint working but also the excuses for separatism.

Another important message of the Blair government is that, in implicit contrast to the medical model, health is a responsibility beyond the NHS. Local government has been given the power (though not the duty) to promote the well-being of its residents by addressing the social, economic and environmental root causes of ill-health. There is a renascence of interest in public health, in a tradition of medical intervention with its roots in local government, the nineteenth century, urbanization and epidemiology. Prevention, rehabilitation and interventions spanning organizational boundaries are seen as a possible solution to such wicked issues as poverty and ill-health. Multi-disciplinary working across agency and sectoral boundaries is the key to a series of clinical networks operating across the country. The government accepts that these networks need time, stability and dependable funding to build trust between and understanding of the several viewpoints. In other words, New Labour is developing a joined-up view of health and an integrated, multi-agency, multi-professional approach to service delivery. The prime beliefs are those of collaboration, integration and interdependence and the dominant mode of governance is a network.

The lexicon of New Labour is organizational and professional interdependence and the need for 'coordination', 'collaboration', 'partnership' and 'integrated' (or 'seamless') service planning, management and delivery. It espouses the beliefs of collaboration not competition, of integration not fragmentation and of networks (based on high-trust, long-term collaborative relationships) not markets (based, essentially, on competition). At another level, New Labour's approach to health is also a commitment to social inclusion. Although it rejects Thatcher's radical economic individualism, anti-collectivism and disparagement of public provision, it does not herald a return to the post-war consensus around the beliefs of collectivism and universalism.

It is, of course, true that New Labour espouses universalism. In setting out its 2001 restructuring of the NHS, the Secretary of State, Alan Milburn (2001: 6) referred to 'strong identification with the NHS as a national service. That', he said, 'is a good thing. The universalism of the NHS helps to cement national cohesion and shape national identity'. However, the principle of universalism typically is expressed now as 'universalizing the best'. It is not a restatement of the universalism of the founders of the NHS. Such beliefs may still exist for some parts of the welfare state – for example, child benefits and pensions – but here real monetary values have been allowed to dwindle significantly to curb rising costs. The NHS remains free at the point of delivery, but no longer for all services. Many must pay for some services – for prescriptions, dental care, optical care. Others are encouraged to pay for private sector care by a combination of fiscal measures and 'rationing' by long NHS waiting lists.

Under New Labour, the NHS and other public services are to be restored in esteem, but not as monopoly providers. The emphasis now falls on developing a mixed economy of health with much greater use made of private sector provision – not only in the nursing and residential home sectors but also for acute specialities in private hospitals. However, there are now interesting differences between England, Scotland, Wales and, to a lesser extent, in Northern Ireland. Increasingly, there are four distinct National Health Services in the UK.

Differentiated health services?

The most significant difference between the Blair reforms in England and policy elsewhere in the UK is the clear belief in Wales and Scotland in replacing competitive quasi-markets by state-organized collective action. Such beliefs are clearly and avowedly closer to the historic roots of the NHS. In some respects, the Welsh NHS Plan (Welsh Assembly 2001) mirrors that in England – notably its stress on partnership, joined-up planning and service delivery by integrated, seamless care. In the Foreword to the Plan, the Minister for Health, Jane Hutt, reasserts 'our unifying purpose which was so damaged by the competitive approaches of the last government' (Welsh Assembly 2001: 4). The expressed need is for 'a culture of partnership and openness to working across boundaries' for collaboration and work in multi-disciplinary, cross-agency and cross-sectoral networks.

What is different, however, is the extent and nature of this partnership. Unlike the English Plan's call for a historic *Concordat* with the private sector, references in the Scottish and Welsh official documentation to the private sector are scant. The Welsh Plan refers to 'strong partnerships between the NHS, local government, communities and the voluntary sector [being] the heart of our new and inclusive approach to health' (Welsh Assembly 2001: 5). And the conclusion refers to the need for the NHS to work 'in concert with local government and the voluntary sector' (*ibid.*: 76).

The Welsh Plan strongly asserts a set of 'basic values' [which] formed the ethical foundation of the National Assembly's approach' (*ibid.*: 19). These include seeing health as a fundamental human right, equity and developing social solidarity in communities. The language is of democratization, a well-functioning civic society and 'community empowerment and collectivism'; the case for 'people collectively to shape the future of the health service is more compelling than ever before' (*ibid.*: 34).

What is notable here is an explicit statement of the beliefs underpinning institutional change with a firm rejection of the beliefs that underpinned the NHS inherited from the Conservative government. There is a clear sense of a return to traditional core beliefs, which 'are not new ... we instinctively know them to be right' (*ibid.*: 18). In Wales, it would seem that the historic beliefs of collectivism and universalism rule again.

Like the Welsh document, the Scottish plan expresses collectivist beliefs and a belief in the virtues of the NHS as a public service. The internal market 'undermined the public service ethos of the NHS' (Scottish Executive 2001). It is clear that the Scottish government is attempting to ground the Plan in a set of reclaimed and reasserted beliefs and principles. 'The NHS was founded on the principle that access to care be based on need and not an ability to pay. That principle remains as important today as when the NHS was founded more than 50 years ago' (*ibid.*: 22).

According to the Plan's authors, the internal market undermined this principle and 'over many years, much of the cohesion and the traditional beliefs of the NHS have been eroded'. 'Since 1997', it is claimed, 'much has been done to sweep away the divisiveness and inefficiency of the internal market'. But central to the task of rebuilding is that 'the traditional public service ethos and beliefs of the NHS must be put back at its core' (*ibid.*: 23).

There are, of course, striking parallels between the English, Welsh and Scottish NHS Plans. All reject the competitive culture, the fragmentation and division that is the perceived legacy of the internal market. All also emphasize replacing such competition with a collaborative culture and developing services as part of integrated networks. In Wales, for example, 'managed clinical networks [will be developed] as the normal way of running clinical services across boundaries' (*ibid.*: 16).

Partnership with a 'big stick'?

It was notable that the 1997 NHS White Paper referred to the government's 'third way' as a system 'based on partnership and driven by performance' (Cm 3807 1997: 7 para. 2.2). There was more than a hint here of the tensions between governing structures. Thus, on the one hand, the government wants to promote cooperation, fostering, at field level, collaboration rather than competition, but it was to do so using hierarchical mechanisms for stronger steering and control of performance. The government promises vertical partnership between itself and localities, but this 'partnership' is backed up with detailed service prescriptions – in, for example, the joint national priorities guidance and National Service Frameworks – and with tighter mechanisms for clinical governance. The experience of local education authorities and schools (with the 'naming and shaming' of those perceived to be 'under-performing') has been a clear warning to other public sector organizations thought to be failing to deliver 'best value' services.

This same tension between modes of governance exists in the English *NHS Plan*. Much is made of the virtues of local autonomy and of the need to rely on local agencies working in partnership to solve jointly identified local problems. Whitehall, it was readily admitted, cannot manage local detail. The Plan represents a restatement of the perceived necessity of central steering and hierarchical control. However, the Plan also introduced the notion of 'earned autonomy'. If local agencies can show they work well together, then they will receive not only financial rewards but also lighter central steering to go with their so-called 'green light' status. Where there is no such evidence, however, authorities will be given 'red light' status and the centre will enforce joint working. There is a clear hierarchy of possible interventions culminating in the removal of local powers by the Secretary of State. Alongside such regulation of managerial performance, New Labour also introduced systematic clinical governance (Department of Health 1998). The wide-ranging quality assurance system is now made up of the National Institute for Clinical Excellence, a Commission for Health Improvement and a framework to ensure that all clinicians are subject to regular clinical audit and performance review.

Once again the rhetoric is of partnership with the professions, but there is a clear threat. In the view of one doctor, if co-operation is not forthcoming, and if the medical profession's ways of regulating itself do not significantly improve, the state will encroach even further into the, until now sacrosanct, heartland of clinical autonomy (Salter 2000).[1]

Conclusion

Traditions persist, most notably the medical tradition, but they also change in response to dilemmas. In this chapter, we argued the Thatcher reforms were a response to the dilemma of state overload. We recognize that British policy-makers confronted other dilemmas in the 1980s and 1990s, but state overload is perhaps the most relevant for understanding the shift from hierarchy to markets to networks in the NHS. The Thatcher government rejected government intervention and corporatism for marketization and managerial rationality. It expanded the scope for markets. New Labour's approach to public sector reform reflects its response not only to inflation and state overload but also the New Right's ideas. New Labour's programme of reform assumes it is possible to make the state work. Its notion of the enabling state envisages a combination of hierarchy, markets and networks, with the latter predominating.

The strongest calls for a return to the beliefs of collectivism, social solidarity and public sector primacy are associated with the coalition governments of Scotland and Wales, not of huge Labour majorities. By contrast, in England, where (between 1997 and 2001) Labour had a large majority at Westminster, the *NHS Plan* represents a much weaker echo of such beliefs. It is based on a restatement of the beliefs inherent in public services and in public service, but there is no presumption of public sector primacy. Co-operation and partnership in networks have primacy over competition in markets, but this partnership is between the public and private and voluntary sectors in a way not envisaged in either Wales or Scotland.

All the constituent countries of the UK exhibit overlapping beliefs and practices in their modes of governing the NHS. In particular, there is the professed determination to maximize the autonomy of networks of local providers. In addition, there is the even clearer determination that such autonomy exists within explicit service frameworks of standards and targets and equally explicit frameworks of performance assessment, performance indicators, performance management and clinical governance. Command and control may not be the first recourse, but detailed prescription and hierarchical means of control (including threatened intervention) are, at least in England, intended to ensure that trusts meet clinical as well as managerial standards, targets and guidelines.

The persistent faith in hierarchy, allied to the endless search for new mechanisms of control, illustrates the unresolved dilemma that confronts the NHS: how to combine some form of clinical autonomy with effective financial management. Alford (1975) described the 1950s and 1960s as a contest between 'professional monopolists' and the 'corporate rationalizers'. The labels change, but the perceived dilemma persists. It is the search to contain inflation and devise effective governing structures writ small. Hierarchy is the refuge of first resort for successive governments frustrated by their inability to impose priorities and get results in time for the next election. Clinical autonomy and the medical model of health are the first refuge for the medical profession. The contest between these two traditions is longstanding and not yet over.

9 Police reform[1]

For police services, organizational reform is no longer an event but a way of life. In the past thirty years, police services in the UK, Canada, the USA and Australia have been subjected to a series of demands for change and reform (on the differences between the change process in the USA and countries such as the UK and Australia, see Edwards 1999: 113–14).

The major agendas for reform have been fuelled variously by demands for efficiency and effectiveness, a concern about the relationship between police and the community they serve, and organized corruption and other abuses of authority (see Bayley 1994; Chan 1997; Fleming and Lafferty 2000; Prenzler and Ransley 2002). In the UK, industrial strife and public disorder provided the impetus for the reforms of the 1980s (Scarman 1986). Latterly, the imposition of structural and organizational reforms has been driven by managerialist concerns about operational effectiveness, efficiency and accountability (Sheehy 1993). In Australia, while the managerialist agenda contributed significantly to police organizational reform, successive inquiries into police misconduct since the late 1980s also provided the momentum for change (Fleming and Lafferty 2000). The same is true of the US reforms since 1972. Reform seems to have become cyclical, with each cycle often given a title of its own; examples include Commissioner Imbert's *Plus* programme in the Metropolitan Police of London and Commissioner's Falconer's *Delta* programme in Western Australia (see Edwards 1999: 112).

Why has police reform become constant? The short answer is because it is plagued with unintended consequences. But why don't the reforms work? Most accounts of police reform stress the conservatism of 'police culture' (see Chan 1997; Reiner 1992; Paoline 2003; Barton 2003). We do not. Serving police officers as well as academics see the reforms of the past twenty years as a shift from command and control bureaucracy through markets to networks. We argue, as in our analysis of governance (see Chapter 4), there is no such inexorable trend. Rather, we must explore the beliefs and practices of individual police officers to understand what happened. At this micro-level of analysis, police officers confront new ideas and the resulting dilemma leads to both unanticipated changes and dynamic conservatism. In this chapter, there is no explicit or implicit argument for or against change, nor is there one for or against bureaucracy, contracts or networks. Our point is that for many police officers the ideas underpinning the various reforms mix like oil and water, posing dilemmas that lead to unintended consequences.

To explore this theme, we examine the beliefs of serving police officers. Through semi-structured interviews with twenty-seven senior officers ranking from Sergeant to Commissioner and senior civilian managers conducted in the UK and Australia in 2003, we explore their beliefs about bureaucracy, markets and networks. We focus on recent reforms, which seek to set up networks of policing under the label 'community policing'. Interviewees were selected randomly, with appropriate rank being the only requirement. As one would expect given the existing gender balance of British and Australian police organizations, only four of the interviewees were women. We look behind the scepticism of managers and sworn officers to show that their belief in the incompatibility of governing structures creates dilemmas that afflict all reforms.

Many readers will not be familiar with police reform, so the first section of this chapter outlines briefly the main reforms of the past twenty years. For all intents and purposes it is but public sector reform in Britain writ small. In the second section, we document the beliefs of several serving police officers with experience of the several reforms. In the third section, we analyse their understanding of the dilemmas posed by the reforms.

From bureaucracy to contracts and markets

Governing structures are often presented as formal institutions, yet they can also be seen as practices of governance embodying webs of beliefs about ways of allocating resources, resolving conflicts and co-ordinating actors. As we have argued, the beliefs of elite actors, that is, politicians and senior public servants, about the relative effectiveness of these governing structures has shifted away from hierarchies to markets or contracts, and more recently to networks or partnerships (see Chapter 5). In this section, we briefly discuss each practice of governance, and its relevance to the police.

The bureaucratic state

The story of bureaucracy is the dominant story of the twentieth century. Its characteristics are well known – hierarchy, rules, merit appointments, permanent, neutral, expert. Bayley (1994: 61) notes that police organizations are structured on authoritarian, paramilitary lines, regulated through strict organizational rules and legislation with an emphasis on internal and vertical communication. There is a premium on compliance rather than initiative – decision-making is 'rarely participative or collegial across rank lines'. Annette Davies and Robyn Thomas (2003: 682–3) even suggest that police organizations are resistant to change because of 'a co-existence of formalized bureaucratic and standardized working practices, with a deeply entrenched and pervasive occupational culture' of hierarchical subordination.

In varying degrees, these characteristics fit many bureaucracies in most advanced industrial democracies. Critics deem bureaucracy to be inherently inefficient, too large and expensive, and lacking the structure of incentives of a market. Bureaucracy was suited to standardized administration, not management, and the management of bureaucracy was obsolete. Even worse, the routines of bureaucracy made it risk averse, discouraging innovation. This risk-adverse culture has perhaps been compounded by the traditional resistance of police to organizational change (Skolnick and Bayley 1986), which has proved a potential barrier to reform. For example, the UK government's police reform in 1992 created an unprecedented wave of resistance from police officers at every level (Reiner 1993). However, while change may be significant, bureaucracy is still with us and remains an integral part of the police forces we studied.

The contract state

The story of the contract state marks a potentially new phase in public sector management. Initially 'managerialism' referred to such reforms as performance measurement, but its scope was rapidly extended to include contracting out. There is now an extensive literature on contracting out in the public sector in both Australia and Britain (see Davis and Wood 1998; Deakin and Walsh 1996; Domberger 1998; Walsh *et al.* 1997). Despite resistance from police personnel, there has been a determined effort to use contracts to deliver police services (Bayley 1994: 130–2; Fleming and Lafferty 2000). For example, governments hold contracts with police services with such general objectives as creating a safer and more secure locality through the contractual provision of police services. Canada has a long history of contracting out police services. Municipalities in Canada 'solicit costing proposals from a range of policing services, both public and private and determine which kinds of organizations would have the best service for the best price' (Wood 2000: 19).

Police contracts focus on crime and safety management, road safety, crime prevention and successful prosecution data. Each service has many, often inconsistent performance indicators (PIs). How, for example, do we reconcile maximizing the number of successful prosecutions with the objective of preventing crime? In effect, there is a quasi-market, with the police under great pressure to show that resources are being used efficiently with each objective maximized simultaneously (Moore 1990: 73). Jan Scott (1998: 283) argues that PIs empower management by 'providing a way of measuring where police resources are being allocated' and increasing levels of managerial accountability. Yet as Mark Moore (1990: 74) points out, such measurements set 'useful benchmarks', but are 'always susceptible to criticism and change'.

We know little about the consequences of contracting for policing. Contracts and PIs are not necessarily conducive to proactive policing strategies. Community policing, for example, can exact 'high internal costs' on police organizations in terms of resources (Edwards 1999: 111–12). It is in tension with the 'lean and mean' emphasis of management in confronting the 'do more with less' corporate culture (O'Malley 1997: 374). Additionally, proactive policing is a long-term strategy, the results of which are not easily reflected in contracts or performance indicators. While accountability at the senior levels may improve, conflicts over the relative priority of objectives can cause tensions in the community itself. Middle management tends to reallocate resources away from community policing initiatives when they are under pressure to handle a high-profile incident or to reach specific targets. This is compounded when officers actively prefer law enforcement strategies that favour reactive, action-based solutions (Scott 1998: 285–7).

The concept of contracting out policing services to the private sector, with its emphasis on satisfying the customer, gives private institutions further scope to thrive. But there are other issues associated with legitimacy and authority. As Ian Loader (1999: 378) suggests:

> The more the police resort to market imperatives as a means of reconfiguring police–public relations, the more difficult it will be for them to speak and act as ultimate guardians of order and security; to stand above the competitive fray and appeal successfully to other principles and loyalties, to 'traditional' modes of authority and expertise.

The network state

The interdependence, trust and reciprocity that are often said to characterize networks may not seem instantly recognizable as characteristics of police organizations. Police organizations like all other organizations consist of informal beliefs, traditions and practices. The 'way we do business' is passed on to all recruits. There is a dominant tradition. Police organizations are seen as insular, secretive and prone to solidaristic practices. As Herman Goldstein (1990: 29) notes, there is 'a prevalent feeling that the public does not really understand what the police "have to put up with" in dealing with citizens'. An 'us and them' perspective is a dominant characteristic of police culture, where 'them' can encompass both citizens and senior management, depending on the context.

The rationale behind networks is often to create partnerships. Participants believe, for example, that care of the mentally ill or the protection of battered wives needs co-operation between several agencies, including the police. They believe if each is to do their job properly, they need to share such resources as staff, information, money, infrastructure and expertise. Attempts to promote such networks are now a well-established feature of British government, locally, regionally and centrally (see, for example, Cm 4310 1999; Cabinet Office 2000; Mulgan 2001; for discussion Bevir 2005: 29–53). Indeed policing through networks, also known as community policing or partnerships or holistic governance or 'whole of government' is established policy in Britain and Australia.[2] Most crime problems and palliative solutions in present-day society are interlinked with other public policies. These policies include the delivery of urban services such as transport, housing and street lighting; educational matters such as school bullying and truancy; health and community welfare issues such as inadequate parenting (Cope 2001; Edwards 1999; Brereton 2000). There is a widespread belief that given these linkages and the prevailing climate of fiscal constraint, crime control needs a 'whole of government approach' and indeed, a cross-sectoral approach involving civil society (Cabinet Office 2000; Garland 2001; Mulgan 2001). This argument suggests that no one agency, especially the police, commands the resources necessary to control crime in modern society. Effective crime management will require community effort, involving both individuals and institutions outside law enforcement, and beyond the public sector. Indeed, Loader (2000: 330) refers to the existence today of 'dispersed, inter-organizational policing networks'. The perceived challenge is to enable the police to identify and manage such networks (see also Benyon and Edwards 1999; Edwards and Benyon 2001).

From where they stand

How do those who manage the police understand public sector reform? This section explores the views of the police on bureaucracy, contracts and networks using data obtained from interviews conducted with senior police officers and civilian managers.

We have taken great care to disguise our respondents and their nationality because they talked frankly and we are mindful of the need to protect reputations and careers. We are not trying to explain patterns of behaviour in a specific force by reference to such variables as local history, geography and the wealth and socio-economic composition of the area. Rather, we analyse twenty-seven semi-structured interviews using the three structures of governance as diagnostic tools to justify the argument that the working of reform depends on police responses to the dilemmas created by what they perceive to be the irreconcilable ideas of bureaucracy, markets and networks. Because fieldwork was carried out in police organizations in both Australia and Britain, we use Australian and British terms interchangeably, opting for Commissioner rather than Chief Constable because it is shorter. Similarly we use the term 'government' to cover central government, state government or local government. In this section, we let the interviewees speak. We selected the passages from the transcripts. Obviously, we provide the organizing concepts that guide the selection. We quote extensively so the reader can make an informed judgement about the plausibility of our interpretation.

On bureaucracy

A pervasive idea throughout the interviews was the continuing importance of bureaucracy – of authority, hierarchy, rules and an *esprit de corps*, 'us and them' stance.

We have practical guidelines for the procedure on how to deal with a mentally disturbed person; animals on the loose; pulling vehicles over; arresting someone – just about everything a police officer does is prescribed by a practical guideline. It's up to them to make sure they know it because if a complaint is made against you the first thing [internal investigations] is going to ask is 'did you stick by the guidelines?' Sometimes we have to create new ones to deal with new legislative requirements or new situations. It's about procedure and policy – how we do things – they are not strategy documents. (Interview 10)

With rules go uniforms to bind and differentiate.

I am a firm believer in promotion through uniform – demonstrating where you are in the police service – telling people what you do. The air force and the army all use it. The bomb people have a little bomb motif on their sleeves and I can think of other examples. It's good for morale and recognizes achievement. (Interview 19)

Whenever a few officers congregate at a scene or anywhere we all quickly establish who has the higher rank and then defer accordingly. (Interview 25)

Inevitably perhaps, the traditional 'command and control' style persists:

Action and results are highly valued by police officers . . . they are competitive about arrests . . . they view success as someone behind bars . . . there is a desire to right wrongs . . . that's what motivates them . . . they are not motivated by a school principle who says they have conducted their community policing duties well. (Interview 1)

It isn't about associating with the community. It's about getting a quick result and moving on to the next job – the sooner they can write off the job or put down 'no further police action', the better. (Interview 27)

And an 'us and them', 'macho' mentality goes with the command and control style.

There is an insularity, defensiveness about them – they make it clear their job is to catch crooks – they often feel unappreciated – there is an 'us and them' attitude . . . they tend to overreact and become authoritarian. (Interview 1)

There is still a command and control mentality within the service and [a sense] that the police have no ownership of what goes on. (Interview 2)

Policing is essentially a blue collar occupation – they are into penalties, overtime, it's the culture. (Interview 4)

There is still an 'us and them' thing here. (Interview 7)

The troops don't trust us though, there is still an us and them mentality and that extends to management. They don't trust us. (Interview 9)

Despite extensive reform, for some little has changed. There is much agreement among senior officers that there is a 'silo mentality' (Interviews 9, 16, 17, 20) and a lack of delegation on management's part. The structure is still centralized.

We have gone back to the rationalized, centralized model – where areas such as traffic and crime prevention are considered as specialized units. . . . There is a lot of slippage too. We are all variously starved of information as to what is happening in these areas. . . . [As a result] we have little flexibility and are unable to micro manage quite as effectively. (Interview 15, see also Interview 24)

With centralization goes respect for rank and caution in dealing with superiors.

They pay a lot of lip service to the notion that we have a corporate mentality – no rank distinction – everyone can say what they want but believe you me when you step out of line, the military line comes right back and if you want to get on you are not going to be part of a frank discussion. (Interview 24)

Two important inferences can be drawn from this material. First, beliefs in the efficacy of rules, uniforms and authority persist after decades of reform and appear as important organizing principles in these accounts. Second, such beliefs persist because they accord with the officers' perceptions of their world. For them, bureaucracy works because it imposes order.

On contracts

Managerialism in both its guises of performance measurement and contracting-out litters the conversation of interviewees. There is much 'management speak' – service deliverers, strategic attainment, corporate governance, streamlining managerial accountability with outcomes, ownership and motivation to achieve desired targets. The language of competition abounds and infiltrates their worldview. Some choke on it.

I am sick and tired of the lip service we pay to service, to crime reduction.

They are just rhetoric, platitudes, shamozzle, scraps of clichés from management textbooks that tell you to do more with less. (Interview 24)

Others offer less trenchant comments.

The competitiveness around managerialism contributes to a silo mentality where senior officers seek to rob each other of resources or officers. (Interview 9)

Many believe they are 'driven by contracts' (Interview 23), and are often fearful those contracts will be awarded elsewhere:

I think the [contract] is up for tender shortly. There is a feeling that we have to safeguard against X getting it. (Interview 25)

Most ire is reserved for the PIs. One senior officer described performance measurement as a 'farce' with little being achieved and most people coming away 'none the wiser' (Interview 24). The fact that no junior officer was aware of his or her output responsibilities or indeed of the performance measurement document suggests that managerialist reforms have not percolated far down the hierarchy (Interview 8). Interviewees insist that performance measurement 'be more flexible' (Interviews 25 and 26). Specific measures call forth derision.

I mean – the number of briefs delivered to the Director of Public Prosecutions. Where did they come up with that figure? Quite honestly, I could do that in a couple of weeks if I had to. As it happens we've exceeded it already but what does that mean? What does it achieve? If I am managing to provide briefs in big numbers, does that mean that crime prevention is not doing its job? Does that mean they have not managed to divert juveniles from crime? Why are we being measured on it? (Interview 18. See also interviews 2 and 20)

As ever, interpretations differ. For some, the shift to the new management style has yet to take place.

The thing is collectively we haven't realized yet we are a business. We have to make decisions. [Senior management] don't make decisions and when they are forced by circumstance to do so they shoot from the hip. . . . A strategic plan still doesn't exist! (Interview 12)

For others, change is gradual but the force is getting there.

When I arrived, in the order of 110 performance measures were being proposed! We got it down to 75 in the end but it was difficult. I couldn't believe it when I saw the rising crime figures and this ongoing preoccupation with things like how many forensic tests we might perform in any one year. There didn't seem to be a concern about crime at all at this point. . . . The excess of performance measures . . . reflected [government] uncertainty with it all – they didn't know what was expected but they knew they didn't want much flexibility. . . . The good thing . . . was . . . we did start to move away from a numbers culture to one based on outcomes. In other words, the debate about staff numbers was not driving the service as it had been previously. Now [government] was starting to become interested in genuine outcomes. . . . In the years that followed the measures have changed. Some of them were still a bit meaningless such as number of warrants served – there was no value in this. . . . [Subsequently] we focused on measures that would provide an outcome. We had six to start with, then four. [We] were pragmatic about indicators that could be measured, that could be verified (Interview 5).

Not all areas of policing are affected by contracts and managerialism.

They (PIs) don't affect us. We have no specific outcomes . . . our job is to filter information for intelligence purposes. (Interview 25)

On networks

Advocates of community policing hope it will be a dramatic departure from traditional policing because it adopts a 'long term strategic approach rather than offering a quick fix to an immediate problem' (Edwards 1999: 112). Community policing is said to be about leadership, partnerships, consultation and 'building trust, within and outside the organization' (Green *et al.* 1994: 107). Community policing also depends on government support and adequate resources – factors that are typically out of the force's control. Edwards (1999: 111–12) suggests that 'community policing exerts a high internal cost on the police service'. It is expensive in terms of budget and human resources.

To varying degrees, managing networks or partnerships is the current trend in the public service and increasingly in policing. So, we spend more time describing the views of police organizations on this reform. First, there is a low level of awareness among officers about what networks, if any, they are involved in. Few of our respondents were aware of the extent of the force's involvement with other government agencies and the voluntary sector. They know about their own links but not those of their colleagues. There was no central database or written collective memory. One officer cynically commented to us that 'corporate memory in this organization is the last meeting you went to'. The force has no idea of how many officers, how many resources it is expending on collaborative work, because it has never asked.

The force has formal consultative links, issue-specific links and informal activity. On the back of these interviews, we came up with the following examples. Formal consultative links cover, for example, domestic violence, working with and in schools, and community consultation. Issue-specific links refer in the main to such agreements as memorandums of understanding or MOUs, which cover partnerships with local taxi firms, mental health, and prisons and corrective services. Even when there is no formal consultative body or MOU, the police still have informal contacts with various sections of the community, especially with local chambers of commerce. However, such informal alliances also extend to everyday citizens. In an effort to 'to get the troops more on side' with community initiatives, one officer recalled:

> I told the mobile team to target the school areas. Constable X comes back to me and says he has written a dozen tickets but has spoken to no one. I told him I didn't care about tickets so much as knowing what the community was thinking about crime and their fear of it. I sent him away. Next day he comes and says he's written a few tickets and issued some cautions but has had a great lunch with the local school, noted their concerns and added, 'some of the mums were ok too"! That's what I want them to be doing. (Interview 7)

There are workshops on youth and ethnic groups, partnerships with non-government organizations (on rape, domestic violence, racial conflict) and informal understandings with government agencies. There may be low levels of awareness of the extent of police involvement, but there is commitment from those who see community networking as the future.

> I think the community policing thing is a good idea – I think it works – the problem of course is that it is hard to keep people in the same place for significant periods, but I think it's good, I think it's good for the community. We come up with lots of initiatives – we are good at that – but we are poor finishers – too many goals really. I think we should hit on three things and do them. (Interview 8)

> I think we've got to start focusing on service more. I can see us becoming one arm in a community consultative board – all inter-locking – family services, youth services for example, all meshing with the departments no longer working in isolation. I don't mean a 1984 scenario but I am coordinating it now. An example, a dysfunctional family is causing all sorts of problems at the housing estate where they live. They come from a lower socio-economic background and the child has learning problems. I got together representatives from the Department of [Housing] and [Social Services] and someone from mental health too and sorted something out. Housing got them somewhere else to live. The same family also had problems with a recidivist offender with a drug problem. We . . . sat down to see what we could do about this lad. In the end the Social Services took it off us but sometimes I wonder why I am doing this

– I suppose that's the lot of community policing. . . . We need to work towards an inter-agency approach – it will be difficult but if you are determined to make it work there is no physical reason why it shouldn't work if you persevere. We need a co-operative focus. (Interview 24)

Even the traditional copper sees some virtue in a more integrated approach.

I don't know if outsourcing is the answer (although we outsource the switchboard). It occurs to me that the public like a uniform – they want someone to help them and I don't think they care whether it is a St John's Ambulance person, a parking attendant or a private security guy. Parking attendants used to look like police officers with their uniforms but they don't now. They deliberately dress unlike police officers. A whole of government approach might consider bringing all services under the police umbrella – ambulance, fire, security. So, for example, if there was a major football game, the events planner could ring one number and organize police officers, St John's Ambulance, private security, traffic coordination. A policy like this would give us a better response to things too. The others might not have the powers but they would have the powers to detain until we arrived or at least provide a liaison point with the police on the ground. It would give us much better surge capacity. (Interview 19)

For some, there is a clear stereotype that the police focus on crime and see networking as a soft option.

I think your biggest problem will be the culture. It's still isolated, a 'boy's own' club – community policing means beat policing to them and they don't do that well. They don't like all this touchy feely stuff. (Interview 16)

Police don't want to get into the crime prevention stuff though. No one wants to do these jobs – they want to leave it to the warm and fuzzies. Police want to wear their underpants on the outside and save the world – they want to make the person pay. Culture has changed to some extent but it is still influenced by older people. People who are attracted to the policing role often have that mindset. (Interview 18)

[The Commissioner] puts a lot of rhetoric into crime prevention but at present it is just a limp-wristed, touch jockey, hug a tree PR job. . . . crime prevention as the band aid solution. (Interview 24)

Even supporters have their doubts.

[The community] have progressive views – for example they are comfortable with the idea of multi-agency work. [On the police side, however] there is a reluctance to co-operate in multi-agency work, although I should say, the higher you go in rank, the more accepting they seem to be. (Interview 1)

Of course, the critics are not just professional sceptics, casting a jaundiced eye on another set of reforms. They have some important points to make.

A common theme is that community policing is starved of resources.

Lots of platitudes but little action. The reactive stuff always takes precedence over the proactive stuff. Forty people in my department is not enough and yet [the Commissioner] still asks me continually whether or not my mix of sworn and administrative staff is the right mix with a view to taking away the sworn officers for more important duties. (Interview 3)

But it is also hard to attract staff.

It's hard to attract the right kind of people to the crime prevention area. We don't want people that just want to knock off at 4.00 doing it. If we force them to go there, many people see it as putting their career on the back burner for 12 months. We need to say to people that they need to demonstrate their diversity and suggest that time in crime prevention is a move forward in their careers. (Interview 17)

And it is scarcely any easier to get community support.

I am not confident about people getting together on these things. . . . I have been saving people's lives; cutting people out of cars and generally looking after the community for 24 years and you barely get a thank you. Nowadays you are more likely to get a civil litigation suit because someone has told them you lifted them wrongly or something. We've been spat on and everything. The community's ideas about whether or not they like you are changeable and can change because of a poor episode of *The Bill*. They ring us up asking us why we don't introduce something they've seen on television the night before and they can be quite arrogant about it. I think we need to continue with our efforts to educate the community but I am a bit of a realist – I think we make as much impact as the anti-smoking media. (Interview 19)

On dilemmas

There is much evidence to suggest that police officers face dilemmas as a result of the conflicting and diverging ideas of how best to run the force. They express these dilemmas in their beliefs about reform, their cynicism about the politics of change, their criticisms of leadership and their explicit understanding that the practices do not mix well.

Reform

For many officers the prospect of even more reform is unwelcome.

> [The force] is change weary. Since 1990, it has been one major upheaval after another. The [last Commissioner] had big ideas, and [so did] the Commissioner before him. They would go around telling it how it was but every time there was a change of management, there was another reorganization. Police are so fed up with this, that the [current] Commissioner has decreed that any further change must be incremental. (Interview 9)

The force is not only weary, but also averse to further change.

> New initiatives will be seen as just another fad – a sense that they will outlive the Commissioner and the fad. While they may be supportive of a new system, senior staff have seen it all before. They know resources will not be given to such a scheme and that this alone will kill it off. They may well pay lip service to it but will know that a change of Commissioner will bring on other changes. (Interview 2)

> The change process never stops; it just constantly evolves – those who say we are change-weary miss the point – change is ongoing. Mintzberg [a leading American academic and management consultant] makes it clear that change is a stop – move forward – constant evolution on all fronts – subject to constant review. We are constantly building strategy so it's nonsense to try to build strategy years ahead – it needs to be constantly renegotiated because the contemporary environment changes. (Interview 7)

> There is a sense at the moment we are enduring 'paralysis by analysis'. All we seem to do is to wait around for reviews to tell us something or committees to make a decision. (Interview 15)

> I mean the current [Commissioner] is concerned with decentralization – we move from decentralization to centralization continually – a new [Commissioner] might take us back to the front end again. This is hard on the organization internally. (Interview 17)

The politics of change

Some officers see change as political, not necessarily serving either police or community interests.

> As you can see, it is all political. Any major changes you want to make or anything that required a change in philosophy would require us to talk to

the [government]. They listen, and if it could be sold to them as an asset, I think they would accept it, but they would expect to be consulted. (Interview 5)

We are a bit conservative at changing the way we do things . . . I think we are always concerned about doing things the right way – incremental – there is a lot at stake and the media are always ready to have a go at police initiatives that go wrong. (Interview 8)

[The Commissioner] finds it difficult balancing the political against the needs of the organization. If we wanted to make any major changes in the organization we would always have to run it past the government first – they would want to think about it in terms of the community. It's not that they don't take our advice about things but they are wary, very wary. (Interview 9)

Interviewees do not believe that the police are masters of their own fortunes. The key to success lies with government, not in the hands of the police.

You must have [government] on board – any change must be backed up by [government]. The agencies would fall in line, culture or no culture if [government] directed it. (Interview 24)

Leadership

Middle management is critical of the top leadership.

[Senior management] don't manage well corporately. You can't get them to sign off on anything . . . Once they lose interest . . . it becomes hard to do anything . . . there is a real command and leadership problem up there. . . . They are splintered as a group, they don't mesh and I've told the [Commissioner] that, they just don't function well as an entity. It makes it difficult for the rest of us. . . . [Senior management] have different personalities, different agendas . . . One of the advantages of a fractured leadership, of course, is that you can hone in on someone and get them to champion a cause for you. (Interview 12)

The communication from the top down is poor. The senior executive does not command a vision – not much doubt about that. (Interview 17)

I had a fully laid out blueprint for them – outlining my needs on a prioritized basis and everything. I am still here waiting for their response! They haven't signed off on it! It's so hard to get anything up and running. I think [senior management] mean well but they are so caught up with politics that they are deflected from the main game. (Interview 18)

The lack of communication is the fault of [senior management] for the most part. Our business plan has been with them since May and has still not been signed off. We just carry on regardless. (Interview 15)

On occasion, their frustrations are leavened with wit.

All the [Commissioners] are different, we had one who used to have dreams and visions and would make decisions accordingly. We had another one who would make all his decisions in isolation – we used to call him Nike – just do it! (Interview 15)

It's the mix that matters

Several managers related their aversion to change and criticisms of the leadership to beliefs about tensions among structures or reforms. One officer makes the point with brutal simplicity: 'Terrorism is a problem – it doesn't go with the ideology of community policing and crime management' (Interview 1). The issues posed by police perceptions of conflicts among bureaucracy, contracts and networks can be drawn together around a discussion of the dilemmas of: competition vs cooperation, accountability vs efficiency, openness vs closure and governability vs flexibility (Jessop 2000: 20–3).

Competition vs cooperation

Scott (1998: 285–7) suggests that an organization that measures itself through targets and surveys – that is, one that has a high performance culture – and which at the same time seeks to introduce sector or community policing, faces several problems. Tensions over the priorities among objectives may well cause competition in the community itself. It is likely that resources will be allocated mainly to those activities that are deemed quantifiable or are a part of a target initiative.

We have already shown the prevalence of a silo mentality within the force, and the frustrations engendered by performance measurement. PIs are tangible and easy to monitor. Subsequent agreements may well increase the number of PIs and the levels at which they are to be measured. There is already competition between the silos. More PIs could foster more competitiveness between senior officers and discourage innovative practices that are not measurable.

Clearly, there is a tension between co-operative behaviour in the form of inter-agency agreements and working with the community and the internal competition for resource allocations linked to performance measurement.

Accountability vs efficiency

PIs may empower management by 'providing a way of measuring where police resources are being allocated' and increasing levels of managerial accountability

(Scott 1998: 283), but they do not necessarily measure police effectiveness (Beyer 1993: 97).

It is difficult to collect data on the effects of PIs. More importantly, there is some evidence that several PIs are inappropriate because they betray a lack of understanding of how policing works. For example, police responsiveness, and the way in which officers respond, has been linked by a number of studies to community satisfaction levels. So, how quickly they arrive, and how they behave when they get there, will affect police evaluations (Percy 1998; Tyler and Yeun 2002). Yet reducing response times does not reduce the crime problem or the probability of an arrest (Beyer 1993: 131). Problem-solving policing cannot be based solely on rapid response times. It puts pressure on officers to move on quickly, often 'writing off jobs' without even investigating them (Interview 27). As David Moore (1994: 213) notes in the Australian context, this superficial understanding of police accountability

> is almost certainly fostering reactive, defensive practices. Yet voices from the same quarters are simultaneously calling for open, proactive approaches to the complex social issues with which police are required to deal. It is little wonder, therefore that senior police managers often provide convoluted, even contradictory, answers when asked about the philosophies informing their police practice. Their responses reflect the contradictory demands made on police agencies.

One more example of PIs undermining efficiency will suffice. In this case, PIs impose rigidities and thwart innovation.

> We need to put more money into IT for updated programmes and more sophisticated software. But of course we haven't planned for this and now they are not happy about having to look at it carefully with a view to spending money we haven't got. And as I said we don't get a lot of input. . . . The budgets are completely out of our hands. . . . It is agreed that the PIs need to be more flexible and less tied to public perception, which can be affected by anything, but that's where it all ends. (Interview 25)

Indicators are here to stay. Governments insist on this form of financial accountability. But for community policing to work, surely police organizations require a more sympathetic set of measures. The boast of increasing accountability to government and the community through outsourcing and PIs will prove meaningless if the police are responsible for setting the targets. Joint service delivery requires joint measurements.

Openness vs closure

Many commentators argue that the community, both individually and collectively, holds expectations of its police service that are impossible to achieve

(Bradley 1998). Edwards (1999: 115–17) suggests that inflated community expectations of the police are a result of the community itself having little interest in, or conception of, the actual business of police work. He exposes the paradox inherent in public complaints of police inefficiency on the one hand, and public demand that police do all manner of non-police work and attend to non-urgent calls on the other. He draws on anecdotal evidence of the types of calls made to the police to demonstrate the way in which the police end up being called both to non-urgent incidents, and to incidents where the public is unsure about the service to call. Edwards explains that other services such as fire brigades, hospitals and a myriad of social support groups, all have specific areas of focus, but that the police are the easy 'catch-all' option for all kinds of problems that may lie between these other services.

It has been widely observed that in response to unrealistic community expectations, some police attempt the impossible by cutting corners, acting improperly or following unwise procedures (Goldstein 1977: 14). Edwards (1999: 116) sees this situation as a significant obstacle for policing generally, and for community policing specifically, because declining non-urgent calls, or those outside the core functions of the police, reduces public trust and confidence in them, and undoubtedly generates further criticism. However, community expectations about crime prevention cannot be met while the tremendous load of non-police work remains at its current levels.

As Goldstein (1977: 14) has suggested, the police should be more open about their capacity to cope with the pressures on them. Such transparency may increase public support for extra resources. It would also increase 'the likelihood that the public would more aggressively explore alternatives for dealing with some of the problems now relegated to the police'.

But openness has costs. First,

> The current [Commissioner's] concentration on crime prevention rather than reactive policing is impacting on our resources. In an era when we have politicians agitating, the [media] on our back questioning the way we do things and questioning our policing methods, it makes delivery difficult. I suppose it would be difficult for [the Commissioner] to go out and tell the community the truth – tell it the way it is. We are reducing numbers on the street and are looking for ways to compensate for this. (Interview 17)

Openness about such cost reduction strategies probably will not be seen as a feasible political option by Commissioners or government. As one officer pointed out, 'you can't publicize to the criminal, look we are not looking at stolen motorbikes anymore'. And partnerships impose unwelcome reciprocal obligations on agencies with crucial authoritative discretion over other actors. The MOU with the local cab company foundered on just this point: 'the Cabs thing didn't work because some cabbies wanted something in return – not be booked, for example – you are always going to get that though, people wanting some thing back' (Interview 17. See also interview 10).

Governability vs flexibility

Many of the people we spoke to have eluded to the difficult situation the Commissioner finds himself in and the difficulties of 'balanc[ing] the needs of the organization with that of [government]'. (Interview 9)

> We had a property crime issue. The [government] went to [the Commissioner] and said fix it. [The Commissioner] comes to us and says we have a problem – we say we don't have the resources, he says well find the resources and fix it. He's in a no-win situation. (Interview 23)

> I think the trouble is that we try to be all things to all people. We say 'yes' to everything, if someone asks us we say 'yes' – we are poll driven, media driven, community driven, government driven. We need to be able to say clearly what we can do and what we can't do . . . the [Commissioner] can't say no to the politicians, we've always got one eye on the [contracts] . . . most of us see the [Commissioner] as a figurehead not running the show. (Interview 25)

> We have to get government on board. We have to say to them that eventually there is going to be substantial discontent out there and they mustn't buckle at the knees. They have to sell it to the public and tell them that while we are not attending a gnome theft or even a burglary, we are doing more on patrol and . . . reducing the opportunities for crime. The stats will hopefully support this approach. That's the way to sell it – to explain that the available resources are being used more effectively elsewhere. (Interview 23)

> We can't say no to politicians. (Interview 25)

So police leadership is compromised by political responsiveness.

Equally, working with other agencies can confound governability.

> We have a drugs programme and one of our measures is to refer people to this programme. The only trouble is that the criteria for them is too narrow. They have to meet five criteria – no criminal record, no violence, they have to fully admit the crime, that sort of thing. Well let's take a kid of 15 who steals money off someone and in the process gives the person a shove. He wants the money for some marijuana. That shove has cost him his place in the drugs programme. It's difficult to get them in and many of them would benefit. . . . We need to loosen the criteria up or expand it in some way – not so prescriptive. (Interview 23)

Conclusions

In short, the police understand the story of reform as a shift from the bureaucracy of the interventionist state of the immediate post-war years and the contract state of the neo-liberals to the network state of partnerships. It is a shift that poses many a dilemma for them. The trick is not learning how to rewrite the rulebook, manage a contract or work with neighbourhood watch. Our interviewees are confident in their ability to manage such tasks. The problem is how to reconcile these ways of working effectively when they see them as conflicting with and undermining one another. They know from at times bitter experience that co-operative practices like working with the community can collapse under the impact of changed priorities. All the officers we interviewed can recite examples of how crises in areas such as family services and mental health can swamp the best of reforming intentions. And that was before there was terrorism! Some officers appreciated the dilemmas they confront and recognized the need to fit their managerial strategies to the context.

> Command and control is situational. In my team, I don't have subordinates. I have team members. Years ago a constable wouldn't speak to a superintendent – this is not the case now. I invite their ideas and input and encourage them to talk to me. If they are happy I have a productive working team. However, as I said, it's situational. Terrorism is a good example. As a commander in a crisis, when I want something done, it isn't up for negotiation, I tell the troops. We have to rely on command and control in these situations. (Interview 7)

The central story of police reform will be the responses of officers to dilemmas they associate with the contradictory demands of management reform and today's crisis, whatever it may be. Although they would never express it so, governance is a process of muddling through, seeking to negotiate the ever-changing mix of markets, hierarchies and networks foisted upon them.

10 Conclusions

We have argued governance arises from the bottom-up. It is a product of diverse practices that are themselves composed of multiple individuals acting on conflicting webs of beliefs rooted in overlapping traditions. Our governance stories only scratch the surface of these diverse practices. To conclude, however, we want to step back from the stories and ask: what do they tell us about British governance and even contemporary governance in general?[1] The answer will be that they challenge the craving for generality that characterizes comprehensive theories and definitions of contemporary governance.[2] The craving for generality appears in attempts to explain the highly diverse practices of contemporary governance in terms of a monolithic social logic or law-like regularity. In contrast, our governance stories explain diverse practices of contemporary governance by reference to various contingent actions rooted in overlapping and competing traditions. The craving for generality also appears in attempts to define contemporary governance by reference to a list of general features or essential properties that are supposed to characterize it in each and every instance. In contrast, our governance stories provide a series of perspectives on different aspects of contemporary governance. They point toward a definition of contemporary governance in terms of a series of family resemblances, none of which need be always present. The craving for generality appears, finally, in the concept of policy advice based on scientific expertise. In contrast, our governance stories point to a conception of policy advice based on stories that enable listeners to see new aspects of governance.

Comprehensive accounts of governance

Many other studies of contemporary governance aspire to be comprehensive (see Chapter 5). They aim to provide a general account of what contemporary governance looks like in Britain and beyond. Contemporary governance is characterized, for example, as multiplying networks replacing bureaucratic hierarchies of the welfare state and the markets promoted by the New Right. These comprehensive accounts of contemporary governance typically latch on to a single defining feature, which becomes the central focus that explains all other aspects of contemporary governance. Spreading networks might explain, for example, the greater reliance of states on a 'diplomatic' style of management, or it might embrace the spread of joint ventures, partnerships and holistic governance.

What do such comprehensive accounts imply about the nature of contemporary governance? They imply, first, that we can define 'contemporary governance' by reference to one or more of its essential properties, such as multiplying networks. They imply, second, that these essential properties are general ones that characterize all cases of contemporary governance. So, if and only if we find a spread of networks, do we find governance in its contemporary guise. They imply, finally, that these essential properties can explain at least the most significant other features of contemporary governance. A comprehensive account of contemporary governance makes sense, even as a mere aspiration, only if these implications are valid. We should seek a comprehensive account only if the way to clarify the nature of contemporary governance is to find a social logic or essential property that is common to all those patterns of governance. But why would we assume that contemporary governance has one or more essential features?

The quest for a comprehensive account appears to arise from a preoccupation with the natural sciences. However, even if it is appropriate in the natural sciences, it is counter-productive in the human sciences. As we argued in Chapter 2, human practices are not governed by social logics or law-like regularities associated with their allegedly essential properties. Rather, they arise out of the contingent activity of individuals. When we seek to explain particular cases of governance, therefore, we should do so by reference to the contingent activity of the relevant individuals, not a social logic or a law-like regularity. We should explain practices, including cases of governance, by means of narratives that unpack the contingent actions that embody beliefs informed by contested traditions and dilemmas. What is more, the contingent nature of the links between traditions and their development undermines the possibility of a comprehensive theory that could relate any one type of practice to a specific set of social conditions as opposed to a historical process.

Because we can not explain cases of contemporary governance by reference to a comprehensive theory, we cannot define contemporary governance in terms of key features. Rather, we can define contemporary governance only in terms of particular cases. However, the absence of a comprehensive theory of contemporary governance also implies that there need be no feature common to all the cases to which we would apply the term. It is futile to search for the essential features of an abstract category that denotes a cluster of human practices. Worse still, the search for allegedly common features can lead political scientists to dismiss the particular cases which alone enable them to understand the abstract category. When we provide a definition or general account of contemporary governance, it should be couched as a set of family resemblances.

Explaining governance

Comprehensive accounts of contemporary governance typically attempt to explain cases of governance by reference to a social logic. In contrast, our interpretive approach prompts us to adopt narrative explanations. As we saw in Chapters 1 and 2, these narrative explanations work by relating actions or practices to the beliefs of the relevant actors, and by situating these beliefs against the background of traditions and dilemmas. Thus, in Chapter 5 we argued that the Tory, Liberal, Whig and Socialist traditions inspired distinctive reforms, which we labelled respectively intermediate institutions, networks of communities, reinventing the constitution and joined-up government (see Table 5.1).

Because our narrative does not purport to be a comprehensive account, the Tory, Liberal, Whig and Socialist traditions do not constitute essential properties that appear in each and every instance of contemporary British governance. To the contrary, a fuller account of British governance requires us to move beyond Westminster and Whitehall, and thereby examine the several actors involved in making and implementing public policy, recognizing that many might not conventionally be seen as part of government. In short, we decentre governance and policy to explore how actors going about their daily business construct both. Our stories provide a series of snap-shots of different aspects of governance. Some aspects we can explain in terms of Tory, Liberal, Whig and Socialist traditions. For example, in Chapter 6, we argued that the Tory, Whig and Socialist traditions led to different understandings of the Blair presidency. Other stories require us to postulate alternative traditions such as the generalist tradition in Chapter 7 and clinical autonomy in Chapter 8.

So, our governance stories contrast sharply with those apparently comprehensive accounts that unpack the essential properties and social logic of contemporary governance. Neither the intrinsic rationality of markets nor the path dependency of institutions decides patterns of governance. Rather, patterns of governance arise as the contingent constructions of several actors inspired by competing webs of beliefs formed against the background of diverse traditions. Our governance stories thus explain shifting patterns of governance by focusing on the beliefs and actions by which a host of people construct varied practices. They explore some of the diverse ways in which situated agents are changing the boundaries of state and civil society by constantly remaking practices as their beliefs change.

Defining governance

To reject the idea of a comprehensive account of contemporary governance means we cannot define 'governance' in terms of essential properties. Rather, we understand general concepts such as governance by using them in actual cases. Their meaning derives from the ways in which we use them in the relevant language games. What is more, the absence of a comprehensive account of contemporary governance suggests there are no set ways in which we must – or must not – use the term. There need be no single feature shared by all those cases or narratives to which we would apply the general term 'contemporary governance'.

We understand governance as a set of family resemblances. Wittgenstein (1972b: 63–9) famously suggested that general concepts such as 'game' should be defined by various traits that overlapped and criss-crossed in much the same way as do the resemblances between members of a family – their builds, eye colour, gait, personalities. He considered various examples of games to challenge the idea that they all possessed a given property or set of properties – skill, enjoyment, victory and defeat – by which we could define the concept. Instead, he suggested that the examples exhibited a network of similarities, at various levels of detail, so that they coalesced even though no one feature was common to them all.

We do not master such family resemblances by discovering a theory or rule that tells us precisely when we should and should not apply a concept. Our grasp of the concept consists in our ability to provide reasons why it should be applied in one case but not another, our ability to draw analogies with other cases, and perhaps our ability to point to the criss-crossing similarities. Our knowledge of 'governance' is analogous to our knowledge of 'game' as described by Wittgenstein (1972a: 18): it is 'completely expressed' by our describing various cases of governance, showing how other cases can be considered as analogous to these, and suggesting that we would be unlikely to describe yet other cases as ones of governance.

No doubt some of the family resemblances apparent in our governance stories derive from our philosophical analysis of meaning in action and situated agency and they thus apply to all patterns of rule or governance. Our interpretive theory highlights, first, a more diverse view of state authority and its exercise. Patterns of rule or governance arise as the contingent products of diverse actions and political struggles informed by the varied beliefs of situated agents. Other accounts of governance rightly suggest the New Right's reinvention of the minimal state and New Labour's rediscovery of networks are attempts to find a substitute for the voluntaristic bonds weakened by state intervention. Our philosophical analysis suggests, in addition, that the notion of a monolithic state in control of itself and civil society was always a myth. The myth obscured the reality of diverse state practices that escaped the control of the centre because they arose from the contingent beliefs and actions of diverse actors at the boundary of state and civil society. The state is never monolithic and it always negotiates with others. Policy always arises from interactions within networks of organizations and individuals. Patterns of rule always traverse the public, private and voluntary sectors. The boundaries between state and civil society are always blurred. Transnational and international links and flows always disrupt national borders. In short, state authority is constantly being remade, negotiated and contested in widely different ways within widely varying everyday practices.

Second, these everyday practices arise from situated agents whose beliefs and actions are informed by traditions and expressed in stories. In every government department, NHS hospital and police force, we can identify departmental traditions, often embodied in rituals and routines. We find them in the government department, ranging from Westminster notions of accountability to the ritual of the tea lady. We find them in the persistent faith of the NHS in hierarchy and financial control. Actors pass on these traditions in large part by telling one another stories about how things are done, and about what does and does not work. As we saw in Chapter 7, civil servants are socialized into the broad notions of the Westminster model, such as ministerial responsibility, as well as the specific ways of doing things around here. They are 'socialized into the idea of a profession', and learn 'the framework of the acceptable'. So, governance is not any given set of characteristics. It is the stories people use to construct, convey and explain traditions, dilemmas and practices.

Our stories also highlight family resemblances that characterize the pattern of governance in contemporary Britain, but might perhaps not be found in other times or places. Here the reforms of the New Right and New Labour have been attempts to redefine the role of the state. One family resemblance highlighted by our governance stories is that these reforms have brought something of a shift from hierarchy to markets to networks. While this shift is widely recognized, our governance stories suggest, crucially, that it takes many diverse forms. Thus, in Chapter 9 we saw that the shift from hierarchy to markets to networks poses many a dilemma for the police. They know how to rewrite the rulebook, manage a contract or work with neighbourhood watch, but they struggle to reconcile ways of working, believing they conflict and undermine one another. However, as we saw in Chapter 8, the equivalent shift poses different dilemmas for doctors, where the key issue is to preserve the medical model of health and medical autonomy from managerial reforms that stress hierarchy and financial control.

A second family resemblance is that the central state has adopted a less hands-on role. Its actors are less commonly found within various local and sectoral bodies, and more commonly found in quangos concerned to steer, co-ordinate and regulate such bodies. Once again, our stories suggest, crucially, that such steering, co-ordination and regulation take many diverse forms. The pre-eminent example is 'joined-up' government as the Blair government seeks to devise policy instruments that integrate both horizontally across central government departments and vertically between central and local government and the voluntary sector.

A recurring paradox runs through our stories of British governance. On one hand, our decentred perspective suggests the Westminster model was an illusion masking the contested and contingent nature of British constitutionalism, while the changes associated with the reforms of the New Right and New Labour have arguably made it even less accurate an illusion than once it was. On the other, many political actors continue to use the language of the Westminster model to describe the past, present and future of British politics. It is part of their everyday language for coping. There are also a handful of recurrent metaphors that run through the specific accounts of governance. We talk about the drama of politics, the stage on which politicians appear and the court politics of the centre. The stories take the form of gossip about the games people play. When our ethnographic tools decentre policy and institutions, we till the soil of everyday games and there could be no clearer example than the court politics of the Blair–Brown duumvirate.

A final family resemblance is thus the way actors cast the dilemmas of change as problems for the Westminster model. For example, they emphasize that multiplying networks pose problems of accountability understood as ministerial accountability to parliament. They do so, moreover, even though the Westminster model is itself variously understood against the background of diverse traditions. For example, tales of the Blair presidency are narrated in ways that echo Tory, Whig and Socialist themes.

History and ethnography

We have highlighted family resemblances that contribute to a general characterization of governance and a more specific characterization of British governance. Yet we should reiterate: there is no logic to the specific forms governance takes in particular circumstances. Here our interpretive approach resolves the theoretical difficulties that beset more positivist versions of British government. It avoids the unacceptable suggestion that institutions fix the actions of individuals rather than being products of those actions. It replaces unhelpful phrases such as path-dependency with an analysis of change rooted in the beliefs and actions of situated agents. And yet it allows political scientists to offer aggregate studies by using the concept of tradition to explain how they come to hold those beliefs and perform those actions (see Chapters 1 and 2).

The approach also opens new research agendas – it is fruitful, progressive and open. To improve our knowledge of contemporary British governance, we need to pursue decentred studies of the diverse practices of which it consists. Typically these decentred studies will rely on textual analysis and ethnography to explore the beliefs and actions not only of politicians, civil servants and public sector managers, but also street-level bureaucrats and citizens. Typically they will rely on historical forms of explanation to make sense of these beliefs and actions by reference to traditions and dilemmas. These decentred studies open a wide range of new areas and styles of research about the beliefs and actions of many political actors – from prime minister to individual citizens – as they preserve and modify traditions and practices – from Toryism and Parliament to, say, New Age travellers and forms of protest.

Sometimes we can explore beliefs through analysis of already written texts. For example, in Chapter 5, we relied on texts, including official reports, to postulate the beliefs that characterize Tory, Liberal, Whig and Socialist constructions of governance. Similarly, in Chapter 8, we focused on official documentation to identify the changing beliefs about the NHS. At other times, however, we can explore beliefs only by using ethnographic research to generate further data. For example, in Chapter 9, we relied on interviews to generate texts we could use to identify the beliefs informing the actions by which officers contributed to the construction of the governance of the police. In Chapter 7, we relied, similarly, on participant observation and related techniques to generate data by which we could postulate the beliefs informing the activities that characterize daily life in a government department.

Ethnographic research has two principal features as a source of data. First, it gets below and behind the surface of official accounts by providing texture, depth and nuance, so the story of the department has richness as well as context. Second, it lets interviewees explain the meaning of their actions, providing insights that can only come from the main characters involved in the story. Interviews and non-participant observation offer a type of political anthropology that yields 'thick descriptions'.

We are all too aware of the limits of ethnography. It is commonly argued, in particular, that ethnographic research on the powerful encounters many difficulties. There is the endemic secrecy of British government. Interviews are said to be an unreliable source of data because interviewees 'unself-consciously project an official self-image' (Lee 1995: 149) and politicians are seen as self-serving to the point of misleading. As Seldon (1995: 126) observes, he 'frequently had reason to wonder whether some former ministers had served in the same administration so at variance were their accounts of the way coordination took place at the heart of Whitehall'. Moreover, there are often no written sources to cross-check the accuracy of interviews and their veracity is perhaps undermined when they are not attributed. Finally, it is claimed that non-participant observation always affects the behaviour of the observed. All these points are valid. None present insurmountable obstacles.

British government may well be excessively secretive, but since 1992 the civil service has sought to encourage academic research. However, even if more research does equate to less secrecy, it is not synonymous with open. We had to take great care to disguise the police force that helped us in Chapter 9. For the research on government departments, it became clear during our negotiations about access that secrecy would be a greater problem when it was time to negotiate our way out of the departments; only now the problem was called 'clearance'. So, we sought to do non-participant observation and the shadowing in departments and police forces that were roughly similar. If there were problems with attributing quotes and describing the behaviour of named officials, politicians and police officers, then we could write, as here, a composite portrait of 'the department', 'its minister' and the 'commissioner'. We chose three middle ranking, domestic service ministries. They could be 'merged' to provide a realistic composite.

With few exceptions, everyone was willing to speak on tape. By the end of six hours of interviewing, most were relaxed, willing to chat about anything, historical or present-day. Almost no one can talk in sentences, with commas and full stops, for any sustained period of time. Equally, few can uphold a public posture over a six-hour interview. Many have a need to talk. As Rawnsley (2001: xi) observes 'they have to tell an outsider because they are so worried about whether it makes sense or, indeed, whether they make sense'. In other words, 'how do I know what I think until I hear what I say?' The interviewer is cast in the role of providing reassurance.

Of course, as we saw in Chapter 2, we often decode the official self-image. We postulate a rhetorical gap between expressed and actual beliefs. Although no method can guarantee we do so correctly, we would mention two heuristic contexts for decoding. First, we can locate the official ethos and language in its context by comparing texts, whether they are official publications, files or interview transcripts. Second, all of us during our everyday lives develop skills in decoding what others mean when they speak by reference to many verbal and body cues, and we do not leave such skills at the door of the interview room.

No doubt it is all too easy to affect the relationship between yourself and the observed, causing them to act differently. Our aim was to remain outsiders, but with lengthy on-site visits and extensive repeat interviews, you have conversations and engage with the people around you. You are sucked into events, even if it is only casual badinage to ease tension. Our stays in departments provided several examples. One permanent secretary reduced his corporate civil service commitments when he saw how much time they took up. One changed his private secretary after an in confidence briefing about the workings of his private office. Always we tried to blend in with the wallpaper, but we were an object of some interest to the private office and the permanent secretary, and they sought to engage with us.

Again, while no method can guarantee the accuracy of data and stories, we might mention heuristic contexts for checking the veracity and reliability of data. First, we interviewed several other members of the departments, officials and politicians, besides the ministers and the permanent secretaries. Second, we had access to the written records of meetings. Finally, the project was not based on elite interviews alone, but also on fieldwork and, as Sanjek (2000: 281) argues, non-participant observation is a useful complement to interviews. Thus, interviews recorded at a different time from the non-participant observation are a way of corroborating the claims of a speaker. The PS's loyalty to his minister was clear from his behaviour; for example, rearranging his day so he and his staff could rally round.

In sum, we have shown that ethnographic methods are a feasible research tool at all levels of government (see also Rhodes 2002) and an effective way of capturing beliefs and practices, just as the historical analysis of traditions is the means for explaining such beliefs and practices.

Lessons for policy

The craving for generality appears also in the concept of policy advice as scientific expertise. We want to highlight, in contrast, three implications of our governance stories for practitioners. First, the contingent nature of human practices challenges the idea of expertise as a basis for policy. It implies, in other words, that comprehensive accounts can not guide policymakers in the way they often purport to. Second, narratives and cases offer a different type of policy advice from the kind of expertise proffered by those who purport to provide comprehensive accounts. Instead of revealing policy consequences through insights into a social logic or law-like regularities, they enable policymakers to see things differently; they exhibit new connections within governance and new aspects of governance. Third, the process of seeing differently is a dialogical one. Typically we see new aspects of a policy area or problem when someone tells us a story that highlights them. Hence policymakers would be well advised to engage in more dialogic modes of policy formation that involve them in conversations with diverse groups of citizens. In short, our governance stories point to policy advice as stories that enable listeners to see governance afresh.

Most policy-oriented work on governance seeks to improve the ability of the state to manage the mix of hierarchies, markets and networks that have flourished since the 1980s. Typically this work treats hierarchies, markets and networks as fixed structures that governments can manipulate using the right tools (see, for example, Salamon 2002). An interpretive approach encourages us, in contrast, to foreswear management techniques and strategies but, and the point is crucial, to replace such tools with learning by telling stories and listening to them.

We are not alone, although the label varies – the argumentative turn, narratives and storytelling. There is now a growing literature on 'the interpretive turn' in organization studies, policy analysis and public administration (and for reviews of the literature see Morgan 1997; van Eeten *et al.* 1996). The behavioural revolution in the social sciences marginalized storytelling, but it is being rediscovered in several disciplines – law, psychology, even economics. In policy analysis, as Dryzek (1993: 222) points out, there are many social science frames of reference. Each frame 'treats some topics as more salient than others, defines social problems in a unique fashion, commits itself to particular value judgements, and generally interprets the world in its own particular and partial way'. And this multiplicity of 'incommensurable analytical frames' dealt a 'devastating' blow to the 'authoritative ambitions' of policy analysis (see also Bobrow and Dryzek 1987). Instead of such ambitions, we have policy analysis through dialogue. Thus Schram (1993: 252) argues for 'those approaches to examining policy that emphasize how the initiation, contestation, adoption, implementation, and evaluation of any policy are shaped by the discursive, narrative, symbolic practices which socially construct our understanding of problems, methods of treatment and criteria of success'.

In similar vein, van Eeten *et al.* (1996) record the rediscovery of storytelling in the subfield of public administration. They distinguish between story-telling by administrators and storytelling by scholars to make the important point that this latest intellectual fashion has its feet firmly on the ground. In both public and private organizations managers use stories not only to gain and pass on information and to inspire involvement, but also as the repository of the organization's institutional memory.

For Rein (1973: 74–5), for example, advice to policymakers is based 'on the use of illustrative stories, or accounts from past experience, which suggest how the future might unfold if certain actions were taken'. In his view, policy narratives present a chronology or sequence of linked events, using a few major characters, and each step in the story 'causes' the next step. There is a story line or, if you will, a beginning, middle and end (although, of course, that 'end' is the start of the next story). The central thread in the story is the metaphor (or making the unfamiliar analogous to familiar situations). 'The simplest stories are proverbs and parables, used to justify policy relevant stories' (*ibid.*: 266). So there is usually a moral to the tale. The validity of stories is assessed by rules that are 'partly aesthetic and partly logical'. The story should be 'the simplest, most comprehensive, internally consistent explanation we can offer'. We should also ask if the explanation in the story could be generalized. The task of the policy analyst, therefore, 'is to invent objectively grounded normative stories, to participate in designing pro-grammes of intervention based upon them and to test the validity of stories that others commend' (*ibid.*: 268).

So, as advocates of an interpretive approach, we are suspicious that an excessive concern with prediction bolsters inappropriate claims to 'scientific expertise'. Nonetheless, we recognize the appeal of useful techniques as ways of making interpretive studies relevant to policymakers. So, we adopt the device of storytelling to build bridges between theory and practice. Again, if we were policy analysts or senior civil servants advising a minister on (say) public service reform, what rules of thumb, what dos and don'ts, could we derive from an interpretive approach? An interpretive approach that had no purchase on such problems would command little attention. Fortunately we can show that storytelling has practical relevance.

'Imaginization' must be a candidate for one of the ugliest neologisms ever. Why Morgan (1993) did not use the more obvious 'thinking in metaphors', or even just plain 'storytelling', is a mystery. Nonetheless, his analysis is instructive and grounded in a thoroughgoing interpretive framework (buried as Appendix A, but accessible for all that). Imaginization is about creating new metaphors, new stories, with which to understand an organization. It aims to: improve our abilities to see and understand situations in new ways; find new images for new ways of organizing; and create shared understandings that empower people and develop their capacities for self-organization (*ibid.*: 2–19). Imaginization is 'the art of framing and reframing'. It uses 'images, metaphors, readings and storylines to cast situations in new perspective and open possibilities for creative action'. Metaphors are central to this process.

They use paradox to 'break the bounds of normal discourse'. They require the 'users to find and create meaning'. But they work only if they 'ring true, hit a chord and resonate' (*ibid.*: 290). In sum, 'organization always hinges on the creation of shared meaning and shared understandings' (*ibid.*: 11).

Morgan employs the techniques of action learning (*ibid.*: Appendix B) to create new meanings and shared understandings. We can illustrate this process with the cautionary tale of Network (paraphrased from Morgan 1993: chapter 6). Network runs community action programmes for young people. The problem is that they are spread too thinly, with inadequate resources, and have problems in setting priorities. They felt they were not really organized. They were 'a blob out of water' and at their most 'blobby' when dealing with the church hierarchy; for example, the bureaucracy was irritated by their views on social justice. Morgan (*ibid.*: 138) helped the staff to come up with new, shared meanings.

> They *were* like the dandelion seeds and supernova. They *were* like an amoeba and chameleon, changing shape and colour in different circumstances. They operated in a loose, expansive, and at times chaotic style, yet . . . they were held together . . . through their strong value base.

The disorganization was better seen as flexibility; staff could operate autonomously but in unison. But it was too late. Their 'blobbiness' got them. The church hierarchy saw them as too chaotic and closed them down. So the story has four messages. It shows the qualities needed for an organization to be flexible. It shows how metaphors can create new meaning; how chaos can be reconceived as flexibility. It shows how an interpretive approach can be applied to helping people run their organization. And it shows the dangers of a clash in organizational styles; most governments, like the church, will find networks fundamentally messy and carp at the mess. As Morgan concludes (*ibid.*: 306) such stories will be more or less effective as interventions if they 'resonate and evoke ideas and personal responses in a wide variety of situations' (see *ibid.*: 307–11 for an extended discussion).

Advice to the practitioner is not confined to telling resonating stories. Weick (1995: chapter 8) identifies six rules of thumb to guide the behaviour of practitioners.

1   *Acting and talking*: You will find out what you think by acting.
2   *Words matter*: The stories you tell and the words you use to tell them will affect what you see and how others see you.
3   *History*: 'Good' decision-makers retrospectively construct a history that appears to have led directly to the decision.
4   *Committees*: Meeting more often is good for you; it makes sense of ambiguity, puzzles and the organization.
5   *Sharing*: Tell stories about shared experiences to foster shared meaning.
6   *Reality*: Reality is up for grabs and expectations are powerful realities.

Obviously we paraphrase, but it is unnecessary to unpack these rules of thumb. We seek to make the simple point that an interpretive approach has techniques (storytelling) which provide guides for managers in the guise of rules of thumb or, if you will, proverbs.

Others still might ask, however, how do you write stories that guide managers? Morgan's (1993: 301–2) basic protocol is to 'get inside a situation and understand it as far as possible on its own terms'; adopt the role of a learner, not expert, and let 'the situation "speak for itself"'; 'create a rich description' of what is said and done; and develop an 'evolving "reading"' or interpretation. He collects three kinds of data: the 'so-called objective facts of a situation'; the social constructions of reality; and the researcher's social constructions of reality. The resulting knowledge can be generalized in two ways. First, it provides 'insights that capture the pattern of event and problems'. Second, it provides 'strategies and tactics through which similar problems . . . can be tackled elsewhere'.

In a similar vein, Weick (1995: chapter 8) suggests that action research studies practices in context; relies on participants' definition of what they are doing and why; observes people at work; generates patterns, not hypotheses; judges patterns by their plausibility, not against prior theories or models; writes thick descriptions; and concentrates on meanings, not statistical frequencies. An interpretive approach enjoins us to unpack individual beliefs and the traditions from which they stem. Morgan and Weick practice ethnographic research, which is one of the many ways of recovering meanings. For present purposes, however, it is enough to show that an interpretive approach has its own techniques (of stories and metaphors) and tools (based on participant and non-participant observation) and that its findings can be translated into practical advice to decision-makers.

Given that much of our argument is general, it is important to bring it down to earth with a thud. Most, if not all, policy advisers will accept that the art of storytelling is an integral part of their work. Such phrases as: 'Have we got our story straight?', 'Are we telling a consistent story?' and 'What is our story?' are common. The basis for much advice is the collective memory of the department, its traditions if you will. It is an organized, selective retelling of the past to make sense of the present. Advisors explain past practice and events to justify recommendations for the future. In short, our stress on storytelling is not an example of academic whimsy. We ground our approach in both an explicit epistemology *and* the everyday practice of advisors.

Our interpretive approach shows that governance has no essential properties. We have argued for specific studies of governance rather than comprehensive accounts. We seek to persuade that our ethnographic and historical studies offers an edifying account of British government. We offer a redefinition of policy analysis as lesson drawing through storytelling that enables listeners to see governance afresh. In short, we have decentred governance.

Notes

1 Introduction: Meaning in action

1 When we follow the logic of decentring or disaggregating concepts like voting or policy network, we end up with micro-level stories of individual actions based on one person's set of beliefs. Although such stories are interesting as cases, there are times when we want to tell more general stories, for example about governance. To do so, we need aggregate concepts like traditions and dilemmas.

2 Interpretation and its others

1 Several colleagues prompted us to clarify and develop our approach. We are grateful to participants in the collaborative project on 'Traditions of Governance', and at panels of the Political Studies Association Annual Conference, University of Lincoln, 6–8 April 2004; the American Political Science Association Annual Conference, Chicago, 1–3 September 2004; and the Australasian Political Studies Association, University of Adelaide, 29 September–1 October 2004.

2 Some critical realists adhere to a thick ontological concept of social structure. They reify structures as if they had an independent existence apart from the activity of individuals (Bhaskar 1998 [1979]). We would demur from that view. Other critical realists grope for a thin concept of social structure, accepting that structures are emergent properties of individual actions (Hay 2002). We would accept such an analysis, arguing only that the term 'practice' is preferable to 'structure' precisely because 'structure' evokes a thicker ontological notion of social context.

3 For such a logic, see Popper (1959). On its early appeal to political scientists, see Ricci (1984: 141–4). For its contemporary place, see Gerring (2003) and Sanders (1995).

3 British political sciences

1 It is also surprising and revealing that, in a text of 511 pages, there is not a single reference in the index to Louis Althusser, Roland Barthes, Manual Castells, Jacques Derrida or Nicos Poulantzas, although there are entries for noted American political scientists such as Robert Dahl and David Easton. The defence could be entered that the book is about British political science, not the Continental version. In which case it is indefensible that there are no entries for

Bob Jessop or Ernesto Laclau – only those with a myopic focus on modernist empiricism and positivism could leave them out.

2 This paragraph paraphrases Hayward (1991b). With various embellishments he repeats this story in Hayward (1986, 1991a, 1999). We should also acknowledge that Hayward (1991b: 320) notes in passing the Continental and Marxist contributions to British political science, but opines they had a 'belated and limited impact' as British political scientists were 'inoculated' against their attractions (1991b: 310–11). In addition to the mainstream account told by political scientists such as Hayward, there is a more historicist but still rather Whiggish narrative of British political science told by intellectual historians such as Stefan Collini (1988, 2001) and Julia Stapleton (1994, 2001), and for critical commentary see Adcock and Bevir (2005).

3 The same story is told about the sub-fields. Traditional Public Administration was essentially institutional and concerned to analyse the history, structure, functions, powers and relationships of government organizations (see Mackenzie 1975: 4, 7–8, 9–10; Rhodes 1997: chapter 4; Robson 1975). It also avoided theory (Mackenzie 1975: 8). The distaste for theory and focus on formal institutions was challenged by the rise of organization theory and policy analysis. Both introduced more positivist theories and methods to the subject. The rise of rational choice and the new public management further contributed to explicit theorizing and purportedly more sophisticated research methods.

4 Of course Blondel is not the only example. The subfield of British election studies is dominated by this approach. Any comprehensive listing would be inordinately long, but for relevant citations see Scarbrough (1987).

5 Rational choice is seen as 'genre' political science. Albert Weale (Essex) is the source of this appellation. At the time he made this statement, he was chair of the 2001 Research Assessment Exercise Panel (RAE), which was responsible for evaluating the research output of all British political scientists. There is little by way of an indigenous literature. We consulted colleagues specializing in rational choice. The criteria for inclusion were a book by a political scientist based in Britain and doing rational choice research. The resulting list was short. Excluding textbooks, the main examples include Boyne (1998), Dowding and King (1995), Dunleavy (1991) and McLean (2001).

6 For discussion of Taylor's time in Britain and his involvement in British intellectual groups, see Smith (2002: 173–83).

7 The first signs of this movement appeared in Skinner (1984: 231–88, 1990: 293–309). It became triumphantly clear in Skinner (1998).

8 See Hobsbawm (1981), and on developments in Anglo-Marxist historiography since the 1970s, see Bevir and Trentmann (2002).

9 In brief, the ESRC priorities are: economic performance and development; environment and human behaviour; governance and citizenship; knowledge, communication and learning; lifecourse lifestyles and health; social stability and exclusion; and work and organizations. See also Donovan (2005).

10 We are sorely tempted to comment that we await our invitation to the Board of a major corporation so we can give them the benefit of our business experience, for we know as much about their work as they know about ours! To do so, of course, would be to fly in the face of today's conventional wisdom that business skills are 100 per cent transferable irrespective of sector, a proposition so palpably false it is hard to know where to begin or whether it is worth beginning.

4   Westminster models

1 These normative themes are all too apparent in the views of the Australian Labor Party, which sees federalism as a conservative form of government. See, for example, Galligan (1995: 56–62), Sawer (1969: 152, 179, 181), Wheare (1963: 235–6) and Wilenski (1983: 82–7). Even less politically aligned critics, see non-decisions where others see conservative bias (see Spann 1975: 65).

2 However, while browsing through the six-volume Official Record of the Debates of the Australasian Federal Convention (1986), we were struck by the diverse views expressed and the unsystematic nature of the analysis compared to the Federalist Papers. It was not just federal theory that was absent, but that there was no substantial measure of agreement or clarity over the notion of ministerial responsibility.

3 There have been arguments about whether Australia is a three-party or two-and-a-half party system, because on the non-Labor side of politics two separate parties (Liberal and National) contest for seats (usually in separate geographical regions). However, they invariably form a single, stable coalition in government and in opposition.

4 The exceptions include Brown (2003a, 2003b), Davis, R. S. (1995), Fletcher (1991), Galligan (1995), Galligan *et al.* (1991), Painter (1998), Sharman (1990), Thompson (1980) and Uhr (1998). The seminal contribution on Australia as a federal republic is Galligan (1995), but see also Davis, R. S. (1995) and Sharman (1990). Some international commentators were astute in their observations. For example, Uhr (2002: 269) points out that Bryce (1921) recognized that the Australian system had many checks and balances on its leadership – a written constitution, federalism, bicameralism, separation of powers and independent judiciary.

5 We paraphrase Kelly (1994) because his was the most influential account of the fall of the Australian Settlement and rise of neoliberal beliefs about economics and government. See also the collection of essays in Smyth and Cass (1998) and Stokes (2004).

6 It is plausible to claim that the pre-eminence of prime ministers during election campaigns is promoted by the media. However, turning from the electoral arena to others such as policymaking and policy implementation, the pre-eminence of prime ministers is much less obvious, especially in a federal system where the senate and the states can frustrate both policy and its implementation (and on Britain see Chapter 6).

7 Indeed, it would find little resonance in European parliamentary democracy (outside Britain) built around coalition politics. Moreover, the problem is not peculiarly Australian. All bicameral systems confront the issue of the powers of the upper house and the implications for accountability.

8 Although the opposition is institutionalized to a far greater extent than in many other Westminster systems, Australia, unlike Britain, does not have an independent vote for the speaker (no opposition member has been speaker of the House or president of the Senate), and there is no tradition of allowing the opposition to chair the public accounts committee or have a majority on this important standing committee.

5 Decentring governance

1 This chapter draws on the ideas about governance in Bevir and Rhodes (2003).

2 How could we fail to note Marks & Spencer's fall from grace, from exemplar of business efficiency in the 1980s to the floundering High Street chain of the 2000s? Yet again, the notion of the private sector as the arbiter of taste in all things managerial falls flat on its face.

6 The Blair presidency

1 On the ethnographic methods see: Dexter (1970), Eckstein (1975), Fenno (1990), Geertz (1973), Hammersley and Atkinson (1983), Sanjek (1990), Silverman (1997, 2000), Strauss *et al.* (1973) and Yin (1994). For applications to British government see: Glennerster *et al.* (1983), Heclo and Wildavsky (1974) and McPherson and Raab (1988).

2 Definitions of the presidentialization thesis vary: cf. Allen (2002: 16), Foley (1993: chapter 1), Pryce (1997: 37, 67) and Mughan (2000: 9–10). They variously emphasize the particular presidential case (Wilson, Thatcher, Blair) and presidentialization trends. We synthesize the argument into the three trends of greater centralization of policymaking, pluralization of advice and personalization of party leadership and elections. The Blair presidency is seen as a defining case supporting the presidentialization thesis. If the evidence for the Blair case is weak, then the evidence for the thesis is weakened. Also, it is not always clear whether the comparison is with presidential systems generally or the American example. On the insurmountable difficulties of the American analogy see Rose (2001: 236–44).

3 When Hugh Heclo and Aaron Wildavsky (1974: 341–3) described the debate about prime ministerial power as one of the 'chestnuts of the constitution', they probably did not expect to see it thriving 35 years later as the presidentialization thesis. Butler and Stokes (1969: 351) published their classic analysis of British elections. They claimed the election of Harold Wilson in 1964 provided hard evidence of the independent effect of party leaders on elections for the first time. Academic debate had been fuelled by Richard Crossman's introduction to Bagehot's *The English Constitution*. He claimed that 'if we mean by presidential government, government by an elective first magistrate then we in England have a president as truly as the Americans' (Crossman 1963: 22–3; reaffirmed in 1972b: 67–8; see also Mackintosh 1968: 627). The terminology varies encompassing prime ministerial government, presidentialism, duumvirate and monocratic government. Heaven forbid we should cover this ground again. For a review see Rhodes (1995) and Smith (1999). For useful collections of articles see King (1969, 1985) and Rhodes and Dunleavy (1995). For a comparative analysis of trends see Campbell (1998), Elgie (1997), Foley (2000), Hargrove (2001), Savoie (1999) and Weller (1985).

4 Although most quotes are from practitioners, we draw on four journalist-historians whose insider sources are as impeccable as they are limitless: Hennessy (1989), Peston (2005), Rawnsley (2001) and Seldon (2004).

5 We illustrate the various positions and arguments with selective quotes. We have not piled quote upon quote to make our point, although we could do so. Also, when we cite other practitioners in support of a particular point, we provide

illustrative, not comprehensive, page references. In many cases there are several relevant citations in the specified text.

6 If there is one dominating impression given by the several diaries of the Wilson era, it is of ministers oppressed by the hurly burly of their everyday life. There is just no time to think about overall strategy, the prime minister's style and the government's overall performance. Such topics are at best *obiter dicta* scattered in the text, not mature reflections. On the workload see, for example, Castle (1980: 317–8, 320, 385). Wilson's (1971) own record leaves the clear impression not only of a crushing workload but also of domestic politics and policies losing out to foreign policy.

7 Tony Benn was Postmaster-General 1964–6, Minister of Technology 1966–70, Secretary of State for Industry 1974–5 and Energy Secretary 1975–9.

8 Under Harold Wilson, Reg Prentice was Minister for Education and Science (1964–6, 1974–5), Public Buildings and Works (1966–7) and Overseas Development (1967–9, 1975–6). In 1977, he defected to the Conservatives and served under Margaret Thatcher as a junior social security minister (1979–81).

9 Foley (1993, 2000, 2002, 2004) is the most prolific academic contributor. Others who identify a trend to presidentialization even as they criticize it include: Allen (2002), Heffernan (2003), Hennessy (1998, 2000a, 2000b, 2002), Kavanagh and Seldon (2000), Mughan (2000), Pryce (1997) and Rose (2001). The most coruscating critic of all things presidential is George Jones. See, for example, Jones (1985, 1995).

10 On the growth of the media and its impact on British politics see Seymour-Ure (2003). On its relevance to the presidential thesis see Foley (1993, 2000, 2002) and Mughan (2000). On New Labour's 'spin doctors' see Jones (1999, 2001).

11 Peston (2005: 57, 58, 60) claims that: the key meeting took place on 15 May at the home of Nick Ryden in Edinburgh, two weeks before the meeting at Granita; Brown was promised 'total autonomy over the social and economic agenda'; and negotiations continued over the next two weeks culminating in the Granita agreement.

12 Peston (2005: 63) disagrees. He cites Nick Brown, a Gordon Brown supporter and former Minister of Agriculture, quoting Gordon Brown immediately after the Granita meeting saying 'Blair promised that he would only fight two elections as leader' and that 'he would endorse Brown as leader when the time came'.

13 If 'heebie-jeebie' refers to a state of nervous apprehension, then 'TeeBee-GeeBees', formed from the respective initials of the two protagonists, refers to their state of apprehensive antagonism and their regular spats.

14 For the oestrogen-fuelled, *Girl's Own*, comic book view of life at the No. 10 court see Beckett and Hencke (2004: chapter 14) and Oborne and Walter (2004).

15 Over the years, it included the likes of Alistair Campbell (Head, SCU), Jonathan Powell (No. 10 Chief of Staff), Jeremy Heywood (PM's principal private secretary), Anji Hunter (Special Adviser), David Miliband (Head of the Policy Unit) and Philip Gould (PM's pollster). Among ministers it included Charlie Falconer (Minister, Cabinet Office) and Peter Mandelson (various).

16 For example, Alan Milburn (Health) had 'grown in competence and ability', Margaret Beckett (Environment and Agriculture) is 'just holding the ring'; Charles Clarke (Education) 'has not developed as expected', Patricia Hewitt (Trade and Industry) does not think strategically and Gordon Brown throws his weight around (Pollard 2005: 27–8). Of course his colleagues reciprocate. John Prescott

(deputy prime minister) is said to hold Blunkett in a mixture of contempt and suspicion, while others grit their teeth at his 'idiotic indiscretion' (*Observer* 12 December 2004).

17 After the 2005 election, Blair reduced the number of cabinet committees to 44. There are 25 new committees, most mergers of existing ones. Their numbers will grow over the life of the government. Blair will chair 15 committees. The rationalization was accompanied by the statement that 'government is a collective exercise and what you need to do is harness the collective responsibilities that different ministers have and also the collective experience they bring with them'. *The Guardian* 24 May 2005. Like Margaret Thatcher before him, Tony Blair has discovered that collective government is a useful security blanket. He just didn't leave it as late!

18 For the 2005 election, Blair recalled Alan Milburn from his retirement to act as election supremo, playing the role that Brown played in 2001. But who stood beside Tony Blair in the first Labour Party electoral broadcast? Who else but Gordon Brown, the pair shot as a happy couple by Anthony Minghella, director of *The English Patient*. The economy was and remained Labour's master card. Milburn retired (again). It was simple. It was brutal. Blair needed Brown and Brown judged it in his interests to cooperate. The wags have it that the Conservatives toyed with the slogan 'Vote Blair, Get Brown' until they realised that is exactly what the electorate wanted! Gordon Brown's key position in the government and the Labour Party is signalled by his return to the National Executive Committee NEC of the Labour Party, from which he was excluded in November 2003.

7 Everyday life in a ministry

1 We should note the more important exceptions. Among political scientists, the work of Heady (1974), Heclo and Wildavsky (1974), Marsh *et al.* (2001) and Rhodes and Dunleavy (1995) are important sources on ministers and their departments. Barberis (1996) filled the gap and wrote a book specifically devoted to permanent secretaries (see also Theakston 1999, 2000). Rhodes and Weller (2001) provide a comparative analysis of departmental secretaries that includes interview material. Bevir and Rhodes (2003: 170–94) and Young and Sloman (1982, 1984) quote extensively from their interviews with top civil servants. Among politicians, Kaufman (1980) is funny as well as informative on being a minister and Bruce-Gardyne's (1986) comparable effort deserves more attention than it gets. The undisputed classics among ministerial diaries are Benn (1988, 1989, 1990), Castle (1984) and Crossman (1975). Among ministerial memoirs, Jenkins (1991) is worth consulting and Lawson's (1992) detailed account of economic policy is impressive. As Gamble (1994: 38) points out, few memoirs set out to describe ministerial policymaking and since 1979 few tomes from Conservative ministers repay the effort of reading them. There is some relevant material in Fowler (1991) and Young (1990). Journalists spend much time and effort on prime ministers, but such doyens of the profession as Andrew Rawnsley (2001), Peter Riddell (1989) and Hugo Young (1989) rarely descend from such Olympian heights. The exceptions include Peter Hennessy's (1989) book on Whitehall, with its incomparable anecdotes, and Jeremy Paxman's (2002) patchy and ultimately commonplace account of ministers and their motivation. There are,

finally, some useful case studies with material on departmental and ministerial decision-making (see Butler *et al.* 1994; Burch and Holliday 1996; Greenaway *et al.* 1992; Rhodes and Dunleavy 1995).

8 National Health Service reform

1 We end our story in 2002. Little has happened to change our general argument. The government announced its policy on patients' choice in Cm 6079 (2003). However, the target of 205,000 patients booking the hospital of their choice through their GPs by December 2004 produced a mere 63 bookings (National Audit Office 2005: 28). On New Labour's conflicts about health policy see Peston (2005).

9 Police reform

1 The Australian Research Council funded part of the research for this chapter (Grant no: LP0346987).
2 On Britain see Davies and Thomas (2003), Edwards and Benyon (2001), Hughes (2002) and Hughes and McLaughlin (2002). On Australia see APMC (2002), Bayley (1986), MAC (2004) and Vernon and McKillop (1990).

10 Conclusions

1 We use the phrase 'contemporary governance' to distinguish between the empirical, contingent properties of contemporary governance and the universal features of 'governance' as conceived in our interpretive approach.
2 We derive the argument that some concepts, including governance, are best elucidated through studies of particular cases that reveal family resemblances rather than essential properties from Wittgenstein's famous discussion of 'game' (Wittgenstein 1972b). In his preliminary sketch of just this discussion, he explicitly contrasts this position with a 'craving for generality' he ascribes to inappropriate attempts to model all knowledge on natural science (Wittgenstein 1972a: 17–20).

References

Adcock, R. and Bevir, M. (2005) 'The history of political science'. *Political Studies Review*, 3: 1–16.

Alford, R. (1975) *Health Care Politics*. Chicago, IL: University of Chicago Press.

Allen, G. (2002) *The Last Prime Minister: Being Honest About the UK Presidency*. London: Politico's.

Anderson, Sir John (1946) 'The machinery of government'. *Public Administration*, 24: 147–56.

APMC [Australian Police Minister's Council] (2002) *Directions in Australasian Policing: 2002–2005*. Canberra: Australian Police Minister's Council, November.

Armstrong, Sir Robert (1985) *The Duties and Responsibilities of Civil Servants in Relation to Ministers*. Note by the Head of the Civil Service. London: Cabinet Office, 25 February.

Bach, S. (2003) *Platypus and Parliament: the Australian Senate in Theory and Practice*. Canberra: Department of the Senate.

Bacon, R. and Eltis, W. (1976) *Britain's Economic Problem: Too Few Producers*. London: Macmillan.

Baker, K. (1993) *The Turbulent Years. My Life in Politics*. London: Faber and Faber.

Bancroft, Lord (1983) 'Whitehall: some personal reflections'. Suntory-Toyota lecture, London School of Economics and Political Science, 1 December.

Bancroft, Lord (1984) 'Whitehall and management: a retrospect'. *Royal Society of Arts Journal*, 132(5): 367–79.

Bang, H. P. and Sørensen, E. (1999) 'The everyday maker: a new challenge to democratic governance'. *Administrative Theory and Praxis*, 21(3): 325–41.

Barberis, P. (1996) *The Elite of the Elite*. Aldershot: Dartmouth.

Barker, R. (1994) *Politics, Peoples and Governments. Themes in British Political Thought Since the Nineteenth Century*. London: Macmillan.

Barry, B. (1999) 'The study of politics as a vocation'. In J. Hayward, B. Barry and A. Brown (eds), *The British Study of Politics in the Twentieth Century*. Oxford: Oxford University Press for the British Academy.

Barton, H. (2003) 'Understanding occupational (sub) culture – a precursor for reform. The case of the police service in England and Wales'. *The International Journal of Public Sector Management*, 16(4/5): 346–59.

Bayley, D. H. (1986) *Community Policing in Australia – An Appraisal*. Working Paper, Australasian Centre for Policing Research (ACPR). South Australia: Payneham.

Bayley, D. H. (1994) 'It's accountability stupid!' In K. Bryett and C. Lewis (eds), *Un-Peeling Tradition: Contemporary Policing*. South Melbourne: CAPSM, Macmillan Education.

Beckett, F. and Hencke, D. (2004) *The Blairs and their Court*. London: Aurum Press.

Beer, S. (1965) *Modern British Politics*. London: Faber. [All page references are to the 1982 edition.]

Benn, T. (1985) 'The case for a constitutional premiership'. In A. King (ed.), *The British Prime Minister*. London: Macmillan.

Benn, T. (1988) *Out of the Wilderness. Diaries 1963–67*. London: Arrow.

Benn, T. (1989) *Office Without Power. Diaries 1968–72*. London: Arrow.

Benn, T. (1990) *Against the Tide. Diaries 1973–76*. London: Arrow.

Benyon, J. and Edwards, A. (1999) 'Community governance of crime control'. In G. Stoker (ed.), *The New Management of British Local Governance*. Basingstoke: Macmillan.

Berger, P. and Luckman, T. (1971) [1966]. *The Social Construction of Reality: A Treatise in the Sociology of Knowledge*. Harmondsworth: Penguin.

Berman, S. (2001) 'Ideas, norms and culture in political analysis'. *Comparative Politics*, 33: 231–50.

Beveridge, Sir W. (1942) *Report on Social Insurance and Allied Services*. Cmnd 6404. London: HMSO.

Bevir, M. (1999) *The Logic of the History of Ideas*. Cambridge: Cambridge University Press.

Bevir, M. (2005) *New Labour: A Critique*. London: Routledge.

Bevir, M. and O'Brien, D. (2003) 'From idealism to communitarianism: the inheritance and legacy of John Macmurray'. *History of Political Thought*, 24: 305–29.

Bevir, M. and Rhodes, R. A. W. (2003) *Interpreting British Governance*. London: Routledge.

Bevir, M. and Trentmann, F. (2002) 'Critique within capitalism: historiographical problems, theoretical perspectives'. In M. Bevir and F. Trentmann (eds), *Critiques of Capital in Modern Britain and America*. Basingstoke: Palgrave Macmillan.

Beyer, L. (1993) *Community Policing: Lessons from Victoria*. Canberra. Australian Institute of Criminology.

Bhaskar, R. (1998) [1979] *The Possibility of Naturalism: A Philosophical Critique of the Contemporary Human Sciences*, 3rd edn. London: Routledge.

Blair, T. (1996) *New Britain: My Vision of a Young Country*. London: Fourth Estate.

Blair, T. (2004) *Tony Blair: In His Own Words* (edited by Paul Richards). London: Politico's.

Blick, A. (2004) *People Who Live in the Dark: The Special Adviser in British Politics* London: Politico's.

Blondel, J. (1969) *Comparative Government*, 1st edn. London: Weidenfeld and Nicolson.

Blondel, J. (1981) *The Discipline of Politics*. London: Butterworth.

Blondel, J. (1985) *Government Ministers in the Contemporary World*. London: Sage.

Blondel, J. (1990) *Comparative Government*, 2nd edn. London: Philip Allan.

Bobrow, D. B. and Dryzek, J. S. (1987) *Policy Analysis by Design*. Pittsburgh, PA: Pittsburgh University Press.

Bogdanor, V. (1999) 'Comparative politics'. In J. Hayward, B, Barry and A. Brown (eds), *The British Study of Politics in the Twentieth Century*. Oxford: Oxford University Press for the British Academy.

Boyne, G. (1998) *Public Choice Theory and Local Government*. London: Macmillan.

Bradley, R. (1998) *Public Expectations and Perceptions of Policing*. London: Home Office.

Brennan, G. and Pincus, J. (2002) 'Australia's economic institutions'. In G. Brennan and F. G. Castles (eds), *Australia Reshaped*. Cambridge: Cambridge University Press.

Brereton, D. (2000) 'Policing and crime prevention: improving the product'. In D. Chappell and P. Wilson (eds), *Crime and the Criminal Justice System in Australia: 2000 and Beyond*. Sydney: Butterworths.

Bridges, Sir Edward (1950) 'Portrait of a profession'. In R. A. Chapman and A. Dunsire (eds), *Style in Administration*. London: Allen & Unwin.

Brown, A. J. (2003a) 'One nation, two federalisms: rediscovering the origins of Australian federal political ideas'. Paper presented at the Australasian Political Studies Association, Hobart, 29 September–1 October.

Brown, A. J. (2003b) 'The frozen continent. The fall and rise of territory in Australian constitutional thought 1815–2003'. Unpublished PhD thesis. Griffith University.

Brown, Lord George (1972) *In My Way*. Harmondsworth: Penguin Books.

Brown, V. (2002) 'On some problems with weak intentionalism for intellectual history'. *History and Theory*, 41: 198–208.

Bruce-Gardyne, J. (1986) *Ministers and Mandarins*. London: Sidgwick & Jackson.

Bryce, J. (1921) *Modern Democracies*. London: Macmillan.

Burch, M. and Holliday, I. (1996) *The British Cabinet System*. Hemel Hempstead: Prentice Hall/Harvester Wheatsheaf.

Burchell, G., Gordon, C. and Miller, P. (eds) (1991) *The Foucault Effect: Studies in Governmentality*. London: Harvester Wheatsheaf.

Butler, D. (1973) *The Canberra Model*. New York: St Martin's Press.

Butler, D. (1991) 'Introduction'. In D. E. Butler and D. A. Low (eds), *Sovereigns and Surrogates: Constitutional Heads of State in the Commonwealth*. London: Macmillan.

Butler, D. and Low, D. A. (eds) (1991) *Sovereigns and Surrogates: Constitutional Heads of State in the Commonwealth*. London: Macmillan.

Butler, D. and Stokes, F. (1969) *Political Change in Britain*. London: Macmillan.

Butler, D., Adonis, A. and Travers, T. (1994) *Failure in British Government. The Politics of the Poll Tax*. Oxford: Oxford University Press.

Cabinet Office (2000) *Wiring It Up*. London: Cabinet Office.

Callaghan, J. (1987) *Time and Chance*. London: Collins.

Campbell, C. (1998) *The US Presidency in Crisis. A Comparative Perspective*. New York: Oxford University Press.

Carrington, Lord Peter (1988) *Reflect on Things Past. The Memoirs of Lord Carrington*. London: Collins.

Castle, B. (1980) *The Castle Diaries 1974–76*. London: Weidenfeld & Nicolson.

Castle, B. (1984) *The Castle Diaries 1964–70*. London: Weidenfeld & Nicolson.

Castle, B. (1993) *Fighting All The Way*. London: Macmillan.

Castles, F. (2002) 'Australia's institutions and Australia's welfare'. In G. Brennan and F. G. Castles (eds), *Australia Reshaped*. Cambridge: Cambridge University Press.

Chabal, P. M. (2003) 'Do ministers matter? The individual style of ministers in programmed policy change'. *International Review of Administrative Science*, 69(1): 29–49.

Chan, J. (1997) *Changing Police Culture: Policing in a Multicultural Society*. Cambridge: Cambridge University Press.

Chapman, L. (1978) *Your Disobedient Servant*. London: Chatto & Windus.

Chapman, R. A. and Greenaway, J. R. (1980) *The Dynamics of Administrative Reform*. London: Croom Helm.

Clark, D. (1997) 'Delivering Better Government from the Bottom Up'. Speech by the Chancellor of the Duchy of Lancaster, at the Queen Elizabeth Conference, London, 17 June.

Clark, W. (1966) *Number 10*. London: Heinemann.

Cmd 6502 (1944) *A National Health Service*. London: HMSO.

Cmnd 3638 (1968) *The Civil Service. Vol. 1 Report of the Committee 1966–68* (Fulton). London: HMSO.

Cmnd 5055 (1972) *National Health Service Reorganization: England*. London: HMSO.

Cm 2627 (1994) *The Civil Service. Continuity and Change*. London: HMSO.

Cm 3807 (1997) *The New NHS. Modern. Dependable*. London: Department of Health.

Cm 4011 (1998) *Modern Public Services for Britain: Investing in Reform. Comprehensive Spending Review: New Public Spending Plans 1999–2002*. London: The Stationery Office.

Cm 4310 (1999) *Modernising Government*. London: The Stationery Office.

Cm 4818-I (2000) *The NHS Plan. A Plan for Investment. A Plan for Reform*. London: The Stationery Office.

Cm 6079 (2003) *Choice, Responsiveness and Equity in the NHS*. London: The Stationery Office.

Collini, S. (1988) '"Disciplinary history" and "intellectual history": reflections on the historiography of the social sciences in Britain and France'. *Revue de Synthese*, 3: 387–99.

Collini, S. (2001) 'Postscript: disciplines, canons, and publics: the history of "The History of Political Thought" in comparative perspective'. In D. Castiglione and I. Hampsher-Monk (eds), *History of Political Thought*. Cambridge: Cambridge University Press.

Cook, R. (2003) *The Point of Departure*. London: Simon & Schuster.

Cope, S. (2001) 'Analysing criminal justice policy-making: towards a policy network approach'. In M. Ryan, S. P. Savage and D. S. Wall (eds), *Policy Networks in Criminal Justice*. Basingstoke: Palgrave.

Crossman, R. H. S. (ed.) (1963) 'Introduction'. In W. Bagehot, *The English Constitution*. London: Collins.

Crossman, R. H. S. (1972a) *A Politician's View of Health Service Planning*. Glasgow: University of Glasgow Press.

Crossman, R. H. S. (1972b) *Inside View: Three Lectures on Prime Ministerial Government*. London: Cape.

Crossman, R. H. S. (1975) *The Diaries of a Cabinet Minister. Volume 1. Minister of Housing*. London: Jonathan Cape.

Dale, H. E. (1941) *The Higher Civil Service of Great Britain*. Oxford: Oxford University Press.

Davies, A. and Thomas, R. (2003) 'Talking COP: discourses of change and police identities'. *Public Administration*, 81(4): 681–99.

Davis, G. (1995) *A Government of Routines*. Melbourne: Macmillan Education.

Davis, G. (1998) 'Australian administrative tradition'. In J. M. Shafritz (ed.), *International Encyclopaedia of Public Policy and Administration*. Boulder, CO: Westview Press.

Davis, G. and Wood, T. (1998) Is there a future for contracting in the Australian public sector? *Australian Journal of Public Administration*, 57(4): 85–97.

Davis, R. S. (1995) *Theory and Reality: Federal Issues in Australia, England and Europe*. St Lucia: Queensland University Press.

De Smith, S. A. (1961) 'Westminster's export models: the legal framework of responsible government'. *Journal of Commonwealth Studies*, 1(1): 3–16.

Deakin, N. and Walsh, K. (1996) 'The enabling state: the role of markets and contracts'. *Public Administration*, 74(1): 33–48.

Dearlove, J. and Saunders, P. (1984) *Introduction to British Politics: Analysing a Capitalist Democracy*. Cambridge: Polity.

Denham, R. (2002) *The Mandarin's Tale*. London: Politico's.

Department of Health (1998) *A First Class Service: Quality in the New NHS*. London: Department of Health.

Department of Health (2000) *For The Benefit of Patients: A Concordat between the Department of Health and the Independent Healthcare Association*. London: Department of Health.

Dexter, L. (1970) *Elite and Specialized Interviewing*. Evanston, IL: Northwestern University Press.

Dicey, A. V. (1914) *Lectures on the Relations between Law and Public Opinion During the Nineteenth Century*. London: Macmillan.

Dogan, M. and Pelassy, D. (1990) *How to Compare Nations: Strategies in Comparative Politics*, 2nd edn. Chatham, NJ: Chatham House.

Domberger, S. (1998) *The Contracting Organization: A Strategic Guide to Outsourcing*, Oxford: Oxford University Press.

Donoughue, B. (1987) *Prime Minister. The Conduct of Policy Under Harold Wilson and James Callaghan*. London: Cape.

Donovan, C. (2005) 'The governance of social science and everyday epistemology'. *Public Administration*, 83:(3): 597–615.

Dowding, K. (2001) 'There must be an end to confusion: policy networks, intellectual fatigue, and the need for political science methods courses in British universities'. *Political Studies*, 49(1): 89–105.

Dowding, K. (2004) 'Interpretation, truth and investigation'. *British Journal of Politics and International Relations*, 6: 136–42.

Dowding, K. M. and King, D. S. (1995) *Preferences, Institutions and Rational Choice*. Oxford: Oxford University Press.

Dryzek, J. S. (1993) 'Policy analysis and planning: from science to argument'. In F. Fischer and J. Forester (eds), *The Argumentative Turn in Policy Analysis and Planning*. Durham, NC: Duke University Press.

Dunleavy, P. (1991) *Democracy, Bureaucracy and Public Choice*. Hemel Hempstead: Harvester Wheatsheaf.

Eckstein, H. (1975) 'Case study and theory in political science'. In F. I. Greenstein and N. Polsby (eds), *Handbook of Political Science. Volume 4. Strategies of Inquiry*. Reading, MA: Addison-Wesley.

Edelman, M. (1961) *The Minister*. London: Hamish Hamilton.

Edwards, A. and Benyon, J. (2001) 'Networking and crime control at the local level'. In M. Ryan, S. P. Savage and D. S. Wall (eds), *Policy Networks in Criminal Justice*. Basingstoke: Palgrave.

Edwards, C. E. (1999) *Changing Policing Theories for 21st Century Societies*. Sydney: The Federation Press.

Efficiency Unit (1988) *Improving Management in Government: The Next Steps*. London: HMSO.

Elgie, R. (1997) 'Models of executive politics'. *Political Studies*, 45: 217–31.

Exworthy, M., Powell, M. and Mohan, J. (1999) 'The NHS: a quasi-market, quasi-hierarchy and quasi-network?' *Public Money and Management*, October–December: 15–22.

Farmer, D. (ed.) (1995) *Papers on the Anti-Art of Administration*. Burke, VA: Chatelaine Press.

Fenno, R. F. (1990) *Watching Politicians: Essays on Participant Observation*. Berkeley, CA: Institute of Governmental Studies, University of California.

Ferlie, E. and Pettigrew, A. (1996) 'Managing Through Networks: Some Issues and Implications for the NHS'. *British Journal of Management*, 7: 81–99.

Finer, S. E. (1970) *Comparative Government*. London: AllenLane/The Penguin Press.

Finer, S. E. (1980) 'Political science: an idiosyncratic retrospect of a putative discipline'. *Government and Opposition*, 15(3/4): 346–63.

Finer, S. E. (1997) *The History of Government from the Earliest Times. Volume I. Ancient Monarchies and Empires. Volume II. The Intermediate Ages. Volume III. Empires, Monarchies and the Modern State*. Oxford: Oxford University Press.

Finn, P. (1987) *Law and Government in Colonial Australia*. Melbourne: Melbourne University Press.

Finnemore, M. and Sikkink, K. (2001) 'Taking stock: the constructivist research program in international relations and comparative politics'. *Annual Review of Political Science*, 4: 391–416.

Fleming, J. and Lafferty, G. (2000) 'New management techniques and restructuring in police organizations'. *Policing: An International Journal of Police Strategy and Management*, 23(2): 154–68.

Fletcher, C. (1991) 'Rediscovering Australian federalism by resurrecting old ideas'. *Australian Journal of Political Science*, 26(1): 79–94.

Flynn, R., Williams, G. and Pickard, S. (1997) 'Quasi-markets and quasi-trust: the social constitution of contracts for community health services'. In R. Flynn and G. Williams (eds), *Contracting for Health: Quasi-Markets and the National Health Service*. Oxford: Oxford University Press.

Foley, M. (1993) *The Rise of the British Presidency*. Manchester: Manchester University Press.

Foley, M. (2000) *The British Presidency*. Manchester: Manchester University Press.

Foley, M. (2002) *John Major, Tony Blair and a Conflict of Leadership*. Manchester: Manchester University Press.

Foley, M. (2004) 'Presidential attribution as an agency of prime ministerial critique in a parliamentary democracy: the case of Tony Blair'. *British Journal of Politics and International Relations*, 6(3): 292–311.

Foucault, M. (1972) *The Archaeology of Knowledge*. London: Tavistock.

Foucault, M. (1980) *Power/Knowledge: Selected Interviews and Other Writings, 1972–77*, edited by C. Gordon. Brighton: Harvester.

Fowler, N. (1991) *Ministers Decide*. London: Chapman.

Galligan, B. (1995) *A Federal Republic*. Cambridge: Cambridge University Press.

Galligan, B., Hughes, O. and Walsh, C. (eds) (1991) *Intergovernmental Relations and Public Policy*. Sydney: Allen & Unwin.

Gamble, A. (1988) *The Free Economy and the Strong State*. London: Macmillan.

Gamble, A. (1994) 'Political memoirs'. *Politics*, 14(1): 35–42.

Gamble, A. (1999) 'Why bother with Marxism?'. In A. Gamble, D. Marsh and T. Tant (eds), *Marxism and Social Science*. London: Macmillan.

Gamble, A., Marsh, D. and Tant, T. (eds) (1999) *Marxism and Social Science*. London: Macmillan.

Garland, D. (2001) *The Culture of Control*. Chicago, IL: University of Chicago Press.

Geertz, C. (1973) *The Interpretation of Cultures*. New York: Basic Books.

Geertz, C. (1983) *Local Knowledge*. New York: Basic Books.

Gerring, J. (1999) 'Does ideology matter? A roll-call analysis of key Congressional votes, 1833–1992'. *Journal of Policy History*, 11: 399–42.

Gerring, J. (2003) 'Interpretations of interpretivism'. *Qualitative Methods*, 1: 2–6.

Gilmour, I. (1978) *Inside Right*. London: Quartet.

Gilmour, I. (1992) *Dancing with Dogma: Britain under Thatcherism*. London: Simon & Schuster.

Glennerster, H., Korman, N. and Marslen-Wilson, F. (1983) *Planning for Priority Groups*. Oxford: M. Robertson.

Goldstein, H. (1977) *Policing a Free Society*. Cambridge, MA: Ballinger Publishing Co.

Goldstein, H. (1990) *Problem Orientated Policing*. New York: McGraw-Hill.

Gourley, P. (2003) 'For the record: let's get our facts straight on the service. In defence of the APS'. *The Public Sector Informant*, February: 10–11.

Green, J. R., Bergman, W. T. and McLaughlin, E. (1994) 'Implementing community policing'. In D. P. Rosenbaum (ed.), *The Challenge of Community Policing: Testing the Promises*. Thousand Oaks, CA: Sage.

Greenaway, J., Smith, S. and Street, J. (1992) *Deciding Factors in British Politics: A Case Study Approach*. London: Routledge.

Greenleaf, W. H. (1983) *The British Political Tradition. Volume 1. The Rise of Collectivism*. London: Methuen.

Griffiths, Sir Roy (1983) *NHS Management Inquiry*. London: Department of Health and Social Security.

Griggs, S. and Howarth, D. (2000) 'New environmental movements and direct action protests: the campaign against Manchester airport's second runway'. In D. Howarth, A. J. Norval and Y. Stavrakakis (eds), *Discourse Theory and Political Analysis*. Manchester: Manchester University Press.

Hall, S. (1980) 'Popular-democratic versus authoritarian populism'. In A. Hunt (ed.), *Marxism and Democracy*. London: Lawrence and Wishart.

Hall, S. (1983) 'The great moving right show'. In S. Hall and M. Jacques (eds), *The Politics of Thatcherism*. London: Lawrence and Wishart.

Hammersley, M. and Atkinson, P. (1983) *Ethnography: Principles in Practice*. London: Routledge.

Hancock, W. K. (1930) *Australia*. London: Benn.

Hargrove, E. C. (2001) 'Presidency and prime ministers as institutions: an American perspective'. *British Journal of Politics and International Relations*, 3(1): 49–70.

Harrison, S. (1994) *National Health Service Management in the 1980s: Policymaking on the Hoof?* Aldershot: Avebury.

Harrison, S., Hunter, D. J. and Pollitt, C. (1990) *The Dynamics of British Health Policy*. London: Unwin Hyman.

Hay, C. (2002) *Political Analysis*. Basingstoke: Palgrave.

Hayward, J. (1986) 'The political science of muddling through: the *de facto* paradigm?'. In J. Hayward and P. Norton (eds), *The Political Science of British Politics*. Brighton: Wheatsheaf Books.

Hayward, J. (1991a) 'Cultural and contextual constraints upon the development of political science in Great Britain'. In D. Easton, J. G. Gunnell and L. Graziano (eds), *The Development of Political Science: A Comparative Survey*. London: Routledge.

Hayward, J. (1991b) 'Political science in Britain'. *European Journal of Political Research*, 20: 301–21.

Hayward, J. (1999) 'British approaches to politics: the dawn of a self-deprecating discipline'. In J. Hayward, B. Barry and A. Brown (eds), *The British Study of Politics in the Twentieth Century*. Oxford: Oxford University Press for the British Academy.

Hayward, J., Barry, B. and Brown, A. (eds) (1999) *The British Study of Politics in the Twentieth Century*. Oxford: Oxford University Press for the British Academy.

Heady, B. (1974) *British Cabinet Ministers*. London: Allen & Unwin.

Healey, D. (1990) *The Time of My Life*. Harmondsworth: Penguin Books.

Heclo, H. and Wildavsky, A. (1974) *The Private Government of Public Money*. London: Macmillan.

Heffernan, R. (2003) 'Prime ministerial predominance? Core executive politics in the UK'. *British Journal of Politics and International Relations*, 5(3): 347–72.

Hennessy, P. (1989) *Whitehall*. London: Secker & Warburg.

Hennessy, P. (1995) *The Hidden Wiring: Unearthing the British Constitution*. London: Victor Gollancz.

Hennessy, P. (1998) 'The Blair style of government'. *Government and Opposition*, 33(1): 3–20.

Hennessy, P. (2000a) 'The Blair style and the requirements of twenty-first century premiership'. *Political Quarterly*, 71: 386–95.

Hennessy, P. (2000b) *The Prime Ministers*. London: Allen Lane/The Penguin Press.

Hennessy, P. (2000c) *The Blair Revolution in Government*. University of Leeds, Institute for Politics and International Studies.

Hennessy, P. (2000d) 'The Blair style of government: three years on'. The Mischon Lecture, University College, London, 18 May.

Hennessy, P. (2002) 'The Blair government in historical perspective: an analysis of the power relationships within New Labour'. *History Today*, 52(1): 21–3.

Heseltine, M. (2000) *Life in the Jungle. My Autobiography*. London: Hodder & Stoughton.

Hill, M. (1993) *The Welfare State in Britain: A Political History Since 1945*. Aldershot: Edward Elgar.

Hobsbawm, E. *et al.* (1981) *The Forward March of Labour Halted*. London: New Left Books.

Holliday, I. (2000) 'Is the British state hollowing out?' *Political Quarterly*, 71(2): 167–76.

Hoskyns, Sir John (1983) 'Whitehall and Westminster: an outsider's view'. *Parliamentary Affairs*, 36: 137–47.

Howarth, D., Norval, A. J. and Stavrakakis, Y. (eds) (2000) *Discourse Theory and Political Analysis*. Manchester: Manchester University Press.

Howe, G. (1994) *Conflict of Loyalty*. London: Macmillan.

Hughes, G. (2002) 'Plotting the rise of community safety'. In G. Hughes and A. Edwards (eds), *Crime Control and Community: The New Politics of Public Safety*. Cullompton: Willan Publishing.

Hughes, G. and McLaughlin, E. (2002) '"Together we'll crack it": partnership and governance of crime prevention'. In C. Glendinning, M. Powell and K. Rummery (eds), *Partnerships, New Labour and the Governance of Welfare*. Bristol: Policy Press.

Inglis, F. (2000) *Clifford Geertz. Culture, Custom and Ethics*. Oxford: Blackwell.

Jackson, R. J. (1995) 'Foreign models and Aussie rules: executive-legislative relations in Australia'. *Political Theory Newsletter*, 7(1): 1–18.

James, S. (1992) *British Cabinet Government*. London: Routledge.

James, S. (1999) *British Cabinet Government*, 2nd edn. London: Routledge.

Jenkins, R. (1991) *A Life at the Centre*. London: Macmillan.

Jessop, B. (1990) *State Theory. Putting Capitalist States in their Place*. Pennsylvania: Pennsylvania State University Press.

Jessop, B. (2000) 'Governance failure'. In G. Stoker (ed.), *The New Politics of British Local Governance*. Basingstoke: Macmillan.

Jessop, B. (2001) 'Institutional re(turns) and the strategic-relational approach'. *Environment and Planning A*, 33: 1213–35.

Jessop, B., Bonnett, K., Bromley, S. and Ling, T. (1988) *Thatcherism: A Tale of Two Nations*. Cambridge: Polity.

Johnson, N. (1975) 'The place of institutions in the study of politics'. *Political Studies*, 23: 271–83.

Johnson, N. (1977) *In Search of the Constitution*. Oxford: Pergamon.

Johnson, N. (1989) *The Limits of Political Science*. Oxford: Clarendon Press.

Jones, G. W. (1985) 'The prime minister's power'. In A. King (ed.), *The British Prime Minister*, 2nd edn. London: Macmillan.

Jones, G. W. (1995) 'The downfall of Margaret Thatcher'. In R. A. W. Rhodes and P. Dunleavy (eds), *Prime Minister, Cabinet and Core Executive*. London: Macmillan.

Jones, N. (1999) *Sultans of Spin: The Media and the New Labour Government*. London: Weidenfeld and Nicholson.

Jones, N. (2001) *The Control Freaks: How New Labour Gets its Own Way*. London: Politico's.

Kampfner, J. (2003) *Blair's Wars*. London: Free Press.

Kass, H. and Catron, B. (eds) (1990) *Images and Identities in Public Administration*. London: Sage.

Kaufman, G. (1980) *How to be a Minister*. London: Sidgwick & Jackson.

Kavanagh, D. (2006) 'The Emergence of an Embryonic Discipline: British politics without political scientists'. In R. Adcock, M. Bevir and S. Stimson (eds), *Modern Political Science: Anglo-American Exchanges since 1880*. Princeton, NJ: Princeton University Press.

Kavanagh, D. and Seldon, A. (2000) *The Powers behind the Prime Minister. The Hidden Influence of Number Ten*. London: HarperCollins.

Keegan, W. (2003) *The Prudence of Mr. Gordon Brown*. Chichester: Wiley.

Kelly, P. (1994) *The End of Uncertainty. Power, Politics and Business in Australia*, rev. edn. St Leonard's, NSW: Allen & Unwin.

Kenny, M. (2006) 'Birth of a Discipline: Interpreting British political studies in the 1950s and 1960s'. In R. Adcock, M. Bevir and S. Stimson (eds), *Modern Political Science: Anglo-American Exchanges since 1880*. Princeton, NJ: Princeton University Press.

Kickert, W. J. M., Klijn, E.-H. and Koppenjan, J. F. M. (eds) (1997) *Managing Complex Networks: Strategies for the Public Sector*. London: Sage.

King, A. (1969) *The British Prime Ministers*, 1st edn. London: Macmillan.

King, A. (1975) 'Overload: problems of governing in the 1980s'. *Political Studies*, 23: 284–96.

King, A. (1985) *The British Prime Ministers*, 2nd edn. London: Macmillan.

Kingdom, J. (1991) *Politics and Government in Britain*. Cambridge: Polity.

Klein, R. (1983) *The Politics of the National Health Service*, 1st edn. London: Longman.

Klein, R. (1989) *The Politics of the National Health Service*, 2nd edn. London: Longman.

Labour Party (2001) *Ambitions for Britain: Labour's Manifesto 2001*. London: The Labour Party.

Laclau, E. (1990) *New Reflections on the Revolution of Our Time*. London: Verso.

Laclau, E. and Mouffe, C. (1985) *Hegemony and Socialist Strategy: Towards a Radical Democratic Politics*. London: Verso.

Lasswell, H. D. and Kaplan, A. (1950) *Power and Society: A Framework for Political Inquiry*. New Haven, CT: Yale University Press.

Lawson, N. (1992) *The View from No. 11*. London: Bantam Press.

Lee, J. M. (1977) *Reviewing the Machinery of Government 1942–1952. An Essay on the Anderson Committee and its Successors*. London: Birkbeck College, mimeo.

Lee, M. (1995) 'The ethos of the Cabinet Office: a comment on the testimony of officials'. In R. A. W. Rhodes and P. Dunleavy (eds), *Prime Minister, Cabinet and Core Executive*. London: Macmillan.

Leys, C. (1983) *Politics in Britain*. London: Heinemann.

Lieberman, R. (2002) 'Ideas, institutions, and political order: explaining political change'. *American Political Science Review*, 96: 697–712.

Lijphart, A. (1999) *Patterns of Democracy Government: Forms and Performance in Thirty-Six Countries*. New Haven, CT: Yale University Press.

Loader, I. (1999) 'Consumer culture and the commodification of policing and security'. *Sociology*, 33(2): 373–92.

Loader, I. (2000) 'Plural policing and democratic governance'. *Social and Legal Studies*, 9(3): 323–45.

Loughlin, M. (1992) *Public Law and Political Theory*. Oxford: Clarendon Press.

Low, D. A. (1988) 'Introduction: Buckingham Palace and the Westminster model'. In D. A. Low (ed.), *Constitutional Heads and Political Crises*. London: Macmillan.

Lowndes, V. (2002) 'The institutional approach'. In D. Marsh and G. Stoker (eds), *Theory and Methods in Political Science*, 2nd edn. Basingstoke: Palgrave-Macmillan.

Lucy, R. (1993) *The Australian Form of Government*. Melbourne: Macmillan.

MAC [Management Advisory Committee] (2004) *Connecting Government. Whole of Government Responses to Australia's Priority Challenges*. Canberra: Commonwealth of Australia.

Mackenzie, W. J. M. (1955) 'Pressure groups in British government'. *British Journal of Sociology*, 6: 133–48.

Mackenzie, W. J. M. (1975) *Explorations in Government: Collected Papers 1951–1968*. London: Macmillan.

Mackintosh, J. (1968) *The British Cabinet*, 2nd edn. London: Stevens.

McAnulla, S. (2004) 'Paving the Rhodes to post-positivism? A critique of the new interpretive approach to British politics – towards a realist alternative'. Paper presented at the Political Studies Association Annual Conference, Lincoln, 6–8 April.

McLean, I. (2001) *Rational Choice and British Politics*. Oxford: Oxford University Press.

McPherson, A. and Raab, C. (1988) *Governing Education*. Edinburgh: Edinburgh University Press.

Mandelson, P. and Liddle, R. (1996) *The Blair Revolution: Can New Labour Deliver?* London: Faber & Faber.

March, J. G. and Olsen, J. P. (1989) *Rediscovering Institutions: The Organizational Basis of Politics*. New York: The Free Press.

Marchant, L. R. (1999) *The Westminster Tradition and Australia: The Parliamentary Democratic System Inherited from Britain*. Carlisle, WA: Hesperian Press.

Marinetto, M. (2003) 'Governing beyond the centre: a critique of the Anglo-Governance School'. *Political Studies*, 51: 592–608.

Marr, D. and Wilkinson, M. (2003) *Dark Victory*. Crows Nest, NSW: Allen & Unwin.

Marsh, D. (1999) 'Resurrecting Marxism'. In A. Gamble, D. Marsh and T. Tant (eds), *Marxism and Social Science*. London: Macmillan.

Marsh, D., Richards, D. and Smith, M. J. (2001) *Changing Patterns of Governance in the United Kingdom*. Basingstoke: Palgrave.

Menzies, Sir Robert (1967) *Central Power in the Australian Commonwealth*. London: Cassell.

Metcalfe, L. and Richards, S. (1991) *Improving Public Management*, 2nd edn. London: Sage.

Milburn, A. (2001) 'Milburn Hands Power to Front Line Staff'. Press Release 2001/0200. London: Department of Health.

Miliband, R. (1969) *The State in Capitalist Society*. London: Weidenfeld & Nicolson.

Miliband, R. (1970) 'The capitalist state: reply to Nicos Poulantzas'. *New Left Review*, 59: 53–60.

Miliband, R. (1977) *Marxism and Politics*. Oxford: Oxford University Press.

Miller, J. D. B. (1959) *Australian Government and Politics*, 2nd edn. London: Duckworth.

Moodie, G. (1984) 'Politics is about Government'. In A. Leftwich (ed.), *What is Politics?* Oxford: Blackwell.

Moore, D. (1994) 'Views at the top, down under: Australian police managers on Australian policing'. *Policing and Society*, 4(3): 191–217.

Moore, M. H. (1990) 'Police leadership: the impossible dream'. In E. C. Hargrove and John C. Glidewell (eds), *Impossible Jobs in Public Management*. Lawrence, KS: University Press of Kansas.

Morgan, G. (1993) *Imaginization*. London: Sage.

Morgan, G. (1997) *Images of Organization*. London: Sage.

Morrison, H. (1959) *Government and Parliament. A Survey from the Inside*. Oxford: Oxford University Press.

Mount, F. (1992) *The British Constitution Now: Recovery or Decline?* London: Mandarin.

Mowlam, M. (2002) *Momentum: The Struggle for Peace, Politics and the People.* London: Hodder and Stoughton.

Mughan, A. (2000) *Media and the Presidentialization of Parliamentary Elections*. Basingstoke: Macmillan.

Mulgan, G. (2001) Speech to the 'Conference on Joined-Up Government', British Academy, London, 30 October.

Mulgan, R. (1996) 'The Australian senate as a "house of review"'. *Australian Journal of Political Science*, 31(2): 191–204.

National Audit Office (2005) *Patient Choice at the Point of GP Referral*. HC 180 Session 2004–2005. London: Stationery Office.

Naughtie, J. (2002) *The Rivals. The Intimate Story of a Political Marriage*, rev. edn. London: Fourth Estate.

Norton, P. (1982) *The Constitution in Flux*. Oxford: Martin Robertson.

Norton, P. (2000) 'Barons in a shrinking kingdom: senior ministers in British government'. In R. A. W. Rhodes (ed.), *Transforming British Government. Volume 2. Changing Roles and Relationships.* London: Macmillan.

Norton, P. (2003) 'The presidentialization of British politics'. *Government and Opposition*, 38(2): 274–8.

Oakeshott, M. (1962) *Rationalism in Politics and Other Essays*. London: Methuen.

Oakeshott, M. (1975) *On Human Conduct*. Oxford: Clarendon Press.

Oborne, P. and Walters, S. (2004) *Alastair Campbell*. London: Aurum Press.

Official Record (1986) Official Record of the Debates of the Australasian Federal Convention. *Volume 1. Sydney, 2 March–9 April 1891. Volume 2. Second Session, Sydney, 2–24 September 1891. Volume 3. Adelaide, 22 March–5 May 1897. Volume 4 and Volume 5. Third Session, Melbourne, 20 January–17 March 1898. Volume 6. The Convention Debates 1891–1898: commentaries, indices and guide.* (Edited by G. Craven). Sydney: Legal Books.

O'Malley, P. (1997) 'Policing, politics and modernity'. *Social and Legal Studies*, 6(3): 363–81.

One Nation Group (1954) *Change is our Ally*. London: Conservative Political Centre.

den Otter, S. (2006) 'The origins of a historical political science in Late Victorian and Edwardian Britain', in R. Adcock, M. Bevir and S. Stimson (eds), *Modern Political Science: Anglo-American Exchanges since 1880*. Princeton, NJ: Princeton University Press.

Painter, M. (1998) *Collaborative Federalism: Economic Reform in Australia in the 1990s.* Cambridge: Cambridge University Press.

Paoline, E. A. (2003) 'Taking Stock: toward a richer understanding of police culture'. *Journal of Criminal Justice*, 31(3): 199–214.

Parker, R. S. (1976) 'The meaning of responsible government'. *Politics*, 11(2): 178–84.

Parker, R. S. (1978) 'The public service inquiries and responsible government'. In R. F. I. Smith and P. Weller (eds), *Public Service Inquiries in Australia*. St Lucia: University of Queensland Press.

Parker, R. S. (1980a) 'Responsible government in Australia'. In P. Weller and D. Jaensch (eds), *Responsible Government in Australia*. Richmond, VIC: Drummond Publishing.

Parker, R. S. (1980b) 'The evolution of British political institutions in Australia'. In A. F. Madden and W. H. Morris-Jones (eds), *Australia and Britain: Studies in a Changing Relationship*. Sydney: Sydney University Press in association with the Institute of Commonwealth Studies, University of London.

Part, A. (1980) *The Making of a Mandarin*. London: Deutsch.

Paxman, J. (2002) *The Political Animal*. London: Michael Joseph.

Percy, S. (1998) 'Response Time and Citizen Evaluation of Police'. In D. H. Bayley (ed.), *What Works in Policing*. New York: Oxford University Press.

Perri 6 (1997) *Holistic Government*. London: Demos.

Peston, R. (2005) *Brown's Britain*. London: Short Books.

Pierre, J. (ed.) (2000) *Debating Governance*. Oxford: Oxford University Press.

Pimlott, B. (1992) *Harold Wilson*. London: HarperCollins.

Pollard, S. (2005) *David Blunkett*. London: Hodder & Stoughton.

Popper, K. (1959) *The Logic of Scientific Discovery*. New York: Basic Books.

Prenzler, T. and Ransley, J. (eds) (2002) *Police Reform: Building Integrity*. Leichhardt, NSW: Hawkins Press.

Pryce, S. (1997) *Presidentializing the Premiership*. New York: St Martin's Press.

Pym, F. (1984) *The Politics of Consent*. London: Hamish Hamilton.

Rawnsley, A. (2001) *Servants of the People. The Inside Story of New Labour*, rev. edn. London: Penguin Books.

Reckwitz, A. (2002) 'The constraining power of cultural schemes and the liberal model of beliefs'. *History of Human Sciences*, 15(2): 115–24.

Reid, G. S. (1981) 'Responsible government and ministerial responsibility'. In G. R. Curnow and R. L. Wettenhall (eds), *Understanding Public Administration: Essays in Honour of Robert Parker and Richard Spann*. Sydney: Allen & Unwin.

Rein, M. (1976) *Social Science and Public Policy*. Harmondsworth: Penguin Books.

Reiner, R. (1992) *The Politics of the Police*. New York: Wheatsheaf.

Reiner, R. (1993) 'Responsibilities and reforms'. *New Law Journal*, 30 July: 1096–7 and 1126.

Rentoul, J. (2001) *Tony Blair: Prime Minister*. London: Little, Brown.

Rhodes, R. A. W. (1988) *Beyond Westminster and Whitehall*. London: Unwin-Hyman.

Rhodes, R. A. W. (1995) 'From prime ministerial power to core executive'. In R. A. W. Rhodes and P. Dunleavy (eds), *Prime Minister, Cabinet and Core Executive*. London: Macmillan.

Rhodes, R. A. W. (1997) *Understanding Governance*. Milton Keynes: Open University Press.

Rhodes, R. A. W. (ed.) (2000) *Transforming British Government. Volume 1. Changing Institutions. Volume 2. Changing Roles and Relationships*. London: Macmillan.

Rhodes, R. A. W. (2002) 'Putting the people back into networks'. *Australian Journal of Political Science*, 37(3): 399–415.

Rhodes, R. A. W. and Dunleavy, P. (eds) (1995) *Prime Minister, Cabinet and Core Executive*. London: Macmillan.

Rhodes, R. A. W. and Weller, P. (eds) (2001) *The Changing World of Top Officials: Mandarins or Valets?* Milton Keynes: Open University Press.

Ricci, D. (1984) *The Tragedy of Political Science: Politics, Scholarship, and Democracy*. New Haven, CT: Yale University Press.

Riddell, P. (1989) *The Thatcher Decade*. Oxford: Blackwell.

Riddell, P. (2001) 'Blair as Prime Minister'. In A. Seldon (ed.), *The Blair Effect*. London: Little, Brown.

Ridley, N. (1991) *My Style of Government*. London: Hutchinson.

Robson, W. A. (1975) 'The study of public administration then and now'. *Political Studies*, 23: 193–201.

Rose, R. (1987) *Ministers and Ministries: A Functional Analysis*. Oxford: Clarendon Press.

Rose, R. (2001) *The Prime Minister in a Shrinking World*. Cambridge: Polity.

Salamon, L. M. (ed.) (2002) *The Tools of Government: A Guide to the New Governance*. Oxford: Oxford University Press.

Salter, B. (2000) 'Change in the governance of medicine: the politics of self-regulation'. In D. Gladstone, J. Johnson, W. G. Pickering, B. Salter and M. Stacy (eds), *Regulating Doctors*. London: Institute for the Study of Civil Society.

Sanders, D. (1995) 'Behavioural analysis'. In D. Marsh and G. Stoker (eds), *Theory and Methods in Political Science*, 1st edn. London: Macmillan.

Sanjek, R. (ed.) (1990) *Fieldnotes: The Making of Anthropology*. Ithaca, NY: Cornell University Press.

Sanjek, R. (2000) 'Keeping ethnography alive in an urbanizing world'. *Human Organization*, 59(3): 280–8.

Savage, S. P. and Atkinson, R. (eds) (2001) *Public Policy under Blair*. Basingstoke: Macmillan-Palgrave.

Savoie, D. (1999) *Governing from the Centre*. Toronto: Toronto University Press.

Sawer, G. F. (1969) *Modern Federalism*. London: Watts.

Scarbrough, E. (1987) 'The British electorate twenty years on: electoral change and election surveys'. *British Journal of Political Science*, 17: 219–46.

Scarman, Lord (1986) *The Scarman Report: the Brixton Disorders 10–12 April 1981*. Harmondsworth: Penguin Books.

Schram, S. F. (1993) 'Postmodern policy analysis: discourse and identity in welfare policy'. *Policy Sciences*, 26: 249–70.

Schwartz-Shea, P. and Yanow, D. (2002) '"Reading", "methods", "texts": how research methods texts construct political science'. *Political Research Quarterly*, 55: 457–86.

Scott, D. (2004) *Off Whitehall: A View from Downing Street*. London: Tauris.

Scott, J. (1998) 'Performance culture: the return of reactive policing'. *Policing and Society*, 8(3): 269–88.

Scottish Executive (2001) *Our National Health. A Plan for Action, A Plan for Change*. Edinburgh: Scottish Executive.

Scruton, R. (1984) *The Meaning of Conservatism*, 2nd edn. London: Macmillan.

Secretaries of State (1989a) *Working for Patients*. London: HMSO.

Secretaries of State (1989b) *Caring for People: Community Care in the Next Decade and Beyond*. London: HMSO

Seldon, A. (1995) 'The Cabinet Office and coordination, 1979–87'. In R. A. W. Rhodes and P. Dunleavy (eds), *Prime Minister, Cabinet and Core Executive*. London: Macmillan.

Seldon, A. (2001a) 'The net Blair effect'. In A. Seldon (ed.), *The Blair Effect*. London: Little, Brown.

Seldon, A. (ed.) (2001b) *The Blair Effect*. London: Little, Brown.

Seldon, A. (2004) *Blair*. London: Free Press.

Seyd, P. (2005) *The Changing Face of Democracy in Contemporary Britain*. Basingstoke: Palgrave Macmillan.

Seymour-Ure, C. (2003) *Prime Ministers and the Media. Issues of Power and Control*. Oxford: Blackwell.

Sharman, C. (1977) 'The Australian senate as a states house'. In D. Jaensch (ed.), *The Politics of the 'New Federalism'*. Adelaide: Australasian Political Studies Association.

Sharman, C. (1990) 'Parliamentary federations and limited government'. *Journal of Theoretical Politics*, 2(2): 205–30.

Sheehy, Sir Patrick (1993) *Inquiry into Police Responsibilities and Rewards*. London: HMSO.

Shore, C. (2000) *Building Europe: The Cultural Politics of European Integration*. London: Routledge.

Short, C. (2004) *An Honourable Deception? New Labour, Iraq and the Misuse of Power*. London: Free Press.

Silverman, D. (ed.) (1997) *Qualitative Research: Theory, Method, Practice*. London: Sage.

Silverman, D. (2000) *Doing Qualitative Research: A Practical Handbook*. London: Sage.

Silverman, D. and Jones, J. (1976) *Organizational Work*. London: Collier-Macmillan.

Sisson, C. H. (1959) *The Spirit of British Administration*. London: Faber & Faber.

Skinner, Q. (1984) 'The idea of negative liberty: philosophical and historical perspectives'. In R. Rorty, J. Schneewind and Q. Skinnner (eds), *Philosophy in History*. Cambridge: Cambridge University Press.

Skinner, Q. (1990) 'The republican ideal of political liberty'. In G. Bock, Q. Skinner and M. Viroli (eds), *Machiavelli and Republicanism*. Cambridge: Cambridge University Press.

Skinner, Q. (1998) *Liberty before Liberalism*. Cambridge: Cambridge University Press.

Skinner, Q. (2003) 'States and Freedom of Citizens'. In Q. Skinner and B. Strath (eds), *States and Citizens: History, Theory, Prospects*. Cambridge: Cambridge University Press.

Skolnick, J. H. and Bayley, D. H. (1986) *The New Blue Line: Police Innovation in Six American Cities*. New York: Free Press.

Smith, M. J. (1999) 'Institutionalising the "eternal": textbooks and the study of British government'. *British Journal of Politics and International Relations*, 1(1): 108–18.

Smith, M. J., Richards, D. and Marsh, D. (1995) 'Central government departments and the policy process'. In R. A. W. Rhodes and P. Dunleavy (eds), *Prime Minister, Cabinet and Core Executive*. London: Macmillan.

Smith, N. H. (2002) *Charles Taylor: Meaning, Morals and Modernity*. Cambridge: Polity.

Smyth, P. and Cass, B. (eds) (1998) *Contesting the Australian Way*. Melbourne: Cambridge University Press.

Snow, C. P. (1964) *Corridors of Power*. London: Macmillan.

Spann, R. N. (1975) 'Responsibility in federal systems'. In R. N. Spann and G. R. Curnow (eds), *Public Policy and Administration in Australia: A Reader*. Sydney: Wiley.

Stapleton, J. (1994) *Englishness and the Study of Politics: The Social and Political Thought of Ernest Barker*. Cambridge: Cambridge University Press.

Stapleton, J. (2001) *Political Intellectuals and Public Identities in Britain since 1850*. Manchester: Manchester University Press.

Stedman-Jones, G. (1996) 'The determinist fix: some obstacles to the further development of the linguistic approach to history in the 1990s'. *History Workshop*, 42: 19–35.

Stoker, G. (ed.) (1999) *The New Management of British Local Governance*. London: Macmillan.

Stoker, G. (ed.) (2000a) *The New Politics of British Local Governance*. London: Macmillan.

Stoker, G. (2000b) 'Urban political science and the challenge of urban governance'. In J. Pierre (ed.), *Debating Governance*. Oxford: Oxford University Press.

Stoker, G. (2004) *Transforming Local Governance*. Basingstoke: Palgrave-Macmillan.

Stokes, G. (2004) 'The "Australian settlement" and Australian political thought'. *Australian Journal of Political Science*, 39(1): 5–22.

Stothard, P. (2003) *30 Days. A Month at the Heart of the Blair War*. London: HarperCollins.

Stowe, Sir Kenneth (1989) *Our Caring for the National Health*. London: The Nuffield Provincial Hospitals Trust.

Strauss, A., Schatzman, L., Ehrlich, D., Bucher, R. and Sabshin, M. (1973) 'The hospital and its negotiated order'. In G. Salaman and K. Thompson (eds), *People and Organizations*. London: Longman for the Open University Press.

Taylor, C. (1964) *The Explanation of Behaviour*. London: Routledge.

Taylor, C. (1967) 'Neutrality in political science'. In P. Laslett and W. Runciman (eds), *Philosophy, Politics, Society*, 3rd series. Oxford: Blackwell.

Taylor, C. (1971) 'Interpretation and the sciences of man'. *Review of Metaphysics*, 25(1): 3–51.

Taylor, C. (1989) 'Cross-purposes: the liberal-communitarian debate'. In N. Rosenblum (ed.), *Liberalism and the Moral Life*. Cambridge, MA: Harvard University Press.

Taylor, C. (1993) *Reconciling the Solitudes: Essays on Canadian Federalism and Nationalism*. Edited by G. Laforest. Montreal: McGill-Queens University Press.

Thatcher, M. (1993) *The Downing Street Years*. London: HarperCollins.

Theakston, K. (1999) *Leadership in Whitehall*. London: Macmillan.

Theakston, K. (2000) 'Permanent secretaries: comparative biography and leadership in Whitehall'. In R. A. W. Rhodes (ed.), *Transforming British Government. Volume 2. Changing Roles and Relationships*. London: Macmillan.

Thompson, E. (1980) 'The "Washminster" mutation'. In P. Weller and D. Jaensch (eds), *Responsible Government in Australia*. Melbourne: Drummond.

Thompson, E. and Tillotsen, G. (1999) 'Caught in the act: the smoking gun view of ministerial responsibility'. *Australian Journal of Public Administration*, 58(1): 48–57.

Timmins, N. (1995) *The Five Giants: A Biography of the Welfare State*. London: Fontana Press.

Tivey, L. (1988) *Interpretations of British Politics*. London: Harvester Wheatsheaf.

Toynbee, P. and Walker, D. (2001) *Did Things Get Any Better? An Audit of Labour's Successes and Failures*. London: Penguin Books.

Trollope, A. (1967) [1873]. *Australia*. Edited by P. D. Edwards and R. B. Joyce. St Lucia: University of Queensland Press.

Tyler, T. R. and Yeun, H. J. (2002) *Trust in the Law*. New York: Russell Sage Foundation.

Uhr, J. (1998) *Deliberative Democracy in Australia*. Cambridge: Cambridge University Press.

Uhr, J. (2002) 'Political leadership and rhetoric'. In G. Brennan and F. G. Castles (eds), *Australia Reshaped*. Cambridge: Cambridge University Press.

UK House of Commons Committee of Public Accounts (1997) *The Former Yorkshire Regional Health Authority: The Inquiry Commissioned by the NHS Chief Executive*. Nineteenth Report, Session 1996–97. London: HMSO.

van Eeten, M. J. G., van Twist, M. J. W. and Kalders, P. R. (1996) 'Verhallen vertellen: van een narratieve bestuurskunde naar een postmoderne beweerkunde?' *Bestuurskunde*, 5(4): 168–89. English translation supplied by Mark van Twist.

Vernon, J. and McKillop, S. (1990) *The Police and the Community*. Canberra: Australian Institute of Criminology.

Walker, P. G. (1970) *The Cabinet*. London: Cape.

Walker, P. (1991) *Staying Power*. London: Bloomsbury.

Walsh, K., Deakin, N., Smith, P., Spurgeon, P. and Thomas, N. (1997) *Contracting for Change. Contracts in Health, Social Care and Other Local Government Services*. Oxford: Oxford University Press.

Wanna, J. and Weller, P. (2003) 'Traditions of Australian governance'. *Public Administration*, 81(1): 63–94.

Ward, R. (1980) [1958]. *The Australian Legend*. Melbourne: Oxford University Press.

Watson, D. (2001) 'Rabbit syndrome. Australia and America'. *Quarterly Essay*, No. 4: 1–59.

Watson, D. (2002) *Recollections of a Bleeding Heart: A Portrait of Paul Keating PM.* Sydney: Knopf.

Webster, C. (1988) *The Health Services Since the War. Volume 1. Problems of Health Care. The National Health Service Before 1957.* London: HMSO.

Weick, K. E. (1995) *Sensemaking in Organizations.* London: Sage.

Weller, P. (1985) *First among Equals: Prime Ministers in Westminster Systems.* Sydney: Allen & Unwin.

Weller, P. (2003) 'Cabinet government: an elusive ideal?' *Public Administration,* 81(4): 701–22.

Weller, P. and Fleming, J. (2003) 'The Commonwealth'. In J. Moon and C. Sharman (eds), *Australian Politics and Government. The Commonwealth, the States and the Territories.* Cambridge: Cambridge University Press.

Welsh Assembly (2001) *Improving Health in Wales: A Plan for the NHS with its Partners.* Cardiff: Welsh Assembly.

Wendt, A. (1999) *Social Theory of International Politics.* Cambridge: Cambridge University Press.

Wettenhall, R. (1987) *Public Enterprise and National Development: Selected Essays.* Canberra: Royal Australian Institute of Public Administration.

Wheare, K. C. (1963) *Federal Government,* 4th edn. Oxford: Oxford University Press.

Wheatcroft, G. (2004) 'The tragedy of Tony Blair'. *The Atlantic Monthly,* June: 56–69.

Wilenski, P. (1983) 'Six states or two nations? In J. Aldred and J. Wilkes (eds), *A Fractured Federation? Australia in the 1980s.* Sydney: Allen & Unwin.

Willetts, D. (1992) *Modern Conservatism.* Harmondsworth: Penguin Books.

Wilson, H. (1971) *The Labour Government 1964–70.* London: Weidenfeld and Nicolson.

Wilson, H. (1977) *The Governance of Britain.* London: Sphere.

Wilson, Sir Richard (2003) 'Portrait of a profession revisited'. *Public Administration* 81(2): 365–378.

Winterton, G. (1983) *Parliament, the Executive and the Governor-General.* Melbourne: Melbourne University Press.

Wittgenstein, L. (1972a) *The Blue and Brown Books.* Oxford: Blackwell.

Wittgenstein, L. (1972b) *Philosophical Investigations.* Translated by G. Anscombe. Oxford: Basil Blackwell.

Wood, J. (2000) *Policing's New Model: Recent 'Waves' and Future Possibilities.* Report prepared for the Ontario Provincial Police.

Yanow, D. (1999) *Conducting Interpretive Policy Analysis.* Newbury Park, CA: Sage.

Yeatman, A. (1996) 'The new contractualism: management reform or a new approach to governance?' In P. Weller and G. Davis (eds), *New Ideas, Better Government.* Sydney: Allen & Unwin.

Yin, R. K. (1994) *Case Study Research: Design and Methods,* 2nd edn. London: Sage.

Young, H. (1989) *One of Us.* London: Macmillan.

Young, D. (1990) *The Enterprise Years. A Businessman in the Cabinet.* London: Headline.

Young, H. and Sloman, A. (1982) *No Minister: An Inquiry into the Civil Service.* London: BBC.

Young, H. and Sloman, A. (1984) *But Chancellor: An Inquiry into the Treasury.* London: BBC.

Young, H. and Sloman, A. (1986) *The Thatcher Phenomenon.* London: BBC.

Index

For Product Safety Concerns and Information please contact our EU
representative GPSR@taylorandfrancis.com
Taylor & Francis Verlag GmbH, Kaufingerstraße 24, 80331 München, Germany

9 780415 459778